Literacy Foundations for English Learners

A Comprehensive Guide to Evidence-Based Instruction

edited by

Elsa Cárdenas-Hagan, Ed.D., CCC-SLP, CDT, CALT, QI
Valley Speech Language and Learning Center
Brownsville, Texas

·P·A·U·L·H·
BROOKES
PUBLISHING CO ®

Baltimore • London • Sydney

Paul H. Brookes Publishing Co.
Post Office Box 10624
Baltimore, Maryland 21285-0624
USA

www.brookespublishing.com

Typeset by BMWW, Baltimore, Maryland.
Manufactured in the United States of America by
Integrated Books International, Dulles, Virginia.

All case examples in this book are composites. Any similarity to actual individuals or circumstances is coincidental, and no implications should be inferred.

Library of Congress Cataloging-in-Publication Data

Names: Cárdenas-Hagan, Elsa, editor.
Title: Literacy foundations for English learners: a comprehensive guide to evidence-based
   instruction / edited by Elsa Cárdenas-Hagan.
Description: Baltimore: Paul H. Brookes Publishing Co., [2020] | Includes bibliographical references
   and index.
Identifiers: LCCN 2019051787 (print) | LCCN 2019051788 (ebook) | ISBN 9781598579659 (paperback) |
   ISBN 9781681250489 (epub) | ISBN 9781681250465 (pdf)
Subjects: LCSH: English language—Study and teaching—Foreign speakers. | Second language
   acquisition. | Literacy.
Classification: LCC PE1128.A2 L5326 2020 (print) | LCC PE1128.A2 (ebook) | DDC 428.0071—dc23
LC record available at https://lccn.loc.gov/2019051787
LC ebook record available at https://lccn.loc.gov/2019051788

British Library Cataloguing in Publication data are available from the British Library.

2024

10   9   8   7

Contents

About the Online Materials

◇◇◇

Literacy Foundations for English Learners: A Comprehensive Guide to Evidence-Based Instruction offers online companion materials to supplement and expand the knowledge and strategies provided in this text. All purchasers of the book may access, download, and print the Appendix: Using Technology to Adapt and Enhance Instruction for English Learners along with select forms from the text. Faculty can also access, download, and print a PowerPoint presentation for each chapter and a sample syllabus to guide course planning.

To access the materials that come with this book,

1. Go to the Brookes Publishing Download Hub: http://downloads.brookespublishing.com
2. Register to create an account or log in with an existing account
3. Filter or search for the book title *Literacy Foundations for English Learners*

About the Editor

Elsa Cárdenas-Hagan, Ed.D., CCC-SLP, CDT, CALT, QI, President, Valley Speech Language and Learning Center, Brownsville, Texas

Dr. Cárdenas-Hagan is a bilingual speech-language pathologist, certified teacher, dyslexia therapist, Certified Academic Language Therapist, and Qualified Instructor. She is President of the Valley Speech Language and Learning Center in Brownsville, Texas, and works with the Texas Institute for Measurement, Evaluation, and Statistics at the University of Houston.

Dr. Cárdenas-Hagan has spent the last 2 decades working with national research teams designing assessments and interventions for English learners who struggle with learning to read. She has a passion for ensuring that every schoolchild in the world has access to a highly qualified educator who can implement effective language and literacy instruction to diverse populations.

Dr. Cárdenas-Hagan has also dedicated her time and expertise to many organizations. She serves as Chairperson of the National Joint Committee on Learning Disabilities and is Past Vice Chairperson of the International Dyslexia Association, Past Chairperson of the Texas State Board for Speech Pathology and Audiology, and Past Chairperson of the Texas State Dyslexia Advisory Board. She has also served as a board member of the Academic Language Therapy Association, Southwest Regional Education Laboratory, and Texas Comprehensive Center at the American Institutes for Research. In addition, Dr. Cárdenas-Hagan has served her local community as Co-Founder of Brownsville READS! She is recognized for her reading reform efforts at the local, state, national, and international levels.

Dr. Cárdenas-Hagan has written many scholarly articles, curricular programs, and book chapters related to language and literacy development among English learners. It is her hope that preservice teachers will have the opportunity to learn evidence-based practices for teaching literacy to all students, including those who are English learners and struggle with learning to read.

Dr. Cárdenas-Hagan has been recognized for her dedication to individuals with dyslexia. She is the recipient of the Margaret Byrd Rawson Lifetime Achievement Award by the International Dyslexia Association, the Dr. Luke Waites Award of Service to people with dyslexia by the Academic Language Therapy Association, and the Champion of Dyslexia Award by the Texas Education Agency.

About the Contributors

◇◇

Coleen D. Carlson, Ph.D., Associate Research Professor, University of Houston, Houston, Texas; Associate Director, Texas Institute for Measurement, Evaluation and Statistics, Houston, Texas

Dr. Carlson is Associate Research Professor and Associate Director of Texas Institute for Measurement, Evaluation, and Statistics at the University of Houston. She has 25 years of experience and expertise in exploratory, evaluative, and randomized controlled trials (RCT) research. She has served as a principal investigator and co-principal investigator on several large-scale program project grants examining the development of language, literacy, and math skills in school-age students and English learners; the mediating effects of effective instruction, teacher knowledge, and professional development programs; and the efficacy of several language and literacy intervention programs.

Linda O. Cavazos, Ph.D., Senior Consultant, American Institutes for Research, Austin, Texas

Dr. Cavazos conducts research and provides technical assistance to states and districts. She assists districts and schools in preparing teachers to effectively work with culturally and linguistically diverse learners with and without exceptionalities. Her extensive experience centers on the intersection of culture, language, and disabilities and providing linguistic and academic interventions for English learners and students in special education. Dr. Cavazos holds a Ph.D. in multicultural special education from the University of Texas at Austin.

Elaine Cheesman, Ph.D., Associate Professor Emerita, University of Colorado at Colorado Springs, Colorado Springs, Colorado

Dr. Cheesman, who has worked in the field of dyslexia education since 1990, earned credentials as a Qualified Instructor of Academic Language Therapists at Columbia University and is certified as a Dyslexia Therapist by the International

Dyslexia Association (IDA). She has presented lectures and workshops throughout the United States, Canada, and Kuwait. An active member of the Global Partners of IDA, Dr. Cheesman received a Fulbright Specialist Grant to develop Institutional Accreditation Standards for dyslexia organizations worldwide.

Virginia Lovelace-Gonzalez, M.Ed., CALT, Educational Diagnostician, Texas Educational Diagnosticians Association, McAllen, Texas

Ms. Lovelace-Gonzalez is an educational diagnostician and a Certified Academic Language Therapist with 30 years' experience in public schools. She previously served for 5 years as the state dyslexia consultant for Texas. Ms. Lovelace-Gonzalez recently served on the Texas Education Agency statewide committee for the 2018 update of *The Dyslexia Handbook*.

Kenneth Nieser, M.A. Project Manager, University of Houston, Houston, Texas

Mr. Nieser is a project manager for the Texas Institute for Measurement, Evaluation, and Statistics at the University of Houston. He has more than 30 years of experience in elementary, bilingual education. He has worked on numerous projects that focus on various aspects of early literacy. He has presented at national and local bilingual conferences and is a national trainer for the Tejas LEE (Paul H. Brookes Publishing Co., 2010) and Esperanza early reading instruments (Valley Speech Language and Learning Center, 2015).

Sharolyn D. Pollard-Durodola, Ed.D., Professor of English Language Learning, College of Education, Department of Early Childhood, Multilingual, and Special Education, University of Nevada, Las Vegas, Nevada

Dr. Pollard-Durodola is a professor in the Early Childhood, Multilingual, and Special Education Department of the School of Education at the University of Nevada, Las Vegas. Her scholarship attends to the prevention/intervention of language and literacy difficulties (Spanish/English) among students at risk of academic difficulties. Central to her scholarship is developing intervention curricula that build on validated instructional design principles, evaluating their impact on the language and reading development of struggling readers, and investigating how to improve the quality of language/literacy practices of teachers and parents of English learners. She is interested in bridging research and practice by examining the feasibility/usability of research-based practices. She has published in peer-reviewed journals such as *Exceptional Children; Journal of Research on Educational Effectiveness; The Elementary School Journal; Language, Speech, and Hearing Services in Schools;* and *Bilingual Research Journal.*

Colleen K. Reutebuch, Ph.D., Senior Project Manager and Researcher, The Meadows Center for Preventing Educational Risk, The University of Texas at Austin, Austin, Texas

Dr. Reutebuch holds a doctorate in special education with experience directing large-scale intervention, evaluation, and professional development projects. She served as a classroom teacher and reading coach before transitioning into higher education. Her areas of research include reading difficulty/disability in children and youth, including those targeting English learners and individuals with autism.

Alessandra Rico, M.Ed., Bilingual Educator, Valley Speech Language and Learning Center, Saint Mary's School, Brownsville, Texas

Ms. Rico is a bilingual educator who works at the Valley Speech Language and Learning Center and Saint Mary's School in Brownsville, Texas. Her expertise includes working with English learners who experience reading difficulties. Most recently, she has specialized in educational technology to incorporate a hybrid model of instruction. She has also served as a co-editor for a curriculum designed to meet the language and literacy needs of bilingual students.

Eric Tridas, M.D., Director, Developmental & Behavioral Pediatrics, Pediatric Epilepsy & Neurology Specialists, Tampa, Florida

Dr. Tridas is Director of Developmental & Behavioral Pediatrics at Pediatric Epilepsy & Neurology Specialists. He is Clinical Associate Professor in Pediatrics at the Morsani College of Medicine at the University of South Florida, a member of the National Joint Committee on Learning Disabilities, and Past President of the International Dyslexia Association. He provides consultation services in areas related to child development and behavior, nationally and internationally.

Foreword

◇◇◇

We know a great deal about how to teach children to read. How is it, then, that there are still more than one in three fourth-graders who lack adequate proficiency in reading? Disappointingly, the rate is even higher for students who are English learners (ELs). How do the challenges of learning to read for ELs differ from students who are not ELs, and what do we need to know to improve their reading success? Dr. Elsa Cárdenas-Hagan to the rescue.

In this book, Dr. Cárdenas-Hagan addresses the literacy foundational skills needed to enhance reading outcomes for the more than 5 million ELs attending public schools in the United States. Establishing our understanding of influences related to literacy acquisition, this book describes the important background information forming the context and characteristics of ELs and their families. Dr. Cárdenas-Hagan also provides necessary details about the federal initiatives and their standards that address ELs. Essential to fully appreciating instruction in the foundations of literacy, as a speech-language therapist, Dr. Cárdenas-Hagan appreciates the oral language knowledge and skills necessary to support literacy instruction and has the expertise for explaining how educators can enhance and support students' oral language and vocabulary in first and second language development. This book also highlights how schools can address accommodations for ELs, including those with dyslexia. Addressing ELs and dyslexia is quite extraordinary and one of the numerous valuable contributions of this text. Many of the critical features of instruction in literacy for ELs—including the cross-linguistic transfer of knowledge of phonological awareness in languages such as Spanish, Arabic, Vietnamese, and Chinese—are presented, as well as practices for instruction in alliteration, syllables, and phonemic awareness.

In addition to discussing the foundational skills, the book addresses reading fluency with specific evidence-based practices as well as how to measure fluency. Entire chapters are devoted to the important foundational skills of spelling and writing—often not adequately addressed considering the reciprocal roles of reading and writing. Essential to a complete book on teaching literacy to ELs is a significant focus on vocabulary instruction, including morphological awareness and word selection—never an easy task for any educator. The book considers how these components contribute to the development of reading comprehension and how research-based practices can be implemented to enhance reading for understanding for ELs. Perhaps of greatest value to many educators seeking answers to improving literacy for ELs are the case studies throughout the book, which illustrate application of the practices.

The success of this book is derived from the extraordinary research-to-practice knowledge and skills of Dr. Cárdenas-Hagan and the team of authors she has selected to support the content of this book. As a bilingual, biliterate professional, Dr. Cárdenas-Hagan has worked tirelessly to develop and implement high-quality instruction in language and literacy for ELs for more than 30 years in some of the most resource-challenged schools and districts in the United States. She has developed instructional materials in English and Spanish, provided professional development for educational stakeholders across the United States who are interested in improving their knowledge and skills for teaching ELs, and conducted randomized control trials funded by the National Institute of Child Health and Human Development and the Institute of Education Sciences. I have worked closely with Dr. Cárdenas-Hagan for 20 years. I continue to learn from her, but even more important, I admire her tireless dedication to improving outcomes for ELs. I am thrilled that Dr. Elsa Cárdenas-Hagan has assembled a book of research-to-practice resources for educational stakeholders interested in improving their background knowledge and educational practices for ELs. This book provides a rare opportunity for educators to learn from Elsa Cárdenas-Hagan and her colleagues.

Sharon Vaughn, Ph.D.
Manuel J. Justiz Endowed Chair in Education
Executive Director of The Meadows Center for Preventing Educational Risk
The University of Texas at Austin

Preface

◇◇◇

Reading and writing are high-level language skills that enable individuals to understand, learn, and share ideas about the world. Every student attending school should have the opportunity to achieve literacy. Yet, as we explore the literacy rates among English learners (ELs), it is evident that far too many of these students do not attain proficient literacy skills. As the number of ELs attending public schools has increased to 9.6% of the population (McFarland et al., 2019), it is imperative that educators provide them with explicit, systematic, and comprehensive literacy instruction.

Only 3% of teachers have specialized training in providing instruction to this diverse population of students (Rahman, Fox, Ikoma, & Gray, 2017). This book was written to serve as a resource to provide evidence-based literacy instruction to ELs. Educators can extend their knowledge for the foundational skills of literacy and learn how to deliver instruction that is linguistically sensitive and appropriate for ELs' individual needs. It is my greatest wish that this book will guide you on your journey in becoming a master literacy teacher among ELs.

Reading is a complex process that involves various foundational skills. One of the skills necessary for successful reading includes oral language proficiency. For ELs, oral language proficiency is a variable for successful reading. Oral language proficiency, for example, is necessary for excellent reading fluency, reading comprehension, and written language skills. Therefore, Chapter 1 (Teaching Literacy Skills to English Learners) and Chapter 2 (Language and Literacy Development), both by Elsa Cárdenas-Hagan, begin Section I of the book with an introduction regarding teaching literacy to ELs. Chapter 3 (Components of Literacy Instruction for English Learners), by Eric Tridas, goes on to describe first and second language development as they relate to literacy.

Section II includes specific chapters for each component of literacy instruction among ELs. Chapter 4 (Phonological Awareness Development Among English Learners), by Virginia Lovelace-Gonzalez, includes examples of phonological awareness activities and specific sounds in various languages that must be processed correctly in order to master phonological awareness. Chapter 5 (Phonics Development Among English Learners), by Ken Nieser and Elsa Cárdenas-Hagan, describes explicit instruction for teaching letter–sound knowledge in addition to the syllable types for decoding and reading. From this chapter, readers will learn how to incorporate similarities and differences across languages for a deeper reflection and understanding of evidence-based practice for teaching reading to ELs. Chapter 6 (Reading Fluency Among English Learners), by Coleen D. Carlson, extends beyond phonics knowledge and describes reading fluency development among ELs. The chapter includes practical strategies and examples on how to monitor reading fluency progress. As students become more fluent readers, they must also have an extensive vocabulary to understand what they are reading. In turn, Chapter 7 (Vocabulary Instruction Among English Learners), by Sharolyn D. Pollard-Durodola, includes the most effective word learning strategies and methods for effective implementation. As it is well known that vocabulary knowledge is a variable for successful reading and is correlated with reading comprehension, Chapter 8 (Reading Comprehension Among English Learners), by Colleen K. Reutebuch, includes principles for effective reading comprehension instruction and provides concrete examples for implementation. Cross-language connections are also described. Chapter 9 (Spelling Development Among English Learners), by Elsa Cárdenas-Hagan and Alessandra Rico, incorporates the similar and unfamiliar spelling patterns across languages with examples for explicit instruction. Chapter 10 (Writing Development Among English Learners), by Linda O. Cavazos and Elsa Cárdenas-Hagan, explores the foundational skills for writing and how to develop writing compositions among ELs. Examples of explicit writing instruction with sample graphic organizers are included. The book concludes with an appendix by Elaine Cheesman (Using Technology to Adapt and Enhance Instruction for English Learners). Information on the use of technology for ELs' literacy instruction is especially necessary, as those who are learning to read in a second language will require additional practice and support for developing literacy.

In summary, this book provides the most evidence-based information for teaching literacy to ELs. It is a comprehensive approach to literacy, which includes the importance of oral language for comprehension and foundational skills such as phonological awareness and phonics. Strategies for improving reading fluency and vocabulary are provided in the chapters that follow. The book extends into writing instruction and includes specific information for developing spelling skills among ELs. Educational technology is also necessary for extending the practice opportunities and support that ELs will need and, thus, only the educational technologies that are most helpful to ELs are provided in this book.

Each chapter begins with learning objectives and includes a vignette for the reader to reflect upon while reading. Specific case studies are also included so the reader can apply recently learned information in a practical manner. Each chapter closes with study questions to help readers determine if they have mastered the content presented. In addition, at the end of each chapter the reader will find suggestions for further reading and ideas to extend subject knowledge.

It is my hope that from this book, each reader will gain essential knowledge for teaching literacy to ELs. This will increase the likelihood of providing successful reading instruction among this diverse population of students.

REFERENCES

McFarland, J., Hussar, B., Zhang, J., Wang, X., Wang, K., Hein, S., . . . Barmer, A. (2019). *The condition of education 2019* (NCES 2019-144). Washington, DC: U.S. Department of Education, National Center for Education Statistics. Retrieved from https://nces.ed.gov/programs/coe/

Rahman, T., Fox, M. A., Ikoma, S., & Gray, L. (2017). *Certification status and experience of U.S. public school teachers: Variations across student subgroups* (NCES 2017-056). Washington, DC: U.S. Government Printing Office.

Acknowledgments

◇◇

I would like to thank Liz Gildea, Acquisitions Editor at Paul H. Brookes Publishing Co., for her unwavering support and guidance during the revision and production process of this book. A special thank you also goes to Astrid Pohl Zuckerman, former Acquisitions Editor at Brookes Publishing, who first approached me regarding creating a proposal for a book. Astrid was always so professional and patient with me. In addition, Savannah Neubert, Editorial Assistant at Brookes Publishing, provided the necessary communication and timelines for the production of the book.

I especially want to thank this book's contributors, who not only accepted an invitation to write a chapter but also responded so positively to each of the suggestions and revisions for the book. Despite their busy schedules, the contributors gave willingly of their time to make sure the content of this book would be so valuable to the readers. I learned so much from each of you.

Finally, I want to thank you, the reader, for your interest in this topic and the likelihood that you will impart your knowledge and skills to others who teach literacy to English learners. We each have a goal in mind: to ensure that every English learner becomes literate and is thus able to achieve his or her own dreams.

With much love and appreciation to
my parents, Renato and Mary Rose,
my wonderful husband, Andy,
our children—Alexandra, James, Emily, and José Luís—
and their children—Andrew, Vivian, and Nicolás—
for their unwavering support and encouragement

I

Introduction to English Learners, Language, and Literacy

1

Teaching Literacy Skills to English Learners

Elsa Cárdenas-Hagan

By completing this chapter, the reader will

- Learn about the profiles and demographics of English learners (ELs) in the United States

- Understand the issues regarding the achievement gap between ELs and native English speakers

- Reflect on the historical perspective of bilingual education in the United States

- Learn how federal initiatives and the Common Core State Standards (CCSS) affect education for ELs

- Examine other considerations for meeting the educational needs of ELs, including multi-tiered systems of support (MTSS) in which students' response to intervention (RTI) and instruction are closely monitored

Victor has just arrived from Honduras with his family. He attended first and second grade in his hometown. His family reports that he made excellent grades in his former school. His family is living with his uncle and adjusting well to living in the United States. Victor tells his teacher that he wants to be a doctor and needs to learn English so that he can read books and one day go to medical school. His teacher is so happy to have a student who is very motivated to learn. She wants to teach him to understand, speak, read, and write in English while also teaching him to understand each of the content standards required of a third-grade student. Fortunately, she has the support of her leadership team. Her school district also provides professional development opportunities to learn the most effective English as a second language strategies to implement in the classroom for students like Victor.

INTRODUCTION

Students such as Victor attend school each day with a desire to learn English and meet their academic goals. Some students have recently arrived from other countries or perhaps their parents or grandparents have continued to speak a language other than English in the home. Although the reasons may vary based on the individual child, in essence, these students have likely experienced limited opportunities for learning English before entering school. Yet, the expected learning outcomes of students such as Victor remain the same as all the other students in the classroom. Students who do not speak English as their native language are known as *English learners (ELs)*; they represent a diverse population of students who speak various native languages and represent various cultures, socioeconomic levels, and educational backgrounds. These individuals may experience challenges in speaking, reading, writing, or understanding English at a level that is commensurate with their native English-speaking peers. ELs also bring with them prior knowledge, experiences, and strengths related to language and learning that educators must find ways to identify and build upon. Teachers must be prepared to meet the educational needs of every student, including ELs. The goal of this book is to close the gap of knowledge and practice for serving the language, literacy, and academic needs of ELs.

DEMOGRAPHICS AND PROFILES

ELs are a fast-growing population in schools (McFarland et al., 2017) and represent a diverse population with varied backgrounds. It is necessary for educators and their school leadership teams to understand and be prepared to meet their educational needs. A first step is to learn about the patterns of growth for this population, the initiatives that support their school services, and the considerations for adjusting instruction in order to achieve positive academic outcomes.

The demographics of the United States are rapidly changing. According to the National Center for Education Statistics (McFarland et al., 2017),

Table 1.1. Languages commonly spoken by English learners in United States

Language	Percentage
Spanish	77%
Arabic	2.3%
Chinese	2.2%
Vietnamese	1.8%
Hmong	0.8%
Somali	0.7%

Source: McFarland et al. (2017).

there has been an increase in the number of ELs living in the United States. As of 2017, there were 4.9 million ELs attending public schools, representing 9.5% of the student population of the United States.

ELs represent varied backgrounds. Spanish-speaking ELs represent close to 80% of the second language learner population. Arabic speakers are the second most common ELs, representing 2.3% of the EL population attending public schools (McFarland et al., 2017). Table 1.1 describes the languages commonly spoken by ELs in the United States. Although ELs are the fastest growing subpopulation of students in public schools, fewer than 3% of teachers have the specialized certification to work with this group of students (Rahman, Fox, Ikoma, & Gray, 2017).

Literacy and English Learners

ELs enter school with varying literacy skills. Some may be able to read and write in their native language, whereas others may only hold oral language skills in their native language. Likewise, some ELs enter school with basic reading and writing skills in English, whereas others present very limited English literacy skills.

As the population of ELs has risen, schools have struggled to implement new practices to meet the needs of these students. As a result, students who speak English as a second language face a 13% chance of not graduating from high school. ELs are almost twice as likely to drop out of high school in comparison to their non-Hispanic White peers (National Assessment of Educational Progress [NAEP], 2019). Furthermore, although Spanish-speaking ELs represent the most common second language learners, they demonstrate significant achievement gaps in literacy. According to the *Nation's Report Card* (NAEP, 2019), Hispanic students in fourth grade are 21 points behind those individuals classified as non-Hispanic Whites in reading achievement. Hispanic students that live in poverty are 28 points behind their English-speaking peers in reading achievement. In addition, only 23% of ELs in fourth grade read at a proficient level, whereas 35% of non-Hispanic White students in the fourth grade read at a proficient level.

In light of these harrowing facts, educators need new approaches, best practices, and evidence-based strategies to address the achievement gap for ELs. This book seeks to provide effective literacy practices to teach this population of students and improve their educational outcomes. Readers will learn the essential components of literacy instruction for teaching ELs, the research base for determining the best practices for instruction, and the resources necessary for successful implementation.

Next, this chapter looks back at the federal legislation that relates to delivering instruction to ELs.

FEDERAL INITIATIVES

Federal initiatives and legislation provide a framework for instructional design among ELs. Teachers and school leaders must understand these guidelines in order to ensure successful implementation and thus positive student outcomes. This section briefly summarizes how the Bilingual Education Act of 1968 (PL 90-247), the No Child Left Behind (NCLB) Act of 2001 (PL 107-110), and the Every Student Succeeds Act (ESSA) of 2015 (PL 114-95) affect instruction for ELs.

Bilingual Education Act

The Bilingual Education Act, Title VII of the Elementary and Secondary Education Act of 1968 (PL 90-247), is one of the most important federal initiatives for ELs. Proposed by Texas Senator Yarborough, it was designed to be the first federal legislation that would address teaching students with limited English proficiency (Stewner-Manzanares, 1988). It stipulated that the federal government would provide school districts with financial assistance to establish and develop innovative educational programs for students with limited English-speaking ability. The Bilingual Education Act was the first attempt to recognize that students with limited English proficiency required specialized instruction and aimed to ensure equal opportunity, provide access to better education, and subsequently increase graduation rates. This was necessary as not to violate the civil rights of students who did not speak English. Notable limitations were that it provided limited funding via competitive grants and was only designed for children between the ages of 3 and 8 with limited English proficiency.

An amendment was established in 1974 as a result of a Supreme Court ruling in *Lau v. Nichols* (1974). *Lau v. Nichols* was a class action suit brought against the San Francisco Unified School District. It alleged that 1,800 Chinese students who did not understand English were not being provided an equal education because the curriculum and resources provided were only in English and no specialized English as a second language techniques were incorporated within the instruction. In 1974, the Supreme Court ruled that providing students who do not understand English with the same facilities, teachers, curriculum, and resources does not constitute equality of treatment. In other words, the students' individual rights were violated. Legally, it was determined that Section 601 of the Civil Rights Act of 1964 (PL 88-352), which prohibits discrimination based on race, color, or national origin in any program or activity receiving federal financial assistance, was violated. The students needed additional language and literacy resources in order to learn the content required of all students, and this was not provided to them.

Soon after the *Lau v. Nichols* ruling, Congress enacted the Equal Educational Opportunities Act of 1974 (PL 93-380). It defined what constitutes a denial of equal educational opportunity and required districts to provide special programs for limited English speakers. In addition, the Bilingual Education Act was not only amended in 1974 but also in 1978, 1984, and 1988. In 1994, the Bilingual Education Act was reauthorized, setting up preferences to programs that promoted bilingualism. Bilingual education programs were described as providing native language instruction and English instruction. In summary, the Bilingual Education Act, and its amendments, was the earliest initiative to address teaching ELs; it was expanded and revised by the No Child Left Behind Act.

No Child Left Behind Act (NCLB)

NCLB reauthorized and restructured the Elementary and Secondary Education Act Amendments of 1968 (PL 90-247). NCLB proposed that school successes should be based on performance measures from standardized tests. Its goal was to ensure that all children demonstrate grade-level proficiency in selected areas, including English literacy, math, and science. The legislation required all public schools receiving federal funding to administer annual statewide assessments to all students.

NCLB had a significant impact on bilingual education and the Bilingual Education Act in the United States, due to its emphasis on monitoring students' progress and testing. As a result of NCLB and its emphasis on testing, the Bilingual Education Act was renamed the English Language Acquisition, Language Enhancement, and Academic Achievement Act (Title III). It allowed states to select how they would address the second language needs of ELs. The individual states would now be required to establish English proficiency standards and quality academic instruction in reading, mathematics, and language arts that was based on scientific evidence for English acquisition. ELs would also be required to take tests that measured their progress compared with monolingual English speakers. These students, however, would be exempt from taking tests in math and reading during their first year in school. States and school districts were required to design plans for providing ELs with the appropriate instruction within their educational budgets. Furthermore, determining the best models of language instruction with the most evidence-based practices would need to be further reviewed because the body of research for this population of students had not been determined.

In addition, the law required each school that received Title I funding through the Elementary and Secondary Education Act of 1965 (PL 89-10) to make adequate yearly progress (AYP). AYP is a measurement to determine how every school in the country is performing academically with each student and student group. In other words, each state could set the expected growth or achievement expected each year and the schools or school districts would be required to meet the expectations. The state objectives needed to be measurable and include various subgroups of students, including students considered to be economically disadvantaged, students with learning disabilities, and students who were identified as limited English proficient. Measures for schools to improve and specific timelines were also required for each school. This was very challenging for states because the meta-analysis for best practices had not been finalized and valid screening measures and assessments for ELs were not available. States began to work on developing the assessments related to their population of students.

Every Student Succeeds Act (ESSA)

ESSA was a later reauthorization of the Elementary and Secondary Education Act of 1965 and replaced NCLB. ESSA is in place at the time of this book's publication, and the law focuses on high academic standards. ESSA also focuses on ELs, students living in poverty, and students with learning disabilities, but it allows each state to determine how they can meet each of the requirements. It expands preschool programs and innovative local programs to meet individual students' needs. ESSA also requires every state to submit a plan and seek approval on how it will meet the legislation requirements, including those related to ELs.

ESSA requires every state to report entrance and exit criteria for ELs' language and learning status in order to secure resources for these students. ESSA also requires states to report the academic outcomes of long-term ELs who have been in the program for more than 5 years. These reporting systems are often referred to as *accountability for quality education.* In addition to the outcomes of long-term ELs, ESSA allows states to report on those students who have attained English proficiency for a maximum of 4 years. Therefore, these students who have successfully attained English proficiency can be identified as a subgroup in the state's reporting system for the purpose of measuring students' progress and educational outcomes. ESSA does allow states to exclude first year ELs in the reporting or accountability system. The test results, however, must still be reported.

ESSA also requires reporting on ELs with disabilities and includes an increase in funding for programs meeting the educational needs of this diverse population. ESSA does provide guidelines regarding the selection of effective approaches for the development of English language proficiency. As such, states are required to design English language proficiency standards as well as academic content standards for each subject area taught in schools. The standards must be designed to meet the educational needs of all students.

CURRICULUM: THE COMMON CORE STATE STANDARDS

As previously discussed, states are required to design proficiency standards under NCLB and ESSA. As this mandate was put into practice, it became clear that allowing states to design their own standards could result in students being held to different standards across various states. To address this concern, the National Governor's Association gathered a group of educational experts to work on developing curriculum standards that could be used by the states. The result of this initiative resulted in the Common Core State Standards (CCSS), published in 2010. The CCSS are designed to provide clear objectives of what students must learn at each of the grade levels. The standards reflect objectives that are relevant to the real world and are designed to help students in public schools prepare for college and careers. Standards were released for mathematics and English language arts on June 2, 2010, with a majority of states adopting the standards in the subsequent months. States were eager to implement the CCSS because the federal grant known as Race to the Top included standards and assessments for students to be college and career ready.

Yet, little research has been completed on the efficacy of the CCSS for ELs. On a related point, many ELs have challenges meeting the demands of CCSS because they must develop their English language skills and English literacy skills while mastering content knowledge. In this book, readers will learn evidence-based strategies for developing language and literacy skills, which can also assist in meeting the guidelines set forth by the CCSS.

PROGRAM MODELS FOR ENGLISH LEARNERS

As educators determine the curriculum standards that are required by their schools, it will be important to understand the educational program models that are currently available and the variables that can affect their language and literacy outcomes (i.e., ELs across the country are provided instruction through various program models). Schools may offer several language of instruction program models, each of which can best serve students at varying levels of their second language development. For example, some schools may be unable to provide native language instruction and therefore may focus on English as a second language, incorporating strategies to increase students' understanding. Other schools may provide English immersion in which all instruction is in English with very little support in the native language. In some settings, students are in a transitional bilingual education program in which the native language is utilized in the first few years. As the student progresses in language and literacy, English becomes a major focus of instruction. Dual language programs provide instruction in the native language and English throughout the students' academic career. The U.S. Department of Education (2016) outlined four program models for ELs that are educationally sound. Each is described next and summarized in Table 1.2.

1. *English as a second language or English language development:* The goal of this model is to teach academic vocabulary to ELs to help them understand instruction in each of the subjects. This requires English language proficiency for listening, speaking, reading, and writing. Instruction is provided primarily in English.

2. *Structured English immersion:* This model is designed to impart English language skills so the EL can make the transition to and succeed in an English-only general education classroom. Instruction is provided primarily in English with strategies to support students' understanding of information.

Table 1.2.   English learner (EL) program models

Program option	Program goal	Language(s) used for instruction
English as a second language or English language development	This program consists of techniques, methodology, and special curricula designed to explicitly teach ELs about the English language, including the academic vocabulary needed to gain access to content instruction, and develop their English language proficiency in all four language domains (i.e., speaking, listening, reading, writing).	Usually provided in English with little use of the ELs' primary language(s)
Structured English immersion	This program is designed to impart English language skills so that the ELs can make the transition to and succeed in an English-only mainstream classroom once proficient.	Usually provided in English with little use of the ELs' primary language(s)
Transitional bilingual education (TBE) (early-exit bilingual education)	TBE is a program that maintains and develops skills in the primary language while introducing, maintaining, and developing skills in English. The primary purpose of a TBE program is to facilitate ELs' transition to an all-English instructional program while the students receive academic subject instruction in the primary language to the extent necessary.	Students' primary language and English
Dual language or two-way immersion	This is a bilingual program in which the goal is for students to develop language proficiency in two languages by receiving instruction in English and another language in a classroom that is usually comprised of half primary English speakers and half primary speakers of the other language.	English and another language

From U.S. Department of Education, Office of English Language Acquisition. (2016). *English learner tool kit* (Rev. ed.). Washington, DC: Author.

3. *Transitional bilingual education (early-exit bilingual education):* This model maintains and develops skills in students' native language while introducing and developing skills in their second language. The purpose of this model is to facilitate the ELs' transition to an all-English instructional program. The students do receive academic subject instruction in their native language, to the extent necessary.

4. *Dual language or two-way immersion:* The goal of this model is for students to develop language proficiency in the native and second language, such as English. Students receive instruction in both languages throughout their academic career. Within a two-way dual language classroom, approximately 50% of students are native English speakers and the other 50% speak another native language. In some schools, a one-way dual language classroom is established in which all students in the classroom are non-native English speakers. The goal for these students, however, continues to be language and literacy proficiency in their native language and English.

The program models to serve ELs are designed to meet a student's language and academic needs in addition to providing guidance to schools for aligning the model to the student. It is important for educators to identify the model that their school or program uses and plan instruction accordingly. When implemented with fidelity, positive student outcomes are expected.

When an EL does not achieve the typical language or literacy skills as his or her peers, then it is necessary to consider providing additional opportunities and support to the student. This can be achieved through multitiered systems of support (MTSS).

MULTI-TIERED SYSTEMS OF SUPPORT: MEETING THE EDUCATIONAL NEEDS OF ENGLISH LEARNERS

A framework for meeting the educational needs of ELs can include a response to intervention (RTI) process within MTSS. This process was first introduced in the Individuals with Disabilities Education Improvement Act (IDEA) of 2004 (PL 108-446). The goal was to identify students with potential learning disabilities during the early years of education using various sources of data in MTSS. In MTSS, students in the general education classroom often meet the educational standards and expectations and are considered to be in Tier 1. Some students will require extra time in a small-group instructional setting to meet the educational standards, which is a Tier 2 level of support. Tier 2 typically requires a minimum of an additional 30 minutes of targeted instruction. The students' progress is closely monitored, and if the RTI is not favorable, then a third tier of support is recommended. Students who require this more intensive intervention are referred to Tier 3 specialized programs. Tier 3 is implemented with more intensity (minimum of 45 min-

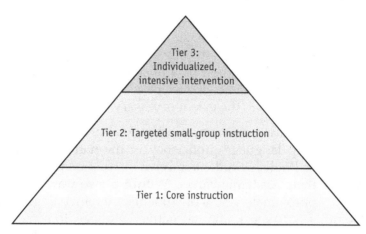

Figure 1.1. Tiered levels of support.

utes per day) to meet the educational standards prescribed by the school
and state. See Figure 1.1 for a summary of the MTSS tiers.

Monitoring an EL's language, literacy, and content knowledge provides
guidance on skills that require more instruction. For example, if the EL is
not meeting the prescribed educational goals at a Tier 1 level of support,
then more opportunity within a small-group setting (Tier 2) can be implemented to further enhance the likelihood that the student can master the
concepts presented during the core instruction within the classroom. Once
these students are identified, their progress monitoring becomes more frequent and their intervention more individualized to meet their needs.

More research must be in place to further understand and improve
upon this service delivery among ELs. For example, educators need to know
which assessment tools should be utilized to determine a student's language
and literacy skills and thus follow his or her progress. These tools must be
valid for ELs and must consider the student's oral language proficiency in
the native language and English. This becomes a complex goal, as there
are many languages and variables to consider when designing an effective
assessment instrument.

This book provides techniques for improving language and literacy
goals among ELs. Students who require more opportunities to achieve their
language and literacy goals should be provided with small-group instruction on a regular basis. The implementation of best practices for language
and literacy development among ELs is necessary so that each of these students can achieve his or her academic goals. The information provided in
this book can benefit typically developing ELs and those who struggle with
reading.

CONCLUSION

This chapter introduced the varying profiles of ELs, the program models
in which they are instructed, and the need for them to achieve high levels

of language and literacy skills. Subsequent chapters in this book address each of the necessary components for the development of literacy skills among ELs.

STUDY QUESTIONS

1. What is the fastest growing population of students in U.S. public schools?

2. What is the most common second language of ELs in the United States?

3. What can be done to improve the number of teachers who are prepared to instruct ELs in public schools?

4. Describe one of the variables related to reading achievement among ELs.

5. What appears to be one of the most essential skills for reading comprehension among ELs?

6. What provisions did the Bilingual Education Act provide?

7. Describe the features of NCLB as related to educating ELs.

8. What are the newer features for ELs in ESSA?

EXTENDED READING AND APPLICATION ACTIVITIES

1. Read the CCSS for literacy standards (http://www.corestandards.org/ELA-Literacy/). With a colleague, discuss the references to ELs within the standards.

2. Read about the waivers for annual yearly progress among ELs in relation to the CCSS. Next, discuss the various challenges reported for achieving positive outcomes among this population of students.

3. Read the literacy briefs on RTI in an MTSS for ELs (https://osepideasthat work.org/osep-model-demonstration-program). Discuss the recommendations for increasing ELs' academic achievement.

REFERENCES

August, D., & Hakuta, K. (Eds.). (1997). *Improving schooling for language-minority children: A research agenda.* Washington, DC: National Academies Press.

Bilingual Education Act of 1968, PL 90-247, 20 U.S.C., §§ 3221-3262 *et seq.*

Civil Rights Act of 1964, PL 88-352, 20 U.S.C. §§ 241 *et seq.*

Common Core State Standards Initiative. (2010). *Common Core State Standards for English language arts and literacy, history/social studies, science, and technical subjects.* Washington, DC: Council of Chief State School Officers and National Governors Association.

Elementary and Secondary Education Act Amendments of 1968, PL 90-247, 20 U.S.C. §§ 877b *et seq.*

Elementary and Secondary Education Act of 1965, PL 89-10, 20 U.S.C. §§ 241 *et seq.*

Equal Educational Opportunities Act of 1974, PL 93-380, U.S.C. § 1701 *et seq.*

Every Student Succeeds Act of 2015, PL 114-95, 20 U.S.C. §§ 1001 *et seq.*

Individuals with Disabilities Education Improvement Act (IDEA) of 2004, PL 108-446, 20 U.S.C. §§ 1400 *et seq.*

Krogstad, J. M. (2014). *Hispanics only group to see its poverty rate decline and incomes rise.* Washington, DC: Pew Research Center.

Lau v. Nichols, 414 U.S. 563 (1974).

McFarland, J., Hussar, B., de Brey, C., Snyder, T., Wang, X., Wilkinson-Flicker, S., . . . Hinz, S. (2017). *The condition of education: 2017* (NCES 2017144). Washington, DC: National Center for Education Statistics.

National Assessment of Educational Progress. (2019). *Nation's Report Card.* Washington, DC: National Center for Education Statistics. Retrieved from https://www.nationsreportcard .gov/about.aspx

No Child Left Behind Act of 2001, PL 107-110, 115 Stat. 1425, 20 U.S.C. §§ 6301 *et seq.*

Rahman, T., Fox, M. A., Ikoma, S., & Gray, L. (2017). *Certification status and experience of U.S. public school teachers: Variations across student subgroups* (NCES 2017-056). Washington, DC: U.S. Government Printing Office.

Stewner-Manzanares, G. (1988). *The Bilingual Education Act: Twenty years later.* Washington, DC: National Clearing House for Bilingual Education.

U.S. Department of Education, Office of English Language Acquisition. (2016). *English learner tool kit* (Rev. ed.). Washington, DC: Author.

2

Language and Literacy Development

Elsa Cárdenas-Hagan

By completing this chapter, the reader will

- Learn the expected native language milestones for young children

- Understand second language acquisition

- Examine the stages of reading development

- Explore the impact of language skills on literacy skills

- Understand the recommended strategies to improve English Learners' (ELs') oral language skills.

Manuel is a 6-year-old student and a recent immigrant from Mexico. He appears to understand information in his native language, and his parents share that Manuel speaks to them in Spanish. Manuel's teacher reports that he understands basic English concepts that she is using in class. For example, he knows English letters and sounds. He is, however, reluctant to communicate verbally in English. Manuel's teacher wants to monitor his language and literacy skill development to make sure he progresses and achieves the milestones expected of an English learner (EL) who is at the beginning stages of English language and literacy skills.

INTRODUCTION

When students like Manuel arrive in the classroom, they bring varied levels of skill and experience in their native language as well as in English. Before planning instruction, educators must understand each students' language and literacy development in both the native and second language. Educators must also identify the language and literacy skills that students need to build.

This chapter discusses how native and second language, as well as literacy skills, develop for typically developing learners. It also provides strategies for building early language skills for ELs. By reading this chapter, educators will be able to set expectations and goals for students like Manuel.

NATIVE LANGUAGE ACQUISITION

Oral language appears to be a rather natural process for human beings. In other words, humans can speak and communicate orally when provided with opportunities and stimulation. Oral language is also a basic skill that is necessary for a higher form of language, which includes reading and writing. Notably, a student must have strong oral language skills in order to achieve high levels of literacy skills. Van Kleeck (1990) described reading as a language-based skill that requires strong oral language skills.

Oral language skills develop in a similar manner across languages. The subsections that follow outline the stages of native language acquisition for typically developing children from birth to age 12 years. Educators who work with ELs need to understand these stages in order to identify what knowledge and skills their ELs hold in their first language. The National Institute on Deafness and Other Communication Disorders (2000) described the following speech and language milestones, which can inform educators and families regarding native language expectations.

Birth to 12 Months

During the first few months of life, infants can listen to and begin to respond to the sounds from within the environment. Early responses may include turning toward sounds and becoming startled by unfamiliar noises. By approximately 3 months of age, infants begin to make noises that are often referred to as *cooing*. By 6 months, infants begin to babble. They can produce some vowel and consonant sounds produced with the lips, such as /b/, /p/, and /m/. One might hear an infant produce /baba/, /mama/, and /papa/ during this stage of development. During the first year of life, children can respond to their name by turning their head when someone uses their name. By the time a child is 12 months, he or she can follow one-step verbal commands such as "Give me the ball," "Touch your nose," or "Drink the water."

1–2 Years

As infants become toddlers, they demonstrate the ability to comprehend three-word phrases or sentences. They can sit and listen to an adult read a simple story to them. They can also identify common and familiar objects such as a comb, toothbrush, or chair and body parts such as the nose, eyes, and mouth. They can also name many of those objects. Their expressive language, which describes how children communicate their wants and needs, expands by approximately 50 words during this stage. By the age of 2, toddlers can combine words to form simple two-word phrases such as "Want ball," "Go out," and "See dog."

2–2.5 Years

At the age of 2, a child can comprehend 500 words and can sit and listen to a 5- or 10-minute story. He or she can also follow a series of two related commands such as "Get the soap and wash your hands." Children within this age range can identify action pictures such as running, eating, or sleeping. In addition, the ability to answer "what" and "where" questions increases (e.g., What animal barks? What do you do with a pencil? Where is the spoon? Where do fish live?).

2.5–3 Years

By the time that a child is 2.5–3 years of age, he or she understands approximately 900 words and can use 500 different words. The child begins to use pronouns such as *I* and *you* (e.g., "I want ball," "You play ball"). The child can also ask simple questions such as, "Want the ball?" The understanding of prepositions such as *in, on,* and *under* is mastered. Speech sounds such as /k/, /g/, /n/, /f/, /t/, and /d/ are mastered.

3–3.5 Years

A child within this age range can comprehend approximately 1,200 words and can use 800 different words. The ability to speak in short sentences continues, and regular plurals such as *cats, dogs,* and *balls* become more consistently used. The child can identify some basic colors and can describe the use of common objects such as a spoon or fork.

3.5–4 Years

By the time that a child is 3.5 years of age, he or she can comprehend approximately 1,500–2,000 words and use 1,000–1,500 words. The child can understand spatial concepts such as *behind, in front of,* or *next to.* The average length of a child's utterance is approximately four words. In addition, a child of 3.5–4 years of age can now understand simple analogies such as

A bird sings and a dog ___ (barks).

An elephant is big and a mouse is ___ (little or tiny).

The ability to understand analogies demonstrates a deeper comprehension of words. That is, the ability to know a word and relate it to another word reflects further command of the word. As such, analogies are often included as one of the measurements for vocabulary knowledge. The child can now answer very simple "who," "what," "where," and "why" questions.

4–5 Years

With exposure to language, the child at this age can comprehend between 2,500 and 2,800 words and use 1,500–2,000 words. The average length of utterance is five words. Children of this age can, however, combine between five and eight words in a sentence. A child in this age range can answer simple "when" questions such as "When do you go to bed?" and "When do you eat breakfast?" The child also begins to tell a story in sequence with more accuracy.

5–6 Years

A 5- to 6-year-old child can comprehend 13,000 words and uses 2,500–3,500 words. The average length of each utterance is six words. Children of this age can, however, combine between six and nine words in a sentence. The ability to use pronouns is more consistent, although occasional errors will occur. The ability to understand antonyms and synonyms increases. The child can now describe objects and define simple words. The child begins to be quite creative and can tell simple stories. Speech is intelligible and most sounds are produced with accuracy, with the exception of sounds such as /l/, /r/, and /th/.

6–7 Years

A child of this age can now comprehend between 20,000–26,000 words. The average length of utterance is seven words. Grammatical structures are more consistent. Yet, occasional errors are still present in the speech patterns. The use of written language increases, as children of this age know the alphabet and the letter–sound correspondences. Their writing may still have letter reversals because this is one of the common error patterns for children of this age range. All speech sounds are mastered.

8–12 Years

Students ages 8–12 continue to increase their knowledge of grammar and more consistently produce complex sentences. They continue to increase their vocabulary levels as they are exposed to formal instruction and various types of texts. Language continues to develop into adolescence. It is during this time that students are more prepared to understand idioms and abstract language. They can also now make inferences and use problem-solving skills.

Variables That Affect Native Language Development

Although the stages and milestones previously outlined are common among most children, they may vary based on home and parental factors. Of note, language develops when students are provided with multiple opportunities for use. Language-rich homes and classrooms can positively benefit students.

Socioeconomic status is one of the more widely known variables that affects language development. Hart and Risley (2003) described a 30 million word gap by the age of 3 between children in professional families and higher socioeconomic status and children in families from lower socioeconomic status, such as those receiving welfare support. In addition, each child's vocabulary consisted of words also recorded in their parents' vocabulary.

The next section shifts to second language acquisition. For ELs, oral language proficiency in the native language affects performance in the second language. A child who has a stronger foundation of oral language is likely to be able to respond well to second language instruction. Educators who recognize skills and strengths that have developed in a student's native language can plan appropriate instruction in the second language.

SECOND LANGUAGE ACQUISITION

Humans have an innate capacity to learn multiple languages. According to Gopnik, Meltzoff, and Kuhl (2000), infants can discriminate sounds from multiple languages, but they lose this capability by 12 months of age if they are not exposed to the language. Yet, if children continue to have opportunities to listen and speak in more than one language, then they can become proficient and multilingual.

Educators should keep the innate nature of multilingualism in mind when setting goals for ELs. ELs can and will learn a second language through evidence-based instruction and appropriate levels of support. The following section outlines the stages of language acquisition. Notably, there are several theories for second language acquisition. This chapter discusses theories by Stephen Krashen and Tracy Terrell (1983) and Jim Cummins (1981). The stages can also serve as a guide for organizing oral language instruction for ELs.

Krashen and Terrell's Five Stages of Second Language Acquisition

Stage I: Silent or Preproduction Stage   As children develop a second language, the first stages developed by Krashen and Terrell (1983) are known as the Silent or Preproduction Stage. It is during this stage that individuals are exposed to the second language and can comprehend approximately 500 words and use some new words in the second language. Responses in the second language, however, typically include gestures or nonverbal language. Although the individual is not very verbal during this stage, he or she is listening to language and may be developing the understanding of many words and phrases.

Stage II: Early Production Stage   During the Early Production Stage, individuals increase their comprehension and begin to communicate in a simple manner. Individuals now comprehend approximately 1,000 receptive words, and oral language includes utterances of one- or two-word phrases. They typically respond to others with short answers and have the ability to answer "who" and "what" questions in addition to "yes" and "no" questions.

Stage III: Speech Emergence Stage   During the Speech Emergence Stage, individuals comprehend approximately 3,000 words. They speak in simple sentences of three to four words and can ask simple questions. Grammatical errors will still be present and are not considered atypical for an individual at this stage of second language acquisition.

Stage IV: Intermediate Language Proficiency Stage   During the Intermediate Language Proficiency Stage, individuals can comprehend approximately 6,000 words. Sentence production includes some complex sentences, and the speaker can ask for clarification and state opinions in the second language. The individual will make few grammatical errors.

Stage V: Advanced Language Proficiency Stage   During the Advanced Language Proficiency Stage, the second language learner can fully participate in an academic setting. Speech includes primarily complex sentences with the appropriate use of grammar. Vocabulary levels are comparable to native speakers.

Cummins' Theory of Second Language Acquisition

Jim Cummins' (1981) theory of second language acquisition describes ELs' native language ability as a common underlying proficiency. In other words, the second language learner has an innate ability to learn a second language. The ability to learn the second language is based on the first language knowledge. Therefore, second language learners can build on the native language to develop their basic interpersonal communication skills, known as *BICS*, in the second language. Cummins described the next level of second language acquisition as cognitive academic language proficiency (CALP). CALP extends on basic language skills to academic skills that require the ability for higher level vocabulary, thinking, and reasoning skills. CALP goes beyond the social, informal, or basic language abilities and is at a level of a more academic and formal language. Cummins described BICS as developing within 1–2 years of instruction, and CALP develops within approximately 5–7 years. As ELs progress and continue their education into middle school or high school, they will require these higher levels of academic language. Teachers must determine each student's current level of second language capabilities and ensure further growth in language and literacy. As educators provide instruction to promote second language acquisition, it will soon become clear that literacy instruction goes hand in hand with language. The connection between language and literacy can be understood in more depth by exploring the typical development of reading. The next section describes reading development stages. Educators who understand first and second language acquisition will be able to design and individualize instruction as they progress students through the stages of reading development.

STAGES OF READING DEVELOPMENT

Oral language development sets the foundation for the development of reading. Reading requires strong language skills in order to comprehend text. In order to plan effective, explicit instruction, educators must understand reading development stages. The stages provide a framework for designing literacy instruction according to each student's level of reading development. Dr. Jeanne Chall (1983) described the following reading stages.

Stage 0: Prereading Stage

By the age of 5 or 6 years, young children understand that the spoken word can be represented in print. At this early stage, children begin to name letters and recognize words. They begin to understand the concepts of rhyming words, alliterations such as "Sally sees seven seagulls," and segmentation of sentences such as counting words and deleting words in a sentence. These are considered foundational skills for reading.

Stage 1: Decoding Stage

During the decoding stage, individuals understand the sound and symbol correlations necessary to begin to read words. They attempt to accommodate and assimilate their error patterns to try to correct any decoding errors they may have made. They analyze the printed words from the individual parts (letters and sounds) into the whole word. They can also analyze words from the whole word into its constituent parts.

Stage 2: Confirmation and Fluency Stage

Between the ages of 7 and 8, individuals have typically mastered their phonological awareness and phonics skills. They focus on reading with more fluency during this stage. *Fluency* is the rapid accurate reading of continuous text with appropriate expression, requiring well-developed word recognition skills (National Institute of Child Health and Human Development, 2000). Therefore, the fluency stage includes reading at an appropriate rate with the appropriate phrasing and expression. As students read with more fluency, they can spend more time understanding the text that they have read.

Stage 3: Reading for Learning Stage

Individuals at this stage have mastered the foundational skills of reading, such as decoding and fluency, and now must read to learn new information. Typically, between the ages of 8 and 14, individuals read text representing various content areas, which increases their word knowledge and vocabulary skills.

Stage 4: Reading From Multiple Viewpoints Stage

Students between the ages of 14 and 18 typically read text from more than one point of view. They can now think and react critically to the text and consider multiple viewpoints. For example, some schools encourage the use of mobile phones in the classroom, whereas others prohibit the use of the phones in the classroom. Students can consider different points of view and look at advantages and disadvantages of the use of phones in the classroom. At this stage of reading development, students can now comprehend and interact with text with many layers of facts.

Stage 5: Construction and Reconstruction Stage

During this stage, individuals are selective about their reading. Readers will choose the text that they prefer to read. Selected texts are perhaps more related to their personal interests and desire for academic knowledge. Readers at this stage construct knowledge for themselves and can form opinions and make judgments.

Understanding first and second language acquisition, as well as reading development stages, can assist educators in designing effective instruction for ELs. Each of the components of language are related to literacy, which is discussed in the following section. Therefore, understanding in more detail how language is specifically related to literacy can help instructors integrate language and literacy skills during instruction.

THE LANGUAGE AND LITERACY CONNECTION

Bloom and Lahey (1978) defined *language* as "a code whereby ideas about the world are represented through a conventional system of arbitrary signals for communication" (p. 4). Ideas and thoughts about the world are therefore shared or communicated through a system that is accepted for communication within a particular context or setting. They described language further into phonology, semantics, syntax, morphology, and pragmatics and related these components into language form, content, and use. For example, components such as phonology and syntax are related to the language form. Semantics is related to the content or meaning of language. Pragmatics is related to language use. Understanding each of the components of language is necessary for integrating language and literacy skills; these components are the building blocks for delivering effective language instruction to ELs. The components of language are described next.

Phonology

Every language consists of sounds and has rules about how sounds can form together to produce words. The word *phonology* literally means the study of sounds. That is, *-ology* is interpreted as the study of, and *phono* means sound. Phonology is related to a language's form (Bloom & Lahey, 1978). Students must be able to process and produce sounds to produce oral language.

Likewise, students' ability to process and produce sounds is necessary for mastering a foundational skill of reading known as *phonological awareness*, which is the ability to process, segment, blend, and manipulate sounds. For example, the word *fish* has three sounds, and /f/ /i/ /sh/ demonstrates the ability to segment a word into its individual phonemes. The ability to blend phonemes can be demonstrated when the student understands that the sounds /ch/ /o/ /p/ can be combined to form the word *chop*. The ability to manipulate sounds can be demonstrated when the student is able to change the /ch/ sound in *chop* to the /sh/ sound, which produces the word *shop*. These skills are foundational for reading in alphabetic and nonalphabetic languages. Therefore, processing and producing sounds is a necessary skill for manipulating and segmenting sounds across many languages (Branum-Martin, Tao, Garnaat, Bunta, & Francis, 2012).

Notably, there appears to be cross-language transfer of phonological awareness skills (Branum-Martin et al., 2012). Students who have the capability to process and manipulate sounds in a first language are likely to do the same in the second language. This topic is discussed in further detail in Chapter 5. One example of cross-language transfer includes the error pattern described in the following example. Liliana is beginning to speak in English and has produced the following sentence:

My mudder and fadder are en the town forr tree days.

Liliana has taken advantage of her native language knowledge and is attempting to produce English with accuracy and precision. It is evident that Liliana can benefit from learning the production of the English voiced /th/ sound. She will also need to learn the short vowel /i/ sound for words such as *in* and *into*. The word *for* does not require a trilled /rr/ sound. These are just a few examples of how phonology can affect second language production and how instructors can analyze ELs' error patterns to design instruction.

Semantics

Every language in the world consists of words that represent meaning. Semantics, the second component of language, is the ability to understand the meanings of words and the various ways words can be used to represent knowledge of the world (Bloom & Lahey, 1978). It is common for an individual to understand more words than he or she can produce. In other words, as we listen and learn words, we then gain the confidence to use them orally or in print. In the classroom, ELs will need explicit instruction to build language acquisition skills related to semantics. For example, they may require many opportunities to understand how some words are more precise in their meaning than others. For instance, Julio, a fifth grader, was asked to explain how his friend was able to retrieve a kite from a tree. Julio said the following:

There was the thing that you fly and it went inside the tree and my friend got something to step up and get the thing down from the tree.

In considering Julio's English language semantics, it is clear that he understands the concept of a kite, but he lacks the precise or exact label for this item. He also understands the concept of a ladder, but he cannot label this item either. It is evident that he understands some concepts, but he cannot use the specific word to express his thoughts. In addition, Julio could have used the word *stuck* to better communicate that the kite was not simply inside the tree but that he was unable to retrieve the kite. Julio will require instruction in word precision, which is related to semantics and is necessary to build his English vocabulary.

Semantics is important for reading comprehension and reading fluency. The more words that ELs understand, the more words they can predict as they read. For example, as students read and have knowledge of words, including their parts of speech, they will be able to better predict the words within sentences. This can positively enhance their individual reading fluency rates (Crosson & LeSaux, 2010). Chapters 7 and 8 of this book, further explore the correlation between semantics and reading.

Morphology

Morphology is the study of language form that includes the ability to understand that there are small units of meaning within a word, which are known as *morphemes* (Bloom & Lahey, 1978). Recognizing morphemes can be very helpful in determining the meaning of words in many languages (Ramirez, 2017). For example, Mario saw the following sentence and recognized some familiar word parts from his native language of Spanish.

My mom said I need to prepare for the geography examination.

Mario observed that the word *geography* had a similar word part, *geo*. The spelling and the meaning of *geo* was the same in his native language and English. The word part *graph* was also similar to *graf*, a word part in his native language of Spanish. Mario also recognized the word *examination* because in Spanish the word is *examinación*. The word parts of *exam* and *-tion* are similar to the Spanish word parts *exam* and *ción*.

The ability to recognize the smaller meaning units within words helps the reader to better understand the words and the general comprehension of the text. ELs can benefit from morphological awareness as many of the morphemes that are of Greek and Latin origin exist in English and other languages (Marinova-Todd, Siegel, & Mazabel, 2013). Chapter 7 explores morphology in greater detail.

Syntax (Grammar)

Every language has rules about how words are used to form phrases and sentences. The American Speech-Hearing-Language Association (ASHA; 2019) described *syntax* as the rules that pertain to the ways in which words can be combined to form sentences in a language. Bloom and Lahey (1978) considered syntax as language form. Students must understand these rules in order to produce words, phrases, and sentences in the correct manner. One example of a Spanish-speaking EL's syntax pattern follows.

My mom, she go to the store yesterday, to get hers paper and pencils.

Consider the syntax errors from the previous example. It is apparent that the student should learn the English verb *went*, which will offer more precision in word choice and prevent using several words to describe this verb. The student could also learn that the pronoun *she* can take the place of the noun. In addition, the student overgeneralizes from Spanish to English the word *hers* for *her* because in Spanish the word would be *sus*.

As they develop literacy skills, students who have intact syntax (grammar) skills are able to read more fluently and write sentences and paragraphs with increased precision. More discussion on this topic is included in Chapter 10.

Pragmatics

Every language has unspoken rules about how to use the language. There are cultural rules, academic rules, and social rules. Some words or phrases are appropriate for a social setting, whereas others are more suited for a formal or academic setting. *Pragmatic language skills* refer to the rules associated with the use of language in conversation and broader social and formal situations (ASHA, 2019), including understanding how to use language in various settings. For example, a student should not say "Hi dude" to a teacher because it is too informal. That greeting may be considered an appropriate greeting in a social setting with a friend. ELs will require opportunities to determine the differences between the social language and the more formal language used in schools. Understanding idioms and higher level or abstract language can also be considered as language use. Language use is important to reading comprehension. Students who have difficulty with the use of implied meaning in conversations are likely to struggle when asked to interpret figurative language, humor, sarcasm, and other less explicitly stated or intended meanings in texts (Nation, Clarke, Marshall, & Durand, 2004).

As students understand more about the use of the language, they can better comprehend and understand the teacher. According to Snow, Burns, and Griffen (1998), excellent reading comprehension is dependent upon students' oral language abilities. It is therefore essential to understand how to further develop ELs' language skills because this can enhance their literacy skills.

LANGUAGE DEVELOPMENT STRATEGIES

The previous sections of this chapter summarized the developmental stages of language and literacy skills and the components of language that provide the basis for those skills. This knowledge serves as a frame for understanding how ELs learn, what skills they bring to the table, and what structure that instruction should take. Next, educators need to identify evidence-based strategies that promote second language acquisition and literacy skills for ELs. Educators should integrate the following strategies (adapted from Cárdenas-Hagan, 2010) into language and literacy instruction.

- Establish routines in the classroom so that students understand what is expected of them. Use gestures and visual supports to further enhance ELs' comprehension.

- Provide native language support when giving oral directions or making connections across languages for ELs.

- Provide opportunities for repetition and rehearsal so the that the new information can be learned and mastered.

- Adjust rate of speech and complexity of language use according to the second language proficiency level of each student.

- Provide multiple opportunities for ELs to practice their second language and literacy skills. The additional practice can be provided in small groups or during cooperative learning settings that include fewer intimidating environments for second language learners to use their newly acquired skills.

- Consider pairing an EL with a more proficient English speaker. Therefore, the student is assured of listening to correct models of the second language.

- Provide extra time, as ELs require more time to process language during the early stages of second language development. They also require more time to formulate their responses.

- Build on ELs' prior knowledge and expand on it in a systematic and explicit manner.

- Provide excellent models of oral language. If an EL creates a simple sentence, then build on this and focus on adding new grammatical structures such as adjectives and adverbs.

- Introduce and practice new learning multiple times. New learning is also more effective when both content and language skills are addressed.

- Use text that includes familiar content. ELs respond best to such text and also understand text when they have opportunities to preview, review, paraphrase, and summarize the information.

When educators consider how they can incorporate language skills during literacy instruction, students can become more proficient speakers and readers. Reading aloud to students and having them retell information will expand the students' background knowledge, vocabulary, and oral language (August & Shanahan, 2006). Expanding this practice with a written summary can also extend the lesson and thus provide a comprehensive approach for listening, speaking, reading, and writing.

CONCLUSION

It is important for educators to understand first and second language development in order to better address the literacy needs of ELs. Incorporating language components such as phonology, semantics, syntax, and pragmatics within the instructional day and creating this as a routine can be beneficial for ELs' language and literacy development. Understanding how reading develops and considering the stages of literacy development during instruction is essential for providing more individualized and appropriate instruction for ELs. This chapter addressed first and second language skill development. Literacy stages have been addressed so teachers can better incorporate language skills with literacy skills. The chapters that follow explore in more depth the components for literacy instruction, including phonological awareness, phonics, fluency, vocabulary, reading comprehension, and writing. A comprehensive approach to language and literacy instruction is provided to the reader.

STUDY QUESTIONS

1. Why is it important to understand native language milestones?

2. What are variables that can affect second language acquisition?

3. A student that is learning English understands letters and sounds. What stage of reading development capabilities do those skills reflect?

4. How will oral language skills affect literacy skills among ELs?

5. What component of language is correlated with reading comprehension? What component of language is correlated with phonological awareness skills?

6. This student is able to read words correctly but primarily reads and understands solely from one point of view. He is at the _____ stage of reading development.

7. This student can read complex text with many layers of facts. She is at the _____ stage of reading development.

EXTENDED READING AND APPLICATION ACTIVITIES

1. Review the description of Krashen and Terrell's (1983) theory of second language acquisition from this chapter. Next, collect examples of students'

expressive language from a class that you work with or a student who you know. Finally, determine which stage of second language acquisition would best describe the majority of your students.

2. Review Dr. Jean Chall's (1983) stages of reading development in this chapter. Working with a single EL, determine the stage that describes his or her reading abilities. Next, determine the set of skills that are necessary for increasing the level of his or her reading abilities.

3. Discuss with a colleague why language development is necessary for literacy development.

4. Discuss students whom you currently work with or have worked with in the past; describe some of the challenges they face(d) for language and literacy development.

5. Review the list of strategies provided in this chapter. With a colleague, discuss how you could implement one or more of the strategies in a daily instructional routine.

REFERENCES

American Speech-Hearing-Language Association. (2019). *Language in brief.* Retrieved from https://www.asha.org/Practice-Portal/Clinical-Topics/Spoken-Language-Disorders/Language-In--Brief/

August, D., & Hakuta, K. (Eds.). (1997). *Improving schooling for language-minority children: A research agenda.* Washington, DC: National Academy Press.

August, D., & Shanahan, T. (2006). *Developing literacy in second-language learners: Report of the National Literacy Panel on Language-Minority Children and Youth.* Mahwah, NJ: Lawrence Erlbaum Associates.

Bloom, L., & Lahey, M. (1978). *Language development and language disorders.* New York, NY: Wiley.

Branum-Martin, L., Tao., S., Garnaat, S., Bunta., F., & Francis, D. J. (2012). Meta-analysis of bilingual phonological awareness: Language, age and psycholinguistic grain size. *Journal of Educational Psychology, 104,* 932–944.

Cárdenas-Hagan, E. (2010). Response to intervention: Implications for Spanish-speaking English language learners. *Perspectives in Language and Literacy, 36*(2), 24–29.

Chall, J. (1983). *Stages of reading development.* New York, NY: McGraw-Hill.

Crosson, A. C., & LeSaux, N. K. (2010). Revisiting assumption about the relationship between fluent reading to reading comprehension: Spanish-speakers text reading fluency in English. *Reading and Writing, an Interdisciplinary Journal, 23,* 435–494

Cummins, J. (1981). The role of primary language development in promoting educational success for language minority students. In California State Department of Education (Ed.), *Schooling and language minority students: A theoretical rationale* (pp. 3–49). Los Angeles: California State University.

Gopnik, A., Meltzoff, A. N., & Kuhl, P. K. (2000). *The scientist in the crib: What early learning tells us about the mind.* New York, NY: HarperCollins.

Hart, B., & Risley, T. (2003, Spring). *The early catastrophe; The 30 million word gap by age 3.* Washington, DC: American Federation of Teachers.

Krashen, S. D., & Terrell, T. D. (1983). *The natural approach: Language acquisition in the classroom.* Oxford, United Kingdom: Pergamon.

Marinova-Todd, S., Siegel, L. S., & Mazabel, S. (2013). *The association between morphological awareness and literacy in English language learners from diverse language backgrounds. Topics in Language Disorders, 33,* 93–107.

Nation, K., Clarke, P., Marshall, C., & Durand, M. (2004). Hidden language impairments in children: Parallels between poor reading comprehension and specific language impairment. *Journal of Speech, Language, and Hearing Research, 47,* 199–211.

National Institute of Child Health and Human Development. (2000). *Report of the National Literacy Panel reports of the subgroups. Teaching children to read: An evidence-based assessment of the scientific research literature on reading and its implications for reading instruction.* Washington, DC: Government Printing Office.

National Institute on Deafness and Other Communication Disorders. (2000). *Speech and language developmental milestones.* Retrieved from https://www.nidcd.nih.gov/sites/default/files/Documents/health/voice/NIDCD-Speech-Language-Dev-Milestones.pdf

Ramirez, G. (2017). Morphological awareness and second language learners. *Perspectives in Language and Literacy, 43*(2), 33–44.

Snow, C.E., Burns, S., & Griffen, P. (1998). Preventing reading difficulties in young children: Committee on the Prevention of Reading Difficulties in Young Children. Washington, DC: National Academy Press.

Van Kleeck, A. (1990). Emergent literacy: Learning about print before learning to read. *Topics in Language Disorders, 10*(2), 25–45.

3

Components of Literacy Instruction for English Learners

Eric Tridas

By completing this chapter, the reader will

- Learn about the National Literacy Panel report and the essential components of literacy instruction for native English speakers

- Understand the need for the research report on literacy development for English learners (ELs) and the key findings for effective literacy instruction

- Reflect on the special considerations necessary for designing effective literacy instruction

Marcos is an English learner (EL) who is in first grade. His kindergarten teacher expressed concern about Marcos' early literacy skills because he was having difficulty with phonological awareness, letter-to-sound knowledge, and vocabulary. The first-grade teacher believes Marcos needs to have the opportunity to listen to more books being read to him. She will provide this opportunity in the classroom and will send bilingual books home for his parents to read to him. The literacy coach who supports all first-grade teachers at the school has determined that students like Marcos need to understand how to read individual words and build fluency skills and vocabulary in order to increase reading comprehension. The coach will model this multidimensional approach for learning to read. It may be necessary to incorporate all recommendations because Marcos needs to establish the foundational skills for reading and he requires more vocabulary skills for comprehension.

INTRODUCTION

Literacy is a necessity and a foundational skill that all education systems have committed to teaching in schools. Yet, schools struggle with ensuring that every student attains high levels of literacy. According to the National Center for Education Statistics (NCES; 2017), fewer than 35% of U.S. students attain a high level of literacy. This pattern appears to have changed very little since 2000. In response to the need to improve literacy and determine the best strategies for teaching reading, the National Institute of Child Health and Human Development (NICHD) gathered a group of reading experts to review the existing research and create a report that would inform educators, parents, legislators, and consumers regarding the best evidence-based practices for reading instruction. This is known as the National Literacy Panel report (NICHD, 2000), and it took 2 years to develop. Since the year 2000, the report has been influential in local, national, state, and international reading reform efforts. In addition to the National Literacy Panel report, Drs. August and Shanahan (2006) coauthored a report for teaching literacy to language-minority children and youth, which explored the special considerations for literacy instruction among this diverse population of students.

This chapter explores the effective literacy practices for native English speakers and ELs by describing the findings from these two national research reports. Each component of the findings is introduced and described in this chapter. The subsequent chapters of this book address each of the key components of literacy and recommendations for instruction. It is important for every teacher to understand the key components of literacy instruction for ELs because the number of ELs attending public schools continues to increase and an achievement gap exists between this population of students and native English speakers (NCES, 2017).

NATIONAL READING PANEL REPORT

In 1997, Congress passed legislation to form a National Reading Panel to review the existing research on reading and determine the effectiveness of different approaches used to teach children to read (NICHD, 2000). The panel convened in 1998 and was comprised of 14 experts who met over the course of 2 years. During this time, the National Reading Panel held five public hearings and received feedback from parents, teachers, administrators, and community leaders on topics to explore. The panel initially explored the topics of phonemic awareness, phonics, oral reading fluency, vocabulary, encouraging children to read, reading comprehension, teacher preparation, computer technology, and reading instruction. After a careful review, the panel decided to focus on five areas of kindergarten through 12th-grade reading that had a significant body of evidence.

1. Phonemic awareness

2. Phonics

3. Oral reading fluency

4. Vocabulary

5. Reading comprehension

Although the skills were listed in this order, the panel did not state that instruction should occur in a sequence. The panel did elaborate on the definition of each of the topics and described the findings for each component. The following sections describe each of these key topics and highlight examples for each component. Subsequent chapters in this book describe in detail each of the key components of literacy and the implications for evidence-based practices in the classroom.

Phonemic Awareness

The National Reading Panel defined *phonemic awareness* as the ability to focus on and manipulate the phonemes (sounds) within words. A *phoneme* is the smallest unit of sound in a language and therefore each word consists of phonemes. The National Reading Panel identified the following skills that make up phonemic awareness:

- *Phoneme isolation* is the ability to identify a sound within a word. For example, the first sound in the word *man* is /m/.

- *Phoneme identity* requires the individual to recognize the common sound in various words. For example, the common sound in the words *lock, loom,* and *lift* is the sound /l/.

- *Phoneme categorization* is the ability to recognize the word with the odd sound in a sequence of three or four words. For example, given the words *do, dinner,* and *run,* the word with the odd sequence is *run.*

- *Phoneme blending* is the ability to blend individual sounds and form words. For example, when provided with the sounds /f/ /a/ /n/, the student can blend them together and form the word *fan.*

The results of the report indicate that phonemic awareness can be taught and is effective in a variety of teaching conditions and with a variety of learners (NICHD, 2000). In other words, phonemic awareness is an essential skill for literacy among children who are typically developing readers, children who are at risk for future reading abilities, and children who experience reading disabilities. Teaching phonemic awareness improves students' word reading abilities and has a positive influence on reading comprehension. Chapter 4 includes detailed information on phonemic awareness and provides examples for cross-linguistic transfer among ELs.

Phonics

Systematic phonics instruction involves explicit instruction on a set of pre-specified associations between letters and sounds; children are taught how to use those sounds and letters to read, typically in texts containing controlled vocabulary (NICHD, 2000). The National Reading Panel found that phonics instruction should take a systematic approach and occur in kindergarten and first grade to be most effective (NICHD, 2000; see Box 3.1).

BOX 3.1. Systematic Instruction Teaches a Definite, Structured Method for a Procedure Carried Out by a Step-by-Step Process (Hougen & Smartt, 2012)

To be effective, systematic phonics instruction introduced in kindergarten must be appropriately designed for learners and must begin with foundational knowledge involving letters and phonemic awareness. Phonics instruction is also effective for younger children at risk for reading problems and those with poor reading performance in the early grades. Findings of the National Literacy Panel report's meta-analysis conclude that systematic phonics instruction produces gains in reading and spelling not only in the early grades (kindergarten and first grade) but also in the later grades (second through sixth grades) and among children having difficulty learning to read. Phonics instruction is discussed further in Chapter 5 of this book. Chapter 5 describes sound and symbol correlations within English and other languages and how instructors can design more efficient phonics lessons among ELs. Lesson procedures and examples are also included in Chapter 5.

Oral Reading Fluency

Fluent readers can read text with speed, accuracy, and proper expression (NICHD, 2000). Fluency depends on an individual's ability to recognize and read words, as well as his or her ability to read with a rate and expression that is similar to his or her oral expression. The National Reading Panel reviewed instructional approaches to fluency development that emphasized repeated oral reading practice or guided repeated oral reading practice. These practices deal with repetition and feedback during oral reading of a specific passage or article. The guided oral reading practice had a moderate impact on reading achievement. The repeated oral reading procedures had a clear impact on the reading ability of readers without reading impairments through at least fourth grade, as well as on students with various kinds of reading difficulties throughout high school. All approaches were associated with positive reading outcomes. These fluency practices were found to be more effective than having students read silently to themselves without feedback or guidance. Chapter 6 describes research on fluency and the effective practices to consider when instructing ELs.

Vocabulary

Word knowledge is an important skill for reading comprehension (NICHD, 2000). The National Reading Panel concluded that vocabulary knowledge is correlated with reading comprehension. Notably, ELs' vocabulary skills lag behind their English-speaking peers' skills. The National Literacy Panel's meta-analysis describes the following results.

- Computer vocabulary instruction shows positive learning gains over traditional vocabulary instruction.

- Vocabulary instruction leads to gains in comprehension. Vocabulary can be learned incidentally in the context of storybook reading or from listening to others read.

- Repeated exposure to vocabulary items is important for learning gains. The best gains were made in instruction that extended beyond single class periods and involved multiple exposures in authentic contexts beyond the classroom.

- Preinstruction of vocabulary words prior to reading can facilitate vocabulary acquisition and comprehension.

- The restructuring of the text materials or procedures facilitates vocabulary acquisition and comprehension (e.g., substituting easy words for hard words).

These findings have many implications for effective reading instruction. The National Literacy Panel suggests the following as implications for practice.

- There is a need for direct instruction of vocabulary items required for a specific text.
- Repetition and multiple exposure to vocabulary items are important. Students should be given items that will be likely to appear in many contexts.
- Learning in rich contexts is valuable for vocabulary learning. Vocabulary words should be those that the learner will find useful in many contexts. When vocabulary items are derived from content learning materials, the learner will be better equipped to deal with specific reading matter in content areas.
- Vocabulary tasks should be restructured as necessary. It is important to be certain that students fully understand what is asked of them in the context of reading, rather than focusing only on the words to be learned. Restructuring seems to be most effective for students who are low achieving or at risk.
- Vocabulary learning is effective when it entails active engagement in learning tasks.
- Computer technology can be used effectively to help teach vocabulary.
- Vocabulary can be acquired through incidental learning. Much of a student's vocabulary will have to be learned in the course of doing things other than explicit vocabulary learning. Repetition, richness of context, and motivation may also add to the efficacy of incidental learning of vocabulary.
- Dependence on a single vocabulary instruction method will not result in optimal learning. A variety of methods can be used effectively that emphasize multimedia aspects of learning, richness of context in which words are to be learned, and the number of exposures to words that learners require for mastery.

Chapter 8 of this book provides research on vocabulary development among ELs and recommendations for instruction.

Comprehension

Comprehension is a multidimensional and complex process. Harris and Hodges (1995) defined *reading comprehension* as the construction of the meaning of a written text through a reciprocal interchange of ideas between the reader and the message in a text. A reader can read a text to learn, find out information, or be entertained. These various purposes of understanding text can be enhanced when the reader uses prior knowledge or experiences and subsequently makes connections for deeper meaning.

The National Reading Panel analyzed 203 studies on instruction of text comprehension and ultimately identified eight effective, evidence-based procedures for improving reading comprehension. The eight types of instruction that appear to be effective and most promising for classroom instruction are as follows:

1. Comprehension monitoring, in which the reader learns how to be aware or conscious of his or her understanding during reading and learns procedures to deal with problems in understanding as they arise

2. Cooperative learning, in which readers work together to learn strategies in the context of reading

3. Graphic and semantic organizers that allow the reader to represent graphically (write or draw) the meanings and relationships of the ideas that underlie the words in the text

4. Story structure, from which the reader learns to ask and answer "who," "what," "where," "when," and "why" questions about the plot and, in some cases, maps out the time line, characters, and events in stories

5. Question answering, in which the reader answers questions posed by the teacher and is given feedback on the correctness

6. Question generation, in which the reader asks him- or herself "what," "when," "where," "why," "what will happen," "how," and "who" questions

7. Summarization, in which the reader attempts to identify and write the main or most important ideas that integrate or unite the other ideas or meanings of the text into a coherent whole

8. Multiple strategy teaching, in which the reader uses several of the procedures in interaction with the teacher over the text; it is effective when the procedures are used flexibly and appropriately by the reader or the teacher in naturalistic contexts

The panel recommended that teachers learn to teach students to use comprehension strategies in natural learning situations. That is, as students are reading, teachers can model and guide students to use a combination of strategies to enhance comprehension. This active engagement of reading will lead to increased comprehension of the text. Finally, the review of the research indicated that more studies are necessary to explore comprehension strategies for various text structures with diverse populations, including those who are ELs and exhibit learning disabilities. Chapter 8 describes comprehension further.

THE NATIONAL LITERACY PANEL REPORT FOR LANGUAGE-MINORITY CHILDREN AND YOUTH

The National Literacy Panel report did not include language-minority children in the reviews for reading research. Language-minority children are those whose first language is not the same language spoken in the school. Because the number of children who speak another native language continues to increase in U.S. schools, it became clear that more research and synthesis was needed about evidence-based practices that are effective for ELs. Therefore, in 2001, the Institute of Education Sciences awarded a contract to SRI International and the Center for Applied Linguistics to convene a National Literacy Panel for Language-Minority Children and Youth. The panel was composed of 14 expert researchers from the fields of reading, language, bilingualism, research methods, and education. They were charged with conducting a comprehensive, evidence-based review of the research literature on the development of literacy among language-minority children and youth. The panel produced a report evaluating and synthesizing more than 2,000 studies to guide educational practice and inform educational policy. They also held two public outreach meetings to gather input regarding important topics from the education community and others interested in literacy development among language-minority children. The review of studies focused on students in preschool through 12th grade.

The panel focused on identifying the differences and similarities in the development of literacy between language-minority and native speakers, understanding the relationship between second language oral proficiency and second language literacy, and discovering the influence of social and cultural factors on literacy attainment of language-minority learners. The major findings are listed next.

- ELs benefit from reading instruction that includes phonemic awareness, phonics, fluency, vocabulary, and text comprehension. Adjustments are necessary, however. One of the major adjustments includes a focus on oral language proficiency, which is often overlooked during instruction.

- Oral language proficiency and literacy in the first language can facilitate the development of English literacy. Therefore, instruction must incorporate the opportunities for using the second language while also learning the structure of the second language for literacy development.

- Individual differences contribute significantly to English literacy development. In other words, some of the individual differences can include one's oral language proficiency, age, previous learning opportunities, cognition, and the similarities and differences between the first language and English.

- Adequate assessments are necessary to determine the ELs' strengths and weaknesses. This is necessary for designing instruction that will meet the needs of the individual student.

- There is limited evidence about the effectiveness of teacher judgment in identifying language-minority students who require intensive reading instruction. Teacher judgment, however, might be more reliable when teachers can respond to specific criteria. Additional research is needed in the areas of assessment and teacher judgment.

- Home language experiences can have a positive impact on literacy achievement. Activities such as reading to a child, singing songs, rhyming, and learning the alphabet can positively affect literacy

- There is little evidence for the correlation between sociocultural factors and student literacy outcomes. Sociocultural factors include immigration status; parent and family influences; district, state, and federal policies; and language status or prestige. It is plausible that there are sociocultural factors that relate to student literacy achievement; however, there is not a body of research that provides empirical support.

The National Literacy Panel on Language-Minority Children and Youth also explored bilingual instruction with English-only instruction. A review of the results indicate that language-minority students instructed in their native language as well as in English perform better on average on measures of English reading proficiency than language-minority students instructed only in English. This was described at the elementary and secondary levels.

The panel also reported that similar proportions of language-minority students and monolingual English speakers are classified as "poor readers." The profiles of poor readers are very similar in that both exhibited difficulties in phonological awareness and working memory. The language-minority children also exhibited reduced English oral language proficiency. Yet, studies reveal that some language-minority students classified as having learning disabilities can achieve grade-level norms when given proper instruction.

The research on the development of English literacy strongly suggests that adequate assessments are necessary for measuring the strengths and weaknesses of language-minority students. Once again, the panel reported that assessments were inadequate to describe the individual needs in most cases.

Reading is a complex process. Learning to read in a second language is also challenging. The National Literacy Panel on Language-Minority Children and Youth systematically examined the research on acquiring literacy in a second language. Recommendations include incorporating foundational skills such as phonemic awareness, phonics, and fluency while developing fluency, vocabulary, and comprehension skills. Special considerations for literacy instruction among ELs include incorporating first language and literacy knowledge and opportunities to further develop oral language, which will contribute positively to reading skills. The subsequent chapters of this book describe in detail the essential components of literacy for ELs and the necessary adjustments to instruction that will ensure their success.

BOX 3.2.   Reflect on the Opening Vignette

Think back to Marcos, the first-grade student from the opening vignette whose teacher wanted him to listen to more books to help him become a better reader. The literacy coach recommended that Marcos learn how to read individual words and build fluency skills and vocabulary in order to increase reading comprehension. Now that you have read the chapter, consider

- Who is more accurate in the process for teaching reading? Are both professionals correct? Why or why not?

- What resources can guide educators to make decisions regarding the best reading methodology?

CONCLUSION

This chapter discussed the major reviews for reading research among monolingual and second language learners and highlighted the key components of literacy that those reviews found. The key components of literacy instruction include phonemic awareness, phonics, fluency, vocabulary, and comprehension (see Table 3.1).

The same five components of literacy instruction that are important for monolingual English speakers are essential for second language learners, with some slight adjustments. Those adjustments include working with developing phonological awareness skills in the second language with an added focus on the sounds that are unfamiliar to the students. Using cross-connections when possible to enhance comprehension of the literacy concepts is also an evidence-based practice. The use of native language for the development of second language vocabulary skills is also recommended. Examples include understanding cognates and word parts that are similar across languages and can assist with vocabulary development, which may also positively affect comprehension skills. It is important for educa-

Table 3.1.   The five components of literacy instruction

Component	Definition
Phonemic awareness	The ability to focus on and manipulate the phonemes (sounds) within words
Phonics	The understanding that there is a predictable relationship between the sounds of spoken language and the letters that represent those sounds in writing
Fluency	The ability to read text with speed, accuracy, and proper expression
Vocabulary	Knowledge about the meaning and pronunciation of words
Comprehension	The ability to construct the meaning of a written text through a reciprocal interchange of ideas between the reader and the message in a text

tors to understand the oral language proficiency levels of ELs and incorporate language opportunities during instruction. Assessments may not provide all the variables affecting an EL's performance, but samples of the student's work and close observation and progress monitoring can help guide instruction.

Each of the five components of literacy and how to provide instruction on each for ELs is explained and explored in Section II.

◇◇

STUDY QUESTIONS

1. What are the five key components for effective literacy instruction as described by the National Literacy Panel report?

2. What are some special considerations necessary for literacy instruction among ELs?

3. Describe some direct and indirect methods for vocabulary instruction from the section on vocabulary instruction methods included in this chapter.

4. Describe eight evidence-based reading comprehension strategies and how instructors can use these strategies among ELs.

5. Describe why oral language proficiency is necessary for reading instruction among ELs.

◇◇

EXTENDED READING AND APPLICATION ACTIVITIES

1. Read the *Teaching Academic Vocabulary and Content Knowledge to English Learners in the Upper Elementary and Middle School Years* practice guide provided by the Institute for Education Sciences, which can be downloaded from https://ies.ed.gov/ncee/wwc/PracticeGuide/19. Create a lesson plan for ELs in your classroom that incorporates the key recommendations from the practice guide for vocabulary and content knowledge.

2. Read *Effective Literacy and English Language Instruction for English Learners in the Elementary Grades,* which can be downloaded from https://ies.ed.gov/ncee/wwc/PracticeGuide/6. Create a lesson plan for ELs in your classroom who are struggling with the foundational skills for literacy and incorporate the key recommendations from this practice guide.

REFERENCES

August, D., & Shanahan, T. (Eds.). (2006). *Developing literacy in second-language learners: Report of the National Literacy Panel on Language-Minority Children and Youth.* Mahwah, NJ: Lawrence Erlbaum Associates.

August, D., & Shanahan, T. (Eds.). (2008). *Developing reading and writing in second-language learners: Lessons from the report of the National Literacy Panel on Language-Minority Children and Youth*. New York, NY: Routledge.

Harris, T. L., & Hodges, R. E. (1995). *The literacy dictionary: The vocabulary of reading and writing*. Newark, DE: International Reading Association.

Hougen, M. C., & Smartt, S. M. (2012). *The fundamentals of literacy instruction and assessment, Pre-K–6*. Baltimore, MD: Paul H. Brookes Publishing Co.

National Center for Education Statistics. (2017). *English language learners in public schools: The condition of education*. Retrieved from https://nces.ed.gov/programs/coe/indicator_cgf.asp

National Institute of Child Health and Human Development. (2000). *Report of the National Reading Panel: Teaching children to read*. Washington, DC: U.S. Government Printing Office.

II

The Components of Literacy and English Learners

4

Phonological Awareness Development Among English Learners

Virginia Lovelace-Gonzalez

By completing this chapter, the reader will

- Learn the components of phonological awareness and how phonological awareness develops among speakers of other native languages

- Understand the research on cross-linguistic transfer of phonological awareness

- Be able to identify and use strategies for improving phonological awareness skills among English learners (ELs)

Josefina is a first-grade student who is learning English. Her mother has informed the school that Josefina is able to read in her native language of Spanish. Students in the first-grade classroom are learning to read and are mastering foundational skills such as phonological awareness. Josefina's teacher will need to determine Josefina's knowledge of phonological awareness and her preparedness for reading in English. The teacher wants to know which English sounds are challenging for Josefina. She will instruct Josefina in a manner whereby Josefina understands how beneficial her native language sound knowledge is for learning to read in English. The teacher will also monitor Josefina's progress.

INTRODUCTION

Students like Josefina come to school with language and literacy skills in their native language; their teachers are tasked with determining what those skills are and how they will transfer to English. Josefina's teacher is particularly interested in her new student's phonological awareness skills because they will have a key impact on other areas of language and literacy development.

Phonology refers to the system of rules that determine how sounds exist and combine in a language (Cárdenas-Hagan, 2018). *Phonological awareness* refers to one's understanding of the sound structure of oral language, such as syllables, onset-rimes, and phonemes. *Phonemes* are the smallest unit of sound in a given language that can be recognized as being distinct from other sounds. Processing and understanding the sounds of a language is a necessary skill for reading in all alphabetic languages (Cárdenas-Hagan & Carlson, 2009). Research has demonstrated that phonological awareness will transfer from one's first language to one's second language (Durgunoğlu, 2002; Shakkour, 2014). It is therefore necessary for educators to understand the similarities and differences of the sound structure across languages in order to incorporate the similarities during instruction and thus increase an English learner's (EL's) phonological awareness.

PHONOLOGICAL AWARENESS

Phonological processing is one's ability to perceive and use the sound structures of words. Every word spoken is processed phonologically. The components of phonological processing include phonological awareness, which is demonstrated by one's understanding of rhyming, alliteration, syllables, and phonemic awareness (Paulson, 2018). Two additional components of phonological processing include phonological memory and phonological naming. These three components are important foundations of literacy acquisition (Paulson, 2018) and are summarized in Figure 4.1.

Of these three components of phonological processing, phonological awareness is the most strongly related to literacy development (Paulson, 2018). The skills of rhyming, alliteration, syllabication, and phonemic awareness can be taught and are discussed in detail next.

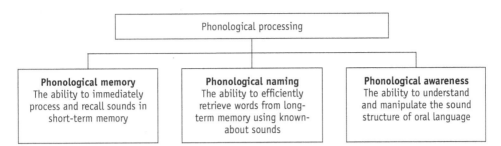

Figure 4.1. The components of phonological processing. (Adapted from Paulson, L. H. [2018]. Teaching phonemic awareness. In J. R. Birsh & S. Carreker [Eds.], *Multisensory teaching of basic language skills* [4th ed., p. 207]. Baltimore, MD: Paul H. Brookes Publishing Co.)

Components of Phonological Awareness and the Linguistic Hierarchy

Phonological awareness is an oral language skill. A student does not have to have any knowledge of letters to demonstrate the developmental components of phonological awareness, which include rhyming, onset-rime, alliteration, syllables, and phoneme awareness.

Rhyming   One of the early signs of emerging sensitivity to this linguistic hierarchy of phonological awareness is the ability to play rhyming games and activities (Paulson, 2018). Researchers have found that early knowledge of nursery rhymes was strongly related to the development of phonological skills as well as emergent reading abilities (Adams, 1990). Examples of nursery rhymes in English for young children might include "Three Blind Mice," "Hey Diddle Diddle," and "The Itsy-Bitsy Spider."

Onset-Rime   Students who can hear rhymes can also recognize the onset, which is the initial phoneme before the vowel. The onset is exchanged for another phoneme in rhyming words. The word *rime* is a linguistic term for the spoken vowel and final consonant(s) (Adams, 1990). Examples of recognizing the onset and rimes in English are as follows:

Onset	Rime
/m/	/an/
/f/	/an/
/p/	/an/
/r/	/an/
/v/	/an/

Alliteration   Alliteration involves matching spoken words with similar onsets, such as *dog, doll,* and *dig.* This requires not only sensitivity to similarities and differences in the overall sounds of words, but also the ability to focus attention on the individual sounds that make words similar or different (Adams, 1990). This skill can also include identifying the common initial sound in an alliteration at the level of a sentence (e.g., *Mary makes marvelous muffins. Sammy saw seven sailors swimming*).

Syllables   Syllable awareness requires the student to build an under-standing that words can be segmented into smaller units. Individual syllables are distinctly marked in the speech stream. Every syllable contains a vowel sound, and these vowel sounds correspond to loudness, providing the speaker cues by which to distinguish one spoken syllable from the next (Adams, 1990). Another cue for identifying syllables for the speaker is the opening and closing of the jaw. Activities for syllable awareness can include having students identify how many syllables exist within a word, blending syllables together to form words, deleting syllables within words, and segmenting words into syllables. For instance, a teacher could use the following scripts for activities on syllable identification and syllable blending:

Syllable identification: *Say* hungry. *How many times did you open your mouth? How many vowel sounds? How many syllables?*

Syllable blending: *Say /ba/ /gel/. The word is* _____. (bagel)

Say toothache. *Now say* toothache *without /ache/. The word is* _____. (tooth)

Phonemes   A *phoneme* is the smallest unit of sound that can change the meaning of a word. Adams (1990) described phoneme awareness as the ability to delete and exchange a unit of sound within words. A student's ability to process and manipulate a phoneme predicts future reading abilities. Tasks at this level are blending individual sounds together to form a word or segmenting a word into its individual sounds (Paulson, 2018). Phoneme identification, phoneme blending, phoneme deletion, phoneme manipulation, and phoneme segmentation are considered tasks that fall under the category of phoneme awareness. Example activity prompts for each of these concepts follow:

Phoneme identification: *Say* man. *Tell me the first sound in* man. (/m/ an)

Phoneme blending: *Say /m/ /e/ /s/. The word is* _____. (mess)

Phoneme deletion: *Say* globe. *Now say* globe *without the /g/ sound.* (lobe)

Phoneme manipulation: *Say* met. *Now change /m/ to /b/. The word is* ____. (bet)

Phoneme segmentation: *Say* run. *Tell me the sounds in the word* run. (/r/ /u/ /n/)

PHONOLOGICAL AWARENESS AND ENGLISH LEARNERS

People possess the ability to learn to communicate and read in multiple lan-guages. Reading in two languages is possible when students' strengths and knowledge base are considered (Cárdenas-Hagan, 2018). Furthermore, studies connecting English to other languages in bilingual student education show that a student's phonological awareness can be transferred, by some extent, to another learned language. According to Peregoy and Boyle (2000), "At a more specific level, transfer of literacy ability from one language to another depends on the similarities and differences between their writing systems, including the unit of speech symbolized by each character" (p. 241).

Although the research on bilingual phonological development is limited, several theories suggest how phonological skills develop in bilingual children. One of several theories is the unified competition theory, which suggests that children are sensitive to common phonological characteristics across languages. This sensitivity results in how bilingual children use knowledge and skills in one language for more accurate productions in the other language; bilingual children transfer knowledge from their native language to their second language. In such situations, both positive and negative transfer might occur in the phonological skills of bilingual phonological development (MacWhinney, 2005). Positive transfer is when knowledge of the native language benefits progression in the second language. Negative transfer is when knowledge of the native language results in errors in the second language. Positive transfer results when phonological development emerges at a more rapid rate in bilingual children than in monolinguals.

Fabiano-Smith and Goldstein (2010) examined the phonological skills of 24 children, including eight monolingual Spanish speakers, eight monolingual English speakers, and eight bilingual Spanish-English speakers. Results of this study demonstrated that bilingual children exhibited a similar rate of phonological acquisition compared with monolingual children. Evidence for negative transfer appears when phonological development emerges at a slower rate in bilingual children than in monolingual children. One characteristic of negative transfer is interference, such as consonants and vowels that are not shared by both languages but are used in the other languages. In addition, Spanish-English speaking children are likely to show evidence of both Spanish-influenced English and English-influenced Spanish. Common errors in Spanish-influenced English include the following:

- Deletion of final consonants, such as /b/ and /v/

- The trilled sound of /rr/ for the English /r/ sound

- The long /e/ sound for the short /i/ vowel sound

- The substitution of /s/ for /z/ because /z/ does not exist in Spanish

- The addition of the short vowel sound /e/ for initial s blends because they do not exist in Spanish

- May substitute the /y/ sound for /j/ because /j/ does not exist in Spanish

Goldstein and Gildersleeve-Neumann (2012) demonstrated that bilingual phonological acquisition is both similar to and different from acquisition in monolingual speakers. Educators should keep in mind the benefits of phonological skills transferring between language while ensuring that their instruction is differentiated enough to address the needs of ELs who may be struggling with negative transfer. The following sections expand on connections of phonological awareness across languages and how this should affect instruction.

CONNECTIONS ACROSS LANGUAGES: UNDERSTANDING THE SIMILARITIES AND DIFFERENCES IN SOUNDS

Learning to read in two languages can be facilitated by incorporating similar and different skills from one language to the next. Teachers can facilitate English language literacy development by providing instruction that builds on native language and literacy knowledge. This knowledge provides a mechanism for making data-informed instructional decisions for meeting the specific needs of ELs (Cárdenas-Hagan, 2018). Connections across languages are provided in the following subsections.

Spanish to English

Spanish is the most common language spoken among ELs in the United States (McFarland et al., 2017). Spanish and English are both alphabetic languages whereby sounds are represented by an alphabetic symbol. The Spanish language consists of 23 phonemes (Cárdenas-Hagan, 2018), and sounds are categorized as vowels or consonants. Spanish consists of five vowels and 18 consonant sounds, including variations in Castilian Spanish /th/, /zh/, and /v/. The English language consists of 44 sounds. These sounds are represented by 26 letters or letter combinations. Many sounds in Spanish and English directly transfer from one language to another. Sounds can be described by the place in the mouth where they are produced, by the voicing or activity of the vocal chords, and by the manner in which they are articulated. The voicing and manner of sounds can be directly related in English and Spanish. These common phonemes facilitate the acquisition of phonology in the two languages. Although Spanish and English have some sounds in common, the orthographic representation of some of the sounds may differ. For example, the /h/ is spelled with the letter *h* in English but with the letters *j* or *g* (before *e* or *i*) in Spanish. Spanish vowels can combine to form diphthongs. Diphthong spellings such as *oy* and *au* directly transfer to the English language (see Table 4.1)

The structure of the Spanish language consists of common syllable patterns. Some of the most common syllable patterns in Spanish are also

Table 4.1. Spanish-to-English diphthong correlations

Spanish	English
ai (*bailarina*)	i (*light, like*)
au (*autobús*)	ou (*out*)
ey (*rey*)	ey (*they*)
ei (*peine*)	a (*pay*)
oi, oy (*oigan, voy*)	oi, oy (*oil, joy*)
ia (*media*)	ya (*yarn*)
ua (*cuando*)	wa (*wand*)
ie (*hielo*)	ye (*yet*)
ue (*cuete*)	we (*went*)
io (*radio*)	yo (*yoke*)
uo (*cuota*)	uo (*quote*)
iu (*ciudad*)	yu (*yule*)
ui (*cuidar*)	we (*week*)

Reprinted from Cárdenas-Hagan, E. (2018). Language and literacy development among English language learners. In J. R. Birsh & S. Carreker (Eds.), *Multisensory teaching of basic language skills* (4th ed., p. 733). Baltimore, MD: Paul H. Brookes Publishing Co.

common syllable patterns in English. The Spanish consonant-vowel (CV) pattern is a basic syllable pattern and can be combined to form consonant-vowel/consonant-vowel (CV/CV) words, such as *mala, sala, masa,* and *pasa.*

Another common pattern is vowel-consonant-vowel (VCV). Spanish words such as *uno, oso,* and *ala* represent this syllable pattern. The word is divided after the first vowel. The English language is also comprised of the VCV syllable pattern in words such as *pilot, token, visit,* and *exit.* In these words, the syllable is divided after the first vowel. This makes the English vowel sound long. Both Spanish and English have the VC/CV pattern in words such as *lista, isla, esta, hasta,* and *norte* in Spanish and in the words *listen, hasten,* and *number* in English. In Spanish, the consonant-vowel-consonant (CVC) syllable pattern is present in words such as *mes, dos, las, son,* and *luz* but is not as common as in English words. In English words, this pattern makes the vowel sound short.

Although open and closed syllables are present in both languages, the EL will need to learn the vowel sound changes in these syllables. Vowel sounds are regular and do not change in Spanish. Vowel sounds do change in English. The English language also includes vowel-pair, vowel-*r*, vowel-consonant-*e*, and final stable syllables. Spanish-speaking children will have difficulty with the vowel-consonant-*e* syllable pattern because they will tend to produce the final *e*. The pattern of a vowel and the letter *r* exists in Spanish, but it is not taught in this manner because the vowel sounds are regular and do not change. Knowing the English syllable types and the similarities and differences between the two languages will assist ELs to read (Cárdenas-Hagan, 2018; see Table 4.2).

Table 4.2.   Spanish-to-English syllable types

English syllable type	Spanish syllable type
Closed syllable *tĕn*	Closed syllable-Vowel sounds do not change *tĕn*
Open syllable *no*	Open syllable-Vowel sounds do not change *no*
Vowel-consonant-*e* *base*	Vowel-consonant-*e* (*e* is pronounced) in Spanish *base*
Vowel-*r* syllable *arc*	Vowel-*r* syllable *arco*
Vowel pair syllable *automobile*	Vowel pair syllable *automóvil*
Final stable syllable *emotion*	Final stable syllable *emoción*

Reprinted from Cárdenas-Hagan, E. (2018). Language and literacy development among English language learners. In J. R. Birsh & S. Carreker (Eds.), *Multisensory teaching of basic language skills* (4th ed., p. 726). Baltimore, MD: Paul H. Brookes Publishing Co.

Arabic to English

The Arabic alphabet has 28 letters that represent the consonants and long vowels. The short vowels are not written but may be specified by additional marks above or below the letters. Written text is horizontal, from right to left on the page, but numerals are written from left to right. The letters within words are joined in a cursive style with the letter before, although a few letters may not be joined with the letter that follows. Letters take a distinctive shape depending on whether they stand alone, start a word, end a word, or connect to other letters within a word. Standard Arabic has 28 consonants and six vowels. There are two standard diphthongs in the Arabic language. All consonants can be used at the beginning, middle, and end of words, with some restrictions governing combinations of consonants within syllables. There are six syllable types, and syllables cannot begin with vowels. CV is the most common syllable, in which C can be any consonant and the V can be any short vowel. The CVV syllable is essentially the same as the CV but includes the long vowels. The CVC syllable pattern is also common and has no restrictions on its consonants. CVVC, CVCC, and CVVCC are somewhat less common or more restricted for location in words.

Vietnamese to English

The Vietnamese alphabet consists of 24 consonants and 11 vowels and is phonemic (i.e., one letter or a specific combination of letters corresponds to one phoneme). The Vietnamese language does not consist of consonant clusters. Consonants may be combined with the sound /w/, but this is the only multiconsonant combination. Common syllable patterns include V, VV, CV, CVV, CVC, CVVC, VC, and VVC. Additional syllable patterns that include /w/ are wV, wVV, wVC, wVVC, CwV, CwVV, CwVC, and CwVVC.

Chinese to English

Cantonese is a dialect of Chinese and consists of 19 consonants, 11 vowels (long and short), and 11 diphthongs. There are six possible syllable structures in Cantonese, including V, C, CV, VC, CVV, and CVC. The existence of tones within the syllable is a major characteristic of Cantonese syllables. Each syllable carries a tone, and syllables are nearly equally stressed. Each syllable usually has a corresponding standard Chinese character. Written Chinese is nonalphabetic and consists of characters that represent lexical morphemes. Chinese words are formed by one or more characters.

PRINCIPLES OF EFFECTIVE PHONOLOGICAL AWARENESS INSTRUCTION FOR ENGLISH LEARNERS

Phonological awareness skills can transfer across languages when students have opportunities to build these skills in their native language and English. The first activity under the category of phonological awareness should be rhyming in the native language and English. Making connections with words that are similar in sound patterns can be helpful. The following sections include alliteration and syllable-level activities as well as phonemic activities (Cárdenas-Hagan, 2018).

For ELs, phonemic activities in English can be complicated by having to recognize sounds in English that do not exist in their native language. Instructionally, it is important for teachers to determine some of the similarities and differences between English and the student's native language to ensure the opportunity to learn. Brown and Ortiz (2014) stated,

> Although precise pronunciation of phonemes is dependent on the age at which they are first heard, acquisition of the sounds of language is not a function of age. For all students, explicit instruction in phonemic awareness is critical and even students at the beginning stages of language acquisition can successfully acquire phonemic awareness skills without much difficulty. Thus, English proficiency is not a necessary precursor to phonemic awareness instruction (Durgunoğlu, Nagy, & Hancin-Bhatt, 1999; Geva, 2006) although the vocabulary used in phonemic activities must also be expressly taught to students. (p. 283)

It is also helpful for ELs to have knowledge of the English vocabulary within which they are to understand phonemes or use preteaching to ensure familiarity prior to the lesson (Brown & Ortiz, 2014).

The National Literacy Panel on Language-Minority Children and Youth found that although ELs need to learn the same five critical areas of reading (i.e., phonological awareness, letter knowledge, phonics, vocabulary, reading fluency, reading comprehension) as English-only students, instruction needs to be adjusted to the EL's proficiency level in the instructional language and his or her cultural knowledge (August & Shanahan, 2006, cited in Brown & Ortiz, 2014). The PLUSS model proposes a systematic enhancement of instructional and intervention programs that specifically address ELs' linguistic, cultural, and experiential needs with a response to intervention framework (Sanford, Brown, & Turner, 2012). The model components

---

BOX 4.1. Sample Teacher Script for Phoneme Segmentation Lesson With Target Sound /th/

Students, today we will learn a new sound in English, /th/.

Say the word *thumb*.

Tell me the sounds of the word *thumb*. (/th/ /u/ /m/)

Look at my thumb. Show me your thumb.

How do you say this word in your home language? Now say it in English. Good job.

The next word is *three*. Tell me the sounds of the word *three*. (/th/ /r/ /e/)

Look as I show you my three fingers. Now you show me three fingers. Very good.

---

include preteaching critical vocabulary, language modeling and opportunities for using academic language, and using visuals and graphic organizers, systematic and explicit instruction, and strategic use of native language and teaching. This model can adapted to English phonological awareness activities.

Features of Lesson

Review Box 4.1. In this activity, students are being introduced to the /th/ sound, which is a new sound for Spanish-speaking ELs. As demonstrated in this example, key features of an effective phonological awareness lesson for ELs are as follows:

- Students are provided with a phoneme awareness task that also addresses a new sound of the English language.

- Students are provided with a model of the word and multiple opportunities to say the word.

- Students are provided with an explicit example of the vocabulary for each word.

- Students are provided with the strategic use of the native language by thinking about the word in the home language.

STRATEGIES FOR TEACHING PHONOLOGICAL AWARENESS TO ENGLISH LEARNERS

The remainder of this chapter discusses instruction of skills and concepts for teaching phonological awareness to ELs. The sections that follow offer

Table 4.3.   Example activity for practicing sound manipulation with Spanish-speaking English learners

Teacher	Students	Teacher	Students	Teacher
(Digan = Say)		(¿Riman? = Do they rhyme?)		Cambiamos . . .por . . . = We change . . . for . . .)
Digan *mía tía*.	mía tía	¿Riman?	Sí	Cambiamos /m/ por /t/.
Digan *sol gol*.	sol gol	¿Riman?	Sí	Cambiamos /s/ por /g/.
Digan *las mas*.	las mas	¿Riman?	Sí	Cambiamos /l/ por /m/.
Digan *sí no*.	sí no	¿Riman?	No	Cambiamos todos los sonidos. (We change all of the sounds.)
Digan *luna cuna*.	luna,cuna	¿Riman?	Sí	Cambiamos /l/ por /k/.

From Cárdenas-Hagan, E. (2018). Language and literacy development among English language learners. In J. R. Birsh & S. Carreker (Eds.), *Multisensory teaching of basic language skills* (4th ed., p. 733). Baltimore, MD: Paul H. Brookes Publishing Co.

specific strategies and activities that can be facilitated by transferring phonological awareness skills from one language to the other.

Strategies for Developing Rhyme Identification Skills

Sound manipulation occurs as children rhyme and is "a necessary step toward achieving a higher level of phonological awareness, such as phoneme manipulation" (Cárdenas-Hagan, 2018, p. 733). An activity for practicing initial sound manipulation with Spanish-speaking ELs is illustrated in Table 4.3. In this activity, the teacher prompts students to say two words and the students repeat the words. Then, the teacher asks if the two words rhyme and explains the initial sound that changed. The teacher could follow this activity with a version in English to encourage students to make connections about the sounds that transfer across languages (see Table 4.4).

The teacher can scaffold this skill using flash cards of the rhyme, keeping in mind the goal for students is to identify the rhyme by listening. The teacher will dictate words that end in the same pattern, such as *-at, -it,* or *-ub.* Some examples of such words are *cat, mat, hat, rat, sat.*

Another goal for rhyming includes the ability to generate rhyming words. Rhyme generation is the ability to produce rhyming words. An activity for practicing rhyme generation could include the teacher offering a word (e.g., *bee)* and asking the student to name a word that rhymes with it (e.g., *me)* (Cárdenas-Hagan, 2018). The teacher can provide models for the students. An additional step to consider for ELs would be to have a closed

Table 4.4.   Example activity with sounds that transfer across Spanish and English

Teacher	Students	Teacher	Students	Teacher
Say *mess, less*.	mess, less	Do they rhyme?	Yes	We changed /m/ to /l/.
Say *den, ten*	den, ten	Do they rhyme?	Yes	We changed /d/ to /t/
Say *boo, soy*	boo, soy	Do they rhyme?	No	We changed all the sounds.

From Cárdenas-Hagan, E. (2018). Language and literacy development among English language learners. In J. R. Birsh & S. Carreker (Eds.), *Multisensory teaching of basic language skills* (4th ed., p. 734). Baltimore, MD: Paul H. Brookes Publishing Co.

set of words and allow students to choose which words rhyme. Another activity may be to provide the ending of the words as previously mentioned and have the student generate different beginning sounds to form additional rhyming words.

Strategies for Developing Alliteration Skills

Children who repeat an alliteration are essentially identifying a common initial sound. The teacher can extend and scaffold this skill by providing the first two words of an alliteration and asking the children to extend the alliteration with words that begin with the same initial sound. For example, a teacher could say, "Sam sees _____" and prompt students to fill in the blank with words such as *seaweed, seals,* or *sandcastles.*

This activity can be extended further by having the student generate an alliteration when provided with the targeted initial sound. For example, if the targeted sound is /d/, then the student can think and produce an alliteration such as *Dan delivers doughnuts daily.* Students will need to understand the vocabulary and grammatical features of the alliteration. It can be helpful to use some of the words that look and sound similar across languages such as Spanish and English (e.g., *Manuel makes mangos*) (Cárdenas-Hagan, 2018).

Strategies for Developing an Understanding of Syllables

The conceptualization of a syllable can occur once students understand that as they open their mouths, they are producing a syllable. This is because every syllable has one vowel sound. Words that are similar across languages can be used when engaging and scaffolding this instruction for ELs. The children can also be engaged with the activity by being asked to watch their mouths or clap their hands as they produce words with more than one syllable. Another activity would be to use counters and move the counters as they listen to words and determine the number of syllables in each word. Students can also practice blending syllables to form words or deleting syllables within words. They can use their fingers to practice counting the number of syllables within a word. Syllable activities for ELs can include an explanation of word meanings to enhance their understanding. For instance, a teacher could print out a word in a large font and cut it into syllables; the students could be prompted to assemble the syllable pieces while saying the word.

Strategies for Developing Phonemic Awareness

Phonemic awareness activities in English can be complicated because students have to recognize sounds in English that do not exist in the their native language. Instructionally, it is important for teachers to informally determine some of the similarities and differences between English and the first language to ensure that instruction is placed on the sounds that do not exist in the first language. Some examples of English sounds that do not exist in Spanish include

- Some long and short vowel sounds, such as /a/ as in *apple,* /i/ as in *inch* or *in,* and /u/ as in *use*

- Diphthongs, such as *audio, paw, out,* and *sue*

- R-controlled vowels, such as *park, perk, cork, turn,* and *bird*

- The sound for *z,* such as *zoo* or *zebra*

It is essential that second language learners have knowledge of the English vocabulary within which they are to understand phonemes. The students can begin with words that have two or three phonemes and then increase this goal to identifying words with four or five phonemes. Students can listen, repeat, and blend sounds to form words. They can use counters or their fingers to illustrate the concept of blending phonemes. In addition to learning the meaning of words, they can discover new sounds and understand how those sounds are represented in print. A teacher could use the following script for this kind of activity:

Students, look in your mirrors.

Repeat these words after me: jaw, paw, saw.

What sound did you hear that was the same?

The sound /aw/.

Can you tell me the sounds of the word jaw? *(/j/ /aw/)*

Can you tell me the sounds of the word paw? *(/p/ /aw/)*

Can you tell me the sounds of the word saw? *(/s/ /aw/)*

Look as I write these words.

The sound is /aw/, and the letters are a *and* w.

In what position do you see the letters a *and* w?

Yes, in the final position.

The sound /aw/ is represented by the letters a *and* w *in the final position.*

Can you touch your jaw? Good job.

Can you look at the picture of the puppy's paw?

Look at the picture of a saw.

Let's pretend that we will use a saw to cut the limb from the tree.

You have learned a new sound and how to segment words.

You have also made a connection to the letters that are representing the sound /aw/.
You also understand some of the words with the sound /aw/.

CONCLUSION

Learning to read in two languages can be facilitated by utilizing similar skills from one language to the new language in a systematic and direct framework such as the PLUSS model. Processing and understanding the sounds of a language is a necessary skill for reading in all alphabetic languages (Cárdenas-Hagan & Carlson, 2009). Research has demonstrated that phonological awareness will transfer from one's first language to one's second language (Durgunoğlu, 2002; Shakkour, 2014). It is therefore necessary for educators to understand the similarities and differences of the sound structure across languages in order to incorporate the similarities during instruction and thus increase ELs' understanding of phonological awareness. In this chapter, the reader learned the components of phonological awareness and how phonological awareness develops among speakers of other native languages. In addition, the use of cross-linguistic features have been described as beneficial for ELs. Strategies such as capitalizing between the similarities of the native language and English have been encouraged, with explicit instruction for the vocabulary of English. Now, it is important to check your understanding of phonological awareness development among ELs.

◇◇

STUDY QUESTIONS

1. What are the components of phonological awareness?

2. What are the typical development patterns of phonological awareness?

3. What are some of the variables that affect the transfer of phonological awareness skills across languages?

4. What is the difference between phonological awareness and phoneme awareness?

5. What are some of the strategies that will assist ELs in developing phonological awareness?

◇◇

EXTENDED READING AND APPLICATION ACTIVITIES

1. Identify the following phonological awareness tasks:

    Little Lisa likes lemons.   _____

    Base-Ball = baseball   _____

    Say "son." Sounds are /s/ /o/ /n/.   _____

Say "match." Change /m/ to /b/.   _____

Say "grain" without /g/.   _____

Say /l/ /e/ /s/, the word is ___.   _____

Say "sailboat" without "sail."   _____

Say two words that rhyme with *mat*.   _____

Say "met." What is the first sound?   _____

Mary makes _____.   _____

2. Maria is in the second grade. She speaks Spanish at home and has been in a classroom focused on developing English as a second language. Her teacher has collected data regarding the status of Maria's phonological awareness skills. It is apparent that Maria is able to create rhymes and alliterations. She understands the concepts of syllables but struggles with phoneme awareness with the new sounds of English. Her vocabulary level in English is at the beginning stages. Design a lesson for the development of Maria's phoneme awareness skills that addresses the new sounds and words of English for Maria.

3. Explore the resources about phonological awareness that are offered on http://www.readingrockets.org and http://www.colorincolorado.org. With a colleague, discuss how you could use the strategies discussed in this chapter paired with the resources on these two web sites to adapt an existing phonological awareness lesson for an EL.

REFERENCES

Adams, M. J. (1990). *Beginning to read: Thinking and learning about print.* Cambridge, MA: The MIT Press.

Brown, J. E., & Ortiz, S. O. (2014). Interventions for English learners with learning difficulties. In J. T. Mascolo, V. C. Alfonso, & D. P. Flanagan (Eds.), *Essentials of planning, selecting, and tailoring interventions for unique learners* (pp. 267–313). Hoboken, NJ: Wiley.

Cárdenas-Hagan, E. (2018). Language and literacy development among English language learners. In J. R. Birsh & S. Carreker (Eds.), *Multisensory teaching of basic language skills* (4th ed., pp. 720–756). Baltimore, MD: Paul H. Brookes Publishing Co.

Cárdenas-Hagan, E., & Carlson, C. D. (2009). *Orthography and ELLs.* Paper presented at Tejas Lee Reading Conference, San Antonio, TX.

Cárdenas-Hagan, E., Carlson, C. D., & Pollard-Durodola, S. D. (2007, July). The cross-linguistic transfer of early literacy skills: The role of initial L1 and L2 skills and language of instruction. *Language, Speech, and Hearing Services in Schools,* 249–259.

Durgunoğlu, A. Y. (2002). Cross-linguistic transfer in literacy development and implications for language. *Annuals of Dyslexia, 52,* 189–204.

Dyson, D. T., & Amayreh, M. M. (2007). Jordanian Arabic speech acquisition. In S. McLeod (Ed.), *The international guide to speech acquisition* (pp. 288–299). Clifton Park, NY: Thomson Delmar Learning.

Fabino-Smith, L., & Goldstein, B. (2010). Phonological acquisition in bilingual Spanish-English speaking children. *Journal of Speech-Language-Hearing Research, 53,* 160–178.

Goldstein, B. A. (2007). Spanish-influenced English speech acquisition. In S. McLeod (Ed.), *The international guide to speech acquisition* (pp. 277–287). Clifton Park, NY: Thomson Delmar Learning.

Goldstein, B. A., & Gildersleeve-Neumann, C. (2012). Phonological development and disorders. In B. A. Goldstein (Ed.), *Bilingual language development and disorders in Spanish-English speakers* (2nd ed., pp. 285–309). Baltimore, MD: Paul H. Brooks Publishing Co.

Hwa-Froelich, D. A. (2007). Vietnamese speech acquisition. In S. McLeod (Ed.), *The international guide to speech acquisition* (pp. 580–591). Clifton Park, NY: Thomson Delmar Learning.

Hwa-Froelich, D. A., Hodson, B. H., & Edwards, H. T. (2002). Vietnamese phonology: A tutorial. *American Journal of Speech-Language Pathology, 11,* 264–273.

Li, G. (2010). *Phonological processing abilities and reading competence: Theory and evidence.* New York, NY: Peter Lang.

MacWhinney, B. (2005). A unified model of language acquisition. In J. Droll & A. De Groot (Eds.), *Handbook of bilingualism: Psycholinguistic approaches* (pp. 49–67). Oxford, England: Oxford University Press.

McFarland, J., Hussar, B., De Brey, C., Snyder, T., Wang, X., Wilkinson-Flicker, S., . . . Hinz, S. (2017). *The condition of education 2017* (NCES 2017-144). Washington, DC: US Department of Education, National Center for Education Statistics. Retrieved from http://nces.ed.gov/pubsearch/pubsinfo.asp?pubid=2017144

Paulson, L. H. (2018). Teaching phonemic awareness. In J. R. Birsh & S. Carreker (Eds.), *Multisensory teaching of basic language skills* (4th ed., p. 207). Baltimore, MD: Paul H. Publishing Co.

Peregoy, S. F., & Boyle, O. F. (2000). English learners reading English: What we know, what we need to know. *Theory into Practice, 39*(4), 237–247.

Roseberry-McKibbin, C. (2014). *Multicultural students with special language needs* (4th ed.). Oceanside, CA: Academic Communication Associates.

Sanford, A. K., Brown, J., & Turner, M. (2012). Enhancing instruction for English learners in response to interventions systems: The PLUSS model. *Multiple Voices for Ethnically Diverse Exceptional Learners, 13*(1), 56–70.

Shakkour, W. (2014). Cognitive skill transfer in English reading acquisition: Alphabetic and logographic languages compared. *Open Journal of Modern Linguistics, 4,* 544–562.

So, L. K. H. (2007). Cantonese speech acquisition. In S. McLeod (Ed.), *The international guide to speech acquisition* (pp. 311–325). Clifton Park, NY: Thomson Delmar Learning.

Wagner K., & Torgesen, J. K. (1987). The nature of phonological processing and its causal role in the acquisition of reading skills. *Psychological Bulletin, 101*(2), 192–212.

5

Phonics Development Among English Learners

Kenneth Nieser and Elsa Cárdenas-Hagan

By completing this chapter, the reader will

- Learn evidence-based phonics instruction strategies for English learners (ELs)

- Understand the six syllable types of English and connections to other languages

- Incorporate adaptations for phonics instruction for ELs

- Determine the skills necessary for phonics knowledge screening tools

- Design phonics instruction lessons for ELs based on data

Julio is in the second grade and is currently in an English as a second language class-room setting. He arrived in the United States 1 year ago. He has learned basic English and can communicate in simple sentences. His parents only speak Spanish, and most of his English language opportunities occur within the school setting. Julio's teacher would like to begin to teach him to read and has determined that he can read in his native language and is beginning to understand English letter–sound correlations. She wants to make sure that each literacy lesson is meaningful for Julio. In order to do this, Julio's teacher will make sure he understands that English is an alphabetic lan-guage like Spanish and will teach him to use his native language and literacy knowl-edge to understand the structure of English literacy. Close monitoring of his progress will be necessary and incorporating connections across languages can be beneficial.

INTRODUCTION

This chapter is designed to assist educators in understanding phonics instruction and the special considerations necessary for effective instruc-tion among English learners (ELs). The chapter begins with a definition of phonics and provides the reader with a description of the skills neces-sary for successful phonics knowledge. As the reader gains knowledge of these components, a description of the necessary adjustments for instruc-tion among ELs is provided. The phonics connections across languages are also included to help the reader understand the importance of using native language knowledge for second language literacy development. This is one of the principles for effective instruction that is described. Finally, a practi-cal guide for implementing effective phonics instruction with ELs and the strategies necessary are comprised within the chapter. Therefore, each com-ponent of phonics instruction is defined, the relevant research is cited, and practical suggestions for effective implementation of each strategy is pre-sented in detail to achieve enhanced literacy instruction for ELs.

PHONICS

The Florida Center for Reading Research (2020) defined *phonics* as "the study of the relationships between letters and the sounds they represent; also used to describe the reading instruction that teaches sound-symbol correspon-dences." In the second case, phonics is a method of instruction that teaches students how to link the letter or symbol to its corresponding sound and blend them together to read words.

Literacy development depends on the ability to understand that let-ters represent the sounds of spoken language. In short, for students to read words, they must know the letter and sound correlations. Experienced read-ers instantly recognize letter and sound correspondences, and they easily blend the letter and sounds together to form syllables and words.

Phonics is differentiated from phonological awareness. Phonological awareness involves identifying, blending, segmenting, deleting, or manipulating sounds in spoken words, whereas phonics requires the student to build a relationship between the sound and the letter or symbol. In short, phonological awareness activities help to build the processing and manipulation of sounds so the individual can subsequently understand sound and symbol correlations. Phonics tasks have a visual component because they involve the use of graphemes. Reading research identifies the following key elements for effective phonics instruction:

- *Letter recognition:* the ability to correctly identify and name the letters of the alphabet

- *Grapho-phonemic knowledge (letter–sound correspondences):* the ability to articulate the correct sound or sounds associated with each letter or symbol

- *Decoding:* the ability to translate a word from print to speech, employing grapho-phonemic knowledge and stable patterns; also called *sounding out* words

- *Morphological awareness:* the ability to understand that smaller meaning units known as *morphemes* exist within many words

This chapter examines each of these key elements.

Letter-Name Knowledge

What do good readers do as they read? Good readers look at the symbol on the page, translate the symbol into its sound correspondence, read the word, and connect the word to its meaning. Ehri and McCormick (2013) described the automaticity of letter recognition as a step toward recognizing the common patterns of letters and then instantly recognizing words through repeated reading opportunities. Chiappe, Siegel, and Wade-Woolley (2002) looked at kindergarten and first-grade students with varying degrees of English language proficiency (native speakers and ELs). The findings identified letter identification in kindergarten as a predictor for decoding skills in first grade among both groups of emergent readers. Results of their study suggested explicit instruction in phonological awareness and phonics as a benefit for children from diverse backgrounds. Schatsneider, Fletcher, Francis, Carlson, and Foorman (2004) described letter-name knowledge as a variable and predictor for reading achievement. Therefore, letter-name knowledge is recommended as a strategy for reading and should be addressed in an explicit manner for ELs.

Grapho-Phonemic Knowledge

As students learn the letters, it is important for them to understand the sound or sounds associated with each letter, which is known as *grapho-phonemic knowledge.* A grapheme is the written symbol, and a phoneme is an individual sound. Grapho-phonemic knowledge is the understanding that the letter (grapheme) has a corresponding sound (phoneme) or sounds associated with it. Share and Stanovich (1995) described how students use their known sound and symbol correspondences and phonological sensitivity to read unknown words. They further develop their reading accuracy with practice, which can lead to more effort spent on the meaning of words. The goal is for students to instantly recognize letters and their corresponding sounds and then blend them together to read words with automaticity. Students who do not read words accurately and with automaticity, continue to have these difficulties 10 years later, which clearly has a negative impact on reading comprehension (Nippold, 2017).

Decoding

Decoding involves accurately translating words from print to speech. Beginning readers use letter–sound correspondences to sound out each grapheme in a word and then blend the sounds together to produce meaning. As these readers become more proficient, they increase their speed and accuracy. Frequently appearing words become part of the readers' sight word repertoire so that cognitive efforts are focused on novel words. This also frees up cognitive abilities that allow readers to attend to the meaning of the text. Decoding is essential because, as Archer and Hughes (2020) stated, "There is no comprehension strategy powerful enough to compensate for the fact you can't read the words."

Morphological Awareness

Morphological awareness is the ability to understand that smaller meaning units known as *morphemes* exist within many words. A morpheme is the smallest unit of meaning in a language. Morpheme knowledge can enhance understanding of words and can assist with reading accuracy, fluency, and comprehension (Ramirez, 2017). For ELs, the greater the overlap across languages, the stronger the association of the skills (Pasquarella, Chen, Gottardo, & Geva, 2014)

PHONICS AND ENGLISH LEARNERS

According to the National Reading Panel report (National Institute of Child Health and Human Development, 2000) and the Center for Instruction (Francis, Rivera, Lesaux, Kieffer, & Rivera, 2006), learning to read requires explicit instruction in phonics that is incorporated with fluency, vocabulary, and comprehension instruction. The National Literacy Panel for Language-Minority Children and Youth (August & Shanahan, 2006) found similar results; however, special considerations regarding oral language proficiency, vocabulary, background knowledge, and attention to addressing new sounds of the language was described as beneficial for ELs. For example, young Spanish-speaking students learning to read in English might make the best progress when given more work with particular phonemes and combinations of phonemes in English that do not exist in their own language. These types of tailored reading interventions make reading instruction more effective.

CONNECTIONS ACROSS LANGUAGES

Phonological awareness and phonics skills are similar across alphabetic languages. For this reason, children can use native language literacy skills to learn to read in the second language. Yet, the amount of transfer depends on several factors. First, alphabetic systems can be either shallow (transparent) or deep (opaque) (Moats, 2009). In shallow alphabetic orthographies, the sound–symbol relationships in the alphabetic writing system are mostly regular and predictable, with one sound represented by one symbol or letter. Examples of shallow languages include Finnish, Italian, and Spanish. Deep alphabetic systems have multiple sounds for letters and/or multiple letters for a single phoneme, such as the English language.

Second, the amount of overlap between the student's native language and English will also determine how much transfer a student can derive from the native language. Many Western European languages share Greek and Latin origins, providing for many points of transfer (shared orthographies, morphologies, and semantics). When the native language has less overlap with the second language, the opportunities for transfer are diminished but still exist (Moats, 2009).

PRINCIPLES OF EFFECTIVE PHONICS INSTRUCTION FOR ENGLISH LEARNERS

Effective phonics instruction needs to be systematic and explicit and should begin with the simplest phonics tasks (letter name/letter sound), then progress to more complex skills as students demonstrate proficiency. Explicit phonics instruction means that the letter–sound relationships are directly taught. Activities should be introduced and modeled several times as a whole group and then be used for guided practice under teacher supervision in small groups or individually. Finally, activities may be moved to centers to be completed independently. Systematic phonics instruction may include teaching the letters/symbols and sound correlations before moving to teaching syllable patterns within words. Building the automaticity of reading words can progress to reading sentences and paragraphs. ELs may have native literacy knowledge that could benefit second language literacy. Therefore, teachers need to be cognizant of the native language skills students may bring into the classroom and take full advantage of these when possible. In these cases, instruction should be focused on areas where the two languages diverge, spending time on new concepts rather than information they already know.

STRATEGIES FOR TEACHING PHONICS TO ENGLISH LEARNERS

The principles of effective phonics instruction previously discussed need to be coupled with evidence-based strategies that can be easily implemented in the classroom during language arts instruction to help students become successful, lifelong readers. The strategies that follow are organized by the elements of phonics previously discussed, starting with the easiest tasks. The step-by step process for each strategy facilitates implementation by the teacher, regardless of experience level. In addition, this guide also provides key information on linguistic differences between languages, with a particular emphasis on English and Spanish (as the vast majority of ELs speak Spanish). Teachers should use this information as a guide to individualize instruction for those students who bring a degree of literacy in the native language to the classroom.

Instructional Strategies to Develop English Learners' Letter Knowledge

Instruction for ELs can begin with opportunities for them to understand that English has 26 letters and those 26 letters represent 44 sounds. Educators should point out differences between the English alphabet and sounds and the alphabet and sounds of the English learners' home language. For example, Spanish has 30 letters if you include the digraphs *ch, ll,* and *rr.* The digraphs are traditionally included in early phonics instruction due to their direct one-to-one correspondence to a single phoneme. Spanish has more one-to-one letter–sound correspondences than English.

Educators who work with ELs do not need to be proficient speakers of each language spoken in their classroom. However, they should endeavor to learn about those phonics systems, so that instruction can be focused on where English and the native languages differ. Online resources can often provide this information. For example, http://www.mylanguages.org offers insights into nearly 100 different languages. The alphabet tab for each language lays out the letter in the native language and the English equivalent where applicable.

To help ELs make connections with their home language, prompt them to compare the letters of their native language with English. The following example compares the English alphabet with Spanish.

English: a, b, c, d, e, f, g, h, i, j, k, l, m, n, o, p, q, r, s, t, u, v, w, x, y, z

Spanish: a, b, c, ch, d, e, f, g, h, i, j, k, l, ll, m, n, ñ, o, p, q, r, rr, s, t, u, v, w, x, y, z

The letters look the same in English and Spanish with the exception of four extra letters and digraphs in the Spanish alphabet. English and Spanish have five letters that represent vowel sounds. In Spanish, the vowel sounds do not change. In English, the vowel sounds do change. For example. the vowel *e* can be produced as a long sound (*be*) or as a short vowel (*met*). In some cases, it is silent when it is at the end of a word in a pattern that has a vowel, a consonant, and a final *e* (*kite*).

Teach students the names of the letters of the English alphabet by having them recite it in sequential order. Another activity to reinforce alphabet knowledge is to have students practice placing the letters in alphabetical order. Distribute paper cutouts or plastic letters of the entire alphabet to students. They can replicate the classroom alphabet strip on their desk or place the letters on top of individual alphabet strips at their desk. This activity has the added benefit of addressing the sequential order of the alphabet.

Another useful letter naming activity is for students to sing the alphabet song in English, while looking at the letters (on individual alphabet strips on their desk) and following along with their fingers as they continue to sing the alphabet. If students have individual plastic letters, then have students place them in sequential order on their desks before beginning the song (using an alphabet strip to assist them if necessary). Students can physically move those letters as they sing, which can provide additional opportunities for learning the English letter names. Another activity for building automaticity of the alphabet is to have students name the letter that occurs before or after a particular letter. For instance, the teacher might prompt

Tell me the letter after h. [waits for student response] *Yes, the letter after* h *is the letter* i.

Tell me the letter before b. [waits for student response] *Yes, the letter before* b *is the letter* a.

Tell me the letter after q. [waits for student response] *Yes, the letter after* q *is the letter* r.

Have students provide their responses in complete sentences. If students have very limited oral proficiency, then provide them with a sentence stem to scaffold their responses. A sentence stem is a set response students can repeat that only lacks the last word or phrase for them to complete independently. For example, as in the previous activity, the teacher might prompt as follows:

Tell me the letter after b. [Waits for student response. If the student responds with only the letter name or no response is forthcoming, then the teacher says the following.] *Repeat after me, "The letter after* b *is* ____."

Guess Who? is another activity to help students learn letter names with the added benefit of building oral language skills. The teacher thinks of a letter and the students try to guess it by asking a series of questions. Model some question stems that students could ask to facilitate the activity and show them how to ask effective questions. For example, "Is this letter a ____ (vowel, consonant)?" and "Does this letter come before the letter ___?" are examples of question stems. For this activity, the teacher would say

I am thinking about a letter that is close to the very beginning of the alphabet.

You can ask three questions, and when you know the letter, you can say it. If you guess the correct letter, then you win the game. If you do not guess the correct letter, then I get a point. The person who achieves 10 points first will win the game.

Some examples of questions could include the following:

- *Is it a vowel?*

- *Is it a consonant?*

- *Is it before the letter___?*

- *Is it after the letter ___?*

- *Is it between the letters___ and ____?*

- *Is it a tall letter?*

- *Is it a round-shaped letter?*

Once again, this activity will help ELs use their language skills by asking questions. You can use sentence stems to assist ELs in creating the necessary questions for this activity. Students can also practice their deductive reasoning skills by determining the targeted letter name in this game-like activity. With practice and teacher demonstrations, students will ask more strategic questions and learn how they can use the information from previous questions to narrow down their search possibilities. Throughout all of these activities, it is important to emphasize that the letter names do not ever change. This is a consistent and reliable concept for ELs.

As students demonstrate a degree of proficiency for at least some of the letter names, it is important for them to learn the sound or sounds associated with those letters. The activities in the next section progress students from letter knowledge to the letter–sound associations, also known as *grapho-phonemic knowledge.*

Instructional Strategies to Develop English Learners' Grapho-Phonemic Knowledge

Emergent readers may not yet understand the alphabetic principle—the concept that letters represent speech sounds or that these sounds are the building blocks of spoken words (Moats, 2009). The following activities help students bridge this gap and provide them with a solid foundation that will assist them at the next level of phonics—decoding. Cárdenas-Hagan (2018) described steps for explicit instruction of letter–sound knowledge for ELs.

1. Teacher says three words that begin with a common sound.

2. Students repeat the words.

3. Students determine the common sound.

4. Teacher discusses the formation of the sound and its features.

5. Teacher leads a discussion regarding the commonalities or differences of the sounds in the native and second languages.

This explicit, step-by-step approach scaffolds children's learning by breaking down the process for learning a new sound into its component parts and making instruction more comprehensible for the students through the use of repetition and multiple examples. The following example shows how a typical lesson might be designed for the sound /b/:

Listen to these words with the common initial or beginning sound: ball, bus, boot.

Repeat the words. (ball, bus, boot)

What was the common sound that you heard? Yes, the sound was /b/.

Let's look at each other or look in a mirror as you determine how to produce the sound. You used your lips. Touch your throat and see if your vocal chords vibrate. Yes, they do. The /b/ sound is a consonant sound that is voiced. The letter name is b *and the sound is /b/.*

Now let's determine if this is a sound you have in your native language. For example, in Spanish you have the sound /b/. It is the same sound as the English sound. It is also a voiced consonant sound. We can use the word bat *to help remember this sound. In Spanish, the word would be* bate. *Say the letter name in English.* B. *Say the keyword.* Bat. *Say the /b/ sound. Good job.*

In the previous example, students reflect on the similarities of the letters and sounds in their native language and English. Table 5.1 describes the letters and sounds that directly or indirectly transfer from Spanish to English. Those that indirectly transfer may have the same letter, but a variation of the sound exists in English. Instructors may consider explicitly highlighting and demonstrating the concepts that directly transfer. For example, in a class that has a native Zulu speaker who has some basic phonics knowledge in his or her native language, the teacher can demonstrate the direct transfer of the /z/ sound by saying

Some letters share the same sound in English and Zulu. You can use what you already know about these letters in Zulu to help you read in English. One of those letters is z. The letter z makes the /z/ sound in English and Zulu.

Table 5.1. Letters and sounds that directly or indirectly transfer from Spanish to English

Spanish letter	English letter	Spanish sound	English sound
a	a	/ah/	/ă/, /ā/, /ŭ/
b	b	/b/	/b/
c	c	/k/	/k/
d	d	/d/	/d/
e	e	/ē/	/ĕ/, /ē/
f	f	/f/	/f/
g	g	/g/ or /h/	/g/ or /j/
h	h	silent	/h/
i	i	/ē/	/ĭ/, /ī/
j	j	/h/	/j/
k	k	/k/	/k/
l	l	/l/	/l/
m	m	/m/	/m/
n	n	/n/	/n/
o	o	/ō/	/ō/ tone difference
p	p	/p/	/p/
q	q	/k/	/kw/
r	r	/rr/	/r/
s	s	/s/	/s/
t	t	/t/	/t/
u	u	/ōō/	/ŭ/, /ū/
v	v	/v/	/v/
w	w	/w/	/w/
x	x	/ks/, /s/, /h/	/ks/, /z/
y	y	/y/	/y/
z	z	/s/	/z/

Next, those concepts that can partially or indirectly transfer can also be explicitly taught. Continuing with the same example with a native Zulu speaker, a partial transfer example prompt could be

The letter c exists in both Zulu and English. In Zulu, however, the c makes the /ch/ sound, whereas in English it will make either the /k/ or /s/ sound. Because this is a difference between our two languages, you will want to be extra careful when reading words with the letter c.

Finally, there are many new reading concepts in English that can be taught in a systematic and explicit manner. For example, for native Spanish speakers, the short vowel sound /ĭ/ will be completely novel. The teacher will need to provide modeling for the correct pronunciation of this new sound and a lot of opportunity for practice.

The explicit and systematic instruction of letter–sound associations previously described serves to facilitate the successful acquisition of this knowledge by ELs, whether there is complete, partial, or no overlap between the native language and English. Once students are armed with this information, they are ready to move on to the next rung on the grapho-phonemic continuum—decoding.

Instructional Strategies to Develop English Learners' Decoding Skills

Decoding words is the foundation on which many higher level reading skills build (accuracy, fluency, and comprehension). A solid knowledge base of letter–sound correspondences discussed in the previous section, along with ample practice to build automaticity, are crucial for students to become proficient at decoding.

Identification of syllable type is a proven strategy for facilitating decoding of words (Moats & Tolman, 2019). The vast majority of words in the English language are comprised of six syllable types (closed, open, vowel-*r*, vowel pair, vowel-consonant-*e*, final stable syllable). Applying the six syllable types to word decoding provides novice readers with information on how to correctly read thousands of unfamiliar words. It also helps teachers organize decoding and spelling instruction (Moats & Tolman, 2019). When this knowledge is combined with syllable division conventions, students learn how to successfully read longer words. The following paragraphs discuss syllable types and syllable division instruction, with modeling and examples provided to facilitate implementation in the classroom.

ELs will need to understand that English has six types of syllables, several of which are discussed next. This is especially necessary for those ELs whose native language is transparent and has reliable letter–sound correlations that do not vary. The concept of a syllable directly transfers across many languages. To explicitly teach this concept or make a connection across languages, teachers can demonstrate the features of a syllable. To do so, the teacher might say

Say the word mom.

How many times did you open your mouth? (one)

How many sounded vowels did you hear? (one)

You heard one.

Every time you open your mouth, you are producing a syllable.

Every syllable has one vowel sound.

Therefore, a syllable is made by opening your mouth. Every syllable has at least one vowel sound.

You have this concept in many languages. For example, a syllable in Spanish is formed by opening the mouth, and every syllable has one vowel sound.

Once students understand the concept of a syllable, they are prepared to learn the syllable types of the English language for correctly reading words. Instructors should teach each syllable type in sequential order, giving students ample practice to identify and practice reading each one individually and then in combined lists that provide various words from the current and previously taught syllable types. Students will then identify the syllable type and decode the words.

Closed Syllable   The English language can be categorized into six types of syllables. The first syllable type is a closed syllable, which has one vowel followed by at least one consonant. The vowel sound will be short. The following example exemplifies how to teach an introductory lesson on closed syllables in an explicit and systematic manner.

Look at these words as I write them on the board: met, son, him, at, hem.

How many vowel sounds do you see in each word? (one)

Yes, you see one vowel.

What is followed by each vowel? (a consonant)

Yes, each word has one vowel followed by at least one consonant.

Every time you produce a consonant sound, your mouth is blocked by the tongue, teeth, or lips.

Consonant sounds close the mouth.

These words end in a consonant, and they are called closed syllables.

A closed syllable has one vowel and at least one consonant.

The vowel sound will be short. You can code it with a breve, which in your language of Spanish or other Latin-based languages means short.

We can also determine the meaning of each of these words because you may not know them in depth in the English language.

Open Syllable   An open syllable ends in one vowel, and the vowel sound is long. Use the following multisensory example to introduce the open syllable concept to students.

Look at these words as I write them on the board: me, so, hi, a, he.

How many vowel sounds do you see in each word? (one)

Yes, you see one vowel.

Take out your mirror, look at your mouth, and say these vowel sounds after me: /ā, ē, ī, ō, ū/

Is your mouth open or closed as you produce these sounds? (open)

Yes, your mouth is open for vowel sounds.

Vowel sounds open the mouth.

Because these words end in a vowel, they are called open syllables.

An open syllable has one vowel, and the vowel sound will be long.

You can code it with a macron, which is a line above the vowel.

We can also determine the meaning of each of these words because you may not know them in depth in the English language.

Once students have learned both the open and closed syllable types, prepare a word list that has both types of words. Ensure that your students can differentiate the words, identifying both the type of syllable and the correct pronunciation of each item. The instructor can have students code the vowel sounds with the markings of a breve or a macron. A breve is a short vowel marking that appears as a curved line above the vowel when coding syllable types. A macron is a long vowel marking that appears as a line above the vowel when coding syllable types.

The breve may be simple for some ELs to understand because the word *breve* in Spanish and other languages reflects something short. A brief list of mixed long and short vowel words follows as an example for syllable type identification, reading, and coding practice.

me	met
so	son
hi	him
a	at
he	hem

Language Connections

An adaption for syllable type instruction among ELs is to have students make a connection to their native language and determine if the syllable patterns are present in both languages. ELs can also benefit from understanding the meanings of the words they are reading. Some of the words in the previous example are cognates, which are words whose spellings and meanings are similar across languages. For example, the word *telephone* is a cognate with many languages. It is spelled in a similar way and has the same meaning. Table 5.2 lists just a few of the many languages that share a cognate for *telephone* with English and can help students as they learn to read and understand words in English.

Table 5.2. Languages that share a cognate for the English word *telephone*

Language	Spelling	Pronunciation
Spanish	teléfono	Tĕ—lay—fo—no
Portuguese	telefone	Tĕ—lee—fon—nee
German	telefon	Tĕ—lĭ—fon
Russian	Телефон	Tay—lay—fohn
Farsi	تلفن	Tĕ—lĕ—fohn
Greek	Τηλέφωνο	Tĕ—lay—fo—no

Instructors can also discuss and practice the pronunciation of the words. In Spanish, the word *a* is pronounced as /ah/. In English, it is pronounced as /ā/. Another question to ask is whether the words are similar in spelling but not in meaning. For example, the word *son* has the same spelling in Spanish and English. Yet, the meaning is different in Spanish. In Spanish, the word *son* means *are*. In English, it means the male child of a parent. The pronunciation in Spanish is /sōn/ with a long *O* sound. In English, it is /sŏn/ with a short vowel sound. Once again, understanding the similarities and the differences between the native language and English can enhance phonics instruction for ELs.

Vowel Pair Syllable   Some words have two vowels next to one another. This makes a pair and is therefore called a *vowel pair syllable*. Each of the English vowel pair syllables must be explicitly taught, especially because some vowel pairs have multiple pronunciations in English. For example the vowel pair *oo* has two pronunciations, and the vowel pair *ea* has three pronunciations. Examples of English vowel pairs are as follows:

   ai, ay, ea, ee, ei, eu, ie, oa, oe, oi, oy, oo, ou, ue

Language Connections

Teachers can help students connect with the different syllable types by pointing out when a particular syllable pattern exists in the students' native language and whether the pronunciation is the same or different. In those cases in which the pronunciation differs, the teacher should determine if the sound exists in both languages but uses different symbols to represent it. The teacher and students can also explore whether words with the pattern are cognates with similar spellings and meanings. If they are not cognates, then they should discuss the meaning of the word in English and compare it with the word in the native language. For instance, the teacher prompts

Say the words boy, toy, soy.

What did you hear at the end of each word? (/oy/)

Look at the words as I write them: boy, toy, soy.

What letters are the same? (oy) *Yes, the letters are* o *and* y.

This is a vowel pair syllable that has two adjacent vowels. Y acts like a vowel in these words.

Does this vowel pair pattern exist in your native or first language?

If so, how do you pronounce it?

Is it the same or different?

Do any words with oy *look the same in your language?*

The word soy *is the same in English and Spanish. The pronunciation is the same in English and Spanish. The meaning is different. In Spanish, the meaning for the word* soy *is* am. *In English, it means a type of sauce for Chinese food.*

Vowel-R Syllable   The English language also has the pattern of a vowel followed by the letter *r*, which is a vowel-*r* syllable. The vowel-*r* syllables must also be taught because the vowel makes various sounds. For example, the vowel-*r* syllable has pronunciations that are challenging to read and produce in the English language, especially when the individual's English language experience has been limited, as in the case of many ELs. Most of the time the vowel-*r* syllable will be produced as /er/ as in the words *her, sir,* and *burn.* Yet, the vowel-*r* syllable for words with *ar* will have various pronunciations.

One way to explain this is to demonstrate how the accent patterns will change the pronunciations. Following is an example of how this might be taught to ELs.

*Today we are going to learn about two different ways to pronounce the vowel-*r *combination of* ar. *Even though there are two ways to read and pronounce the combined letters* a *and* r, *the good news is that the rules are dependable and you can easily learn how to correctly read these words. Let's take a look at the following list that has one of the pronunciations.*

Say the words car, far, bar.

What was the common sound that you heard? (/ar/)

Look at the letters in the words as I write them.

What letters did I use? (a *and* r)

Yes, the letters a *and* r.

*This is a vowel-*r *syllable.*

*Do you have this vowel-*r *pattern in your native or first language?*

If so, is it pronounced in the same way?

In the case of Spanish, you trill the letter r, *unlike the sound in English.*

Do any of the words look the same in your native or first language? (yes)

The word bar *looks the same in Spanish and English.*

The pronunciation is different because the letter r *is trilled in Spanish and not in English.*

Is the meaning the same or different?

The meaning is the same.

Once students understand the first pronunciation of vowel-*r* combination *ar* as /ar/, the teacher should pivot the lesson to words in which the vowel-*r* combination appears in the unstressed syllable and has the pronunciation of /er/. To provide instruction on this concept, the teacher could prompt

Now say these words after me: collar, dollar, polar.

What was the common sound? (/er/)

Look at the letters in the words as I write them.

What letters did I use? (*a* and *r*)

Yes, the letters a *and* r.

So, when the vowel-r combination is written within a word and it is in the unaccented syllable, then it is produced as /er/.

Do you have this unaccented syllable ar *pattern in your native or first language?*

In Spanish, the letters a *and* r *can be in the unaccented syllable (e.g.,* dólar). *Yet, the pronunciation remains the same, /arr/.*

Now that the rules for both pronunciations have been introduced and understood by the students, the teacher might ask the class to compare a variety of words with this pattern:

car	collar
dart	dollar
lard	liar

In the first column, each vowel-*r* combination appears in the accented syllable and the pronunciation is /ar/. In the second column, each vowel-*r* combination appears in the unaccented syllable and the pronunciation is /er/. Next, the teacher can ask students to compare words with the pattern *or* such as

born	valor
storm	doctor
cord	harbor

In the first column, vowel-*r* combination *or* appears in the accented syllable and the pronunciation is /or/. In the second column, each vowel-*r* combination *or* appears in the unaccented syllable and the pronunciation is /er/. The teacher should then ask, "Do you have this unaccented syllable pattern in your native or first language?" In Spanish, words such as *valor* and *doctor* represent the vowel-*r* pattern. The pronunciation for the letters *o* and *r* does not change in Spanish and is produced as /orr/. To explain a final pattern of *or*, the teacher could share

Words such as worth, worthy, *and* world *have the vowel-r combination* or *followed by the letter* w. *In this case, the pronunciation of vowel-r combination is /er/, despite the fact the* or *appears in the accented syllable.*

Do you have a similar pattern for words that have a letter w *before the* or*? If so, explain the pattern.*

To summarize, the vowel-*r* syllable type in English is complex but has several dependable rules that facilitate correct pronunciation.

- *er, ir, ur*—always pronounced /er/
- *ar*—pronounced /ar/ when in the stressed syllable (or single-syllable words); pronounced /er/ when in an unstressed syllable
- *or*—pronounced /or/ when in the stressed syllable (or single-syllable words); pronounced /er/ when in an unstressed syllable (*doctor, tutor*) but with several important exceptions (*world, word*)

Final Stable Syllable   A final stable syllable is another syllable type in the English language and occurs at the end of words. Many of the final stable syllables have the pattern of a consonant followed by -*le*. Following are examples of final stable syllables with a consonant-*le* pattern.

- Bubble
- Uncle
- Candle
- Ruffle
- Angle
- Ankle
- Apple
- Hassle
- Castle

Other final stable syllables can be endings such as -*dure*, -*ture*, -*sion*, and -*tion*, which occurs in words such as

- Procedure
- Picture
- Vision
- Nation

A lesson introducing the final stable syllable type might begin as follows:

Say these words after me: purple, dimple, apple.

What did you hear that was the same in each of these words? (-ple)

Look at these words as I write them on the board: purple, dimple, apple.

What letters do you see at the end of each word? (-ple)

Yes, -ple. In what position of the word do you see -ple? (final)

Yes, it the final position of the word.

-Ple is considered a final stable syllable. A final stable syllable appears at the end of words.

The syllable before is accented.

Does this pattern exist in your native or first language?

If so, please describe. Is the pronunciation the same or different?

Are there any words that look similar and have the same meaning? Please explain.

Syllable Division Patterns

As students learn the syllable types in English, it will be important for them to read words with multiple syllables. This requires the student to not only understand the six syllable types of English, but also to understand how to divide the words into their syllable types for reading multisyllabic words. Some students may be able to read monosyllabic words but struggle with reading multisyllabic words and will require explicit instruction in this area (Nippold, 2017). ELs need instruction to help them understand the most common patterns for syllable division and determine the similarities and differences in their native language and English.

VCCV Syllable Division Pattern   Instruction in syllable division assists students with decoding longer words. Moats and Tolman (2019) stated, "Without a strategy for chunking longer words into manageable parts, students may look at a longer word and simply resort to guessing what it is—or altogether skipping it." Familiarity with the syllable types and how to correctly divide longer words into syllables helps students read more accurately and fluently and also helps them solve spelling problems. Instruction in syllable division patterns should start with the most common type of word in English—the vowel-consonant-consonant-vowel (VCCV) pattern. The following example demonstrates how to introduce this pattern (Moats & Tolman, 2019):

Look at the following words as I write them on the board: intend, mascot, bronco.

We will find the vowels and label them with the letter v.

Next, we will find the consonants and label them with the letter c.

What pattern do we have within these words? (VCCV pattern)

Yes, we have a VCCV pattern.

Divide the words between the two consonants.

What type of syllables do we have? (closed syllables)

Yes, we have closed syllables.

Code the vowels according to the syllable type.

Read the word.

Is this a word you know?

Do you have any of these words in your native language?

If you speak Spanish, then each of these words looks very similar to Spanish and you divide them according to the same pattern.

Did you pronounce the word correctly? Is the accent on the correct syllable?

Use the word in a sentence.

It is important to teach students to be flexible when dividing words into the various syllable division patterns. Words with the VCCV pattern are typically divided between the two consonants. The accent is most often on the first syllable, but English also has words that will be accented on the second syllable. Once ELs have mastered this syllable pattern, it will be important to also teach that some words in English will require the division to occur after the first vowel. Words such as *matron, between* and *decline* are some examples of this pattern.

VCV Syllable Division Pattern   The vowel-consonant-vowel (VCV) pattern is another common syllable division pattern in English (e.g., *total, rebel, navel*). The syllables in VCV words are normally divided after the first vowel. The following script is a discovery inquiry lesson for students to learn how to divide this syllable pattern:

Look at these words as I write them on the board: legal, final, omit.

We will find the vowels and label them with the letter v.

Next, we will find the consonants and label them with the letter c.

What pattern do we have within these words? (VCV pattern)

Yes, we have a VCV pattern.

Divide the words after the first vowel.

What type of syllables do we have? (open and closed syllables)

Yes, we have an open syllable and a closed syllable.

Code the vowels according to the syllable type.

Read the word.

Is this a word you know?

Do you have any of these words in your native language?

If you speak Spanish, then each of these words looks very similar to Spanish and you divide them according to the same pattern.

Did you pronounce the word correctly? Is the accent on the correct syllable?

Use the word in a sentence.

It is important to teach students to be flexible when dividing words into the various syllable division patterns. Words with a VCV pattern are typically divided after the first vowel. The accent is most often on the first syllable, but English can also have words that will be accented on the second syllable. Once ELs have mastered this syllable pattern, it will be important to also teach that some words in English will require the division to occur after the consonant. Words such as *tremor, modest* and *solid* are some examples of this pattern.

VCCCV Syllable Division Pattern   The vowel-consonant-consonant-consonant-vowel (VCCCV) pattern is the final syllable division pattern included in this chapter. The lesson that follows suggests a manner to introduce this concept to students.

Look at these words as I write them on the board: nostril, ostracize, monstrous.

We will find the vowels and label them with the letter v.

Next, we will find the consonants and label them with the letter c.

What pattern do we have within these words? (VCCCV pattern)

Yes, we have a VCCCV pattern.

Divide the words after the first consonant.

What is the first type of syllable? (closed syllable)

Yes, we have a closed syllable.

Code the vowels according to the syllable types within the word.

Read the word.

Is this a word you know?

Do you have any of these words in your native language?

Did you pronounce the word correctly? Is the accent on the correct syllable?

Use the word in a sentence.

Although the rules outlined here are fairly regular and dependable, there are exceptions that should be pointed out to students. Students need to know that they must be flexible in their approach to syllable division. If their initial attempt following the rules outlined does not result in sensible syllables, then they should attempt an alternative point of dividing the word. For example, words with a VCCCV pattern are typically divided after the first consonant. The accent is most often on the first syllable, but English also can have words that will be accented on the second syllable. Once ELs have mastered this syllable division pattern, it will be important to also teach that some words in English will require the division to occur after the second consonant. Words such as *handshake, sandbox,* and *hindleg* are some examples of this pattern.

Instructional Strategies to Develop English Learners' Morphological Awareness

Instructors can incorporate morphological awareness as a strategy for increasing word reading accuracy and comprehension of word meanings. Many morphemes in European languages share the same Latin and Greek roots, which means that there is considerable overlap (and more important for ELs, significant opportunity for transfer from the native language). For instance, the word *telephone* is comprised of two Greek roots: *tele* (meaning distant) and *phone* (meaning sound). As shown in the example earlier in this chapter, many languages employ these same Greek affixes to form words. By systematically teaching Greek and Latin morphemes, educators add an additional strategy for developing ELs' phonics knowledge in addition to their word knowledge. Approximately 60% of words in English have Greek or Latin roots, and this percentage is even higher for many European languages (Dictionary.com, 2019).

Morphemes can either exist as a prefix, root, base word, or suffix. A prefix is a morpheme that is added to a root or base word and can change its meaning. For example, the prefix *re-* can change the meaning of the word *turn* when it is added to the beginning of the word, as in the word *return.* Many prefixes are common across languages in their form and meaning. A root is a morpheme that can have either another root or base word added to it, as in the words *monograph* or *telephone.* A root can also have a prefix added to it, as in the words *revert* or *construct.* A root can also have a suffix added to it, as in the words *stricken* or *visor.*

Teaching morphemes to ELs will assist them in reading words with accuracy and understanding the word meanings because many of the morphemes are common across languages.

Table 5.3 provides an example of common word parts across languages such as English, Spanish, French, Catalan, Italian, and Portuguese. Keep in mind that many of these same affixes will be valid for languages beyond those listed. To teach morphemes, a teacher could prompt

Today you will learn a word part that will help you read and understand words.

Say these words after me: artist, pianist, dentist.

What did you hear that was the same in each of these words? (-ist)

Look at the words as I write them on the board.

What are the letters used for this word part? (-i-s-t)

In what position of the word do we find this word part? (final position)

This word part is in the final position and is considered a suffix.

Table 5.3. Common morphemes across languages

English		Spanish		French	
Word part	Meaning	Word part	Meaning	Word part	Meaning
tri-	three	tri-	tres	tri-	trois
bi-	two	bi-	dos	bi-	duex
con-	with	con-	con	con-	avec
graph	written	graf	escribir	graph	écrit
phone	sound	fono	sonido	phone	bruit
-ist	sound	-ista	alguien que	-iste	celui qui
-itis	one who	-itis	inflammacion	-ite	inflammation

Catalan		Italian		Portugese	
Word part	Meaning	Word part	Meaning	Word part	Meaning
tri-	tres	tri-	tre	tri-	três
bi-	dos	bi-	due	bi-	dois
con-	amb	con-	con	con-	com
graf	escrita	graf	scrivere	grafo	escrito
fon	sona	fono	suono	fone	som
-ista	el que	-ista	colui che	-ista	aquele que

From Cárdenas-Hagan, E. (2000). *Esperanza training manual.* Brownsville, TX: Valley Speech Language and Learning Center; adapted by permission.

A suffix is a morpheme added to the end of a word or root and can change its form or meaning.

Does this suffix exist in your native language? If so, describe it.

Read the base word.

Read the suffix.

Read the entire word together with fluency.

Do you know the meaning of -ist?

An artist is the person who can draw or paint.

A pianist is the person who can play the piano.

A dentist is the person who can care for your teeth.

So, the meaning of -ist is the person who.

Do you have these words in your native language?

We will practice reading more words with this suffix.

We will also review the meanings of each of the words that we read.

In summary, morphological awareness can enhance students' ability to read and understand words. Many of the morphemes transfer across languages and can help ELs to become more efficient in learning to read English. ELs can benefit from this instruction when it is taught in an explicit and systematic manner.

PROGRESS MONITORING

Progress monitoring is the regular, ongoing scientifically based assessment of students' academic performance. It has two main purposes—to determine the effectiveness of instruction that has been provided to the student and to adjust instruction based on student progress and/or devise more effective programs for students not benefiting from the program provided (Mellard & Johnson, 2008). It is important to monitor ELs' knowledge of phonics so teachers can make continual adjustments in ongoing instruction to maximize the effectiveness of instructional time. Such progress monitoring might begin with examining students' letter knowledge. For example, an instructor might progress monitor the learner's mastery of the English alphabet every few weeks to ensure that he or she achieves adequate progress. Many commercial progress monitoring assessments exist for early literacy skills, and/or such tools may be a part of the reading series adopted by the instructor's school district. Progress monitoring tools are also quite easy to develop so that they closely match the ongoing classroom instruction.

To monitor ELs' letter–sound knowledge, the instructor can develop a simple assessment tool to collect data regarding the consonant and vowel sounds already introduced to the students. Figure 5.1 is a simple example of a partial sound monitoring sheet. Sounds not yet introduced are in dark shading. This table can be extended to cover more complex sounds such as diphthongs and blends.

Next, the teacher should monitor if the students can read words with the six syllable types. It is important to know if the students can read words with multiple syllables and divide the words appropriately. To collect this data, teachers could develop targeted word flashcards (or a word list) and a simple progress monitoring chart (similar to the one for sounds) with the words assessed and dates to track student progress. Another example of a progress monitoring tool is to measure if students understand that words have word parts that can assist them with reading and understanding English. Figure 5.2 is a sample from the *Working With English Language Learners* progress monitoring tool (Cárdenas-Hagan, 2016). Once instructors gather

Letter	Sound	9/5	9/12	9/19	9/26	10/3	10/10	10/17	10/24
Yes	Yes	✓	✓	✓					
A	ā								
B									
C	k	X	X	✓					
C	s								
D	d	✓	✓						
E	ĕ (fed)		✓						

Figure 5.1. Example of a partial sound monitoring sheet.

Progress Monitoring
Teacher Form

Student School ID # _____

Last Name _____   First Name _____

Sex: ____ Male   ____ Female

Date of Birth _____ / _____ / _____   Age _____
             MM   DD   YYYY

School _____

Teacher _____

Date of Testing _____ / _____ / _____
              MM   DD   YYYY

Grade ____

Examiner's Name _____

Phonological Awareness

1. Say the word *sip*.	Change /s/ to /z/.	The word is ____. (*zip*)
2. Say the word *they*.	Change /th+/ to /r/.	The word is ____. (*ray*)
3. Say the word *ram*.	Change the /r/ to /j/.	The word is ____. (*jam*)
4. Say the word *lend*.	Change /ĕ/ to /ŏ/.	The word is ____. (*lond*)
5. Say the word *come*.	Change /k/ to /th/.	The word is ___. (*thumb*)
6. Tel me the sounds in the word *quit*.		/kw/ /ĭ/ /t/
7. Tell me the sounds in the word *ring*.		/r/ /ī/ /ng/
8. Tell me the sounds in the word *live*.		/l/ /ī/ /v/

Expected score 6–8 correct

Phonics
Read each letter. Say the name of the letter and its sound in English.

	Correct	Incorrect		Correct	Incorrect
1. H	_____	_____	6. NG	_____	_____
2. Ĭ	_____	_____	7. TH+	_____	_____
3. QU	_____	_____	8. R	_____	_____
4. J	_____	_____	9. Ŭ	_____	_____
5. Z	_____	_____	10. Ă	_____	_____

Expected score 8–10 correct

Incorrect Letters _____

Incorrect Sounds _____

Figure 5.2. The Working With English Language Learners progress monitoring tool.

(continued)

From Cárdenas-Hagan, E. (2016). *Working With English Language Learners 2 (WELLS) training manual.*
Brownsville, TX: Valley Speech Language and Learning Center; reprinted by permission.
In *Literacy Foundations for English Learners: A Comprehensive Guide to Evidence-Based Instruction,*
edited by Elsa Cárdenas-Hagan. (2020, Paul H. Brookes Publishing Co., Inc.)

Read the following words.

	Correct	Incorrect		Correct	Incorrect
1. help	_____	_____	6. quiz	_____	_____
2. add	_____	_____	7. box	_____	_____
3. lip	_____	_____	8. jump	_____	_____
4. thank	_____	_____	9. ring	_____	_____
5. that	_____	_____	10. jazz	_____	_____

Expected score 8–10 correct

Score _____

Letter-sounds read incorrectly _____

Vocabulary

Themes of Transportation, Clothing, and Places

1. I am like a short coat that you wear to keep you warm. I rhyme with the word packet. I am a _____ (jacket).
2. I am the place where airplanes can land and take you to far off destinations. I am an _____ (airport).
3. I am a large powerful vehicle that can be used to pull farm equipment. I am a _____ (tractor).
4. I am a type of aircraft with spinning metal blades attached to the very top. I am a _____ (helicopter).
5. You wear me at night so you can sleep comfortably in the bed. I am _____ (pajamas).

Expected score 4–5 correct

Fluency/Comprehension

Jim is content with his six rings. (7)
Zac is content with his red pots. (7)
Ren is content with his job singing. (9)
Bob is fond of his dog. (6)
Beth is fond of the cat. (6)
Jim, Zac, Ren, Bob, and Beth want to be content.

Number of words read correctly _____/45

Percent correct _____

Questions

Who likes the red pots? (Zac)
Who is a jeweler? Why?
Who likes animals? (Beth and Bob)
What is Ren's job?
What is Beth fond of?

Comprehension Score _____

Figure 5.2.   *(continued)*

From Cárdenas-Hagan, E. (2016). *Working With English Language Learners 2 (WELLS) training manual.*
Brownsville, TX: Valley Speech Language and Learning Center; reprinted by permission.
In *Literacy Foundations for English Learners: A Comprehensive Guide to Evidence-Based Instruction,*
edited by Elsa Cárdenas-Hagan. (2020, Paul H. Brookes Publishing Co., Inc.)

the data from progress monitoring tools, lessons can be modified to specifically target those concepts not yet mastered.

CONCLUSION

ELs can benefit from explicit phonics instruction. Phonics lessons can begin with a focus on learning the names of the English letters and the letter–sound correspondences. Cross-language connections for letters and sounds can be helpful to ELs. These students can then learn the six syllable types of the English language and practice reading words with each of the syllable types. Understanding the various syllable division patterns will also assist ELs when reading words with multiple syllables. Finally, instructors can capitalize on morphological awareness and its potential similarities with native language structure which will aid ELs' reading accuracy and understanding of English words.

STUDY QUESTIONS

1. Why is it important to teach letter names in English? Likewise, why is it important to teach letter–sound correspondences in English?

2. What are the modifications or adjustments that an educator can include when teaching letter–sound correlations to ELs?

3. Describe each of the six syllable types and strategies to teach them to ELs.

4. What special considerations are important for phonics instruction among ELs?

5. What considerations are important for syllable division instruction among ELs?

6. What is morphological awareness, and how can it assist ELs' decoding skills?

7. How does ongoing progress monitoring benefit both teacher and student?

EXTENDED READING AND APPLICATION ACTIVITIES

1. Learning the alphabet is one of the early skills for building letter knowledge. Classrooms often have students from various language backgrounds. Consider your current classroom or a previous class that you have worked in, determine if the languages are alphabetic, and make a comparison with the English alphabet. Next, reflect on how this knowledge should influence instruction for this class.

2. Understanding the English syllable types can enhance decoding skills. Determine the syllable patterns of the various home languages spoken by your students. Next, understand if any similarities can be incorporated into your lessons for the six syllable types of English.

3. Good readers understand that words can have smaller units of meaning within each word. Determine which word parts exist in the home languages of your students and incorporate this morpheme connection during instruction for decoding and vocabulary.

REFERENCES

Archer, A., & Hughes, C. A., (2020) *Explicit instruction* [video clip]. Retrieved from https://explicitinstruction.org/video-elementary/elementary-video-11/

August, D. & Shanahan, T. (2006). *Developing literacy in second language learners: Report of the National Literacy Panel on Language-Minority Children and Youth.* Mahwah, NJ: Lawrence Erlbaum Associates, Publishers.

Cárdenas-Hagan, E. (2000). *Esperanza training manual.* Brownsville, TX: Valley Speech Language and Learning Center.

Cárdenas Hagan, E. (2016). *Working With English Language Learners 2 (WELLS) training manual.* Brownsville, TX: Valley Speech Language and Learning Center.

Cárdenas-Hagan, E. (2018). Cross language connections for English learners' literacy development. *Intervention in School and Clinic, 54*(1) 14–21.

Chiappe, P., Siegel, L., & Wade-Woolley, L. (2002). Linguistic diversity and the development of reading skills: A longitudinal study. *Scientific Studies of Reading, 6*(4) 369–400.

Dictionary.com. (2019). *What percentage of English words are derived from Latin?* Retrieved from https://www.dictionary.com/e/word-origins

Ehri, L. C., & McCormick, S. (2013). Phases of word learning: Implications for instruction with delayed and disabled readers. In D. E. Alvermann, N. J. Unrau, & R. B. Ruddell (Eds.), *Theoretical models and process of reading* (6th ed., pp. 339–361). Newark, DE: International Reading Association. doi:10.1598/0710.12

Florida Center for Reading Research. (2020). *Teacher resource guide: Glossary.* Retrieved from http://www.fcrr.org/curriculum/pdf/GK-1/TRG_Final_Part3.pdf

Francis, D., Rivera, M., Lesaux, N., Kieffer, M., & Rivera, H. (2006). *Practical guidelines for the education of English language learners: Research-based recommendations for the use of accommodations in large-scale assessments* (Under cooperative agreement grant S283B050034 for U.S. Department of Education). Portsmouth, NH: RMC Research Corporation, Center on Instruction.

Mellard, D. F., & Johnson, E. (2008). *RTI: A practitioner's guide to implementing response to intervention.* Boston, MA: Corwin Press.

Moats, L. C. (2009). *LETRS module 1: The challenge of learning to read* (2nd ed.). Longmont, CO: Sopris West Educational Services.

Moats, L., & Tolman, C. (2019, July 17). *Six syllable types.* Retrieved from https://www.reading rockets.org/article/six-syllable-types

Mylanguages.org (2019, July 17). *Language lessons.* Retrieved from http://www.mylanguages.org

National Center for Education Statistics. (2017). *English language learners in public schools: The condition of education.* Retrieved from https://nces.ed.gov/programs/coe/indicator_cgf.asp

National Institute of Child Health and Human Development. (2000). *Report of the National Reading Panel: Teaching children to read* (00-4769). Washington, DC: U.S. Government Printing Office.

Nippold, M.A. (2017). Reading comprehension deficits in adolescents: Addressing underlying language abilities. *Language, Speech, and Hearing Services in Schools, 48*(2), 125–131.

Pasquarella, A., Chen, X., Gottardo, A., & Geva, E. (2014). Cross language transfer of word reading accuracy and word reading fluency in Spanish-English and Chinese-English bilinguals: Script universal and script specific processes. *Journal of Educational Psychology, 107,* 96–110.

Ramirez, G. (2017). Morphological awareness and second language learners. *Perspectives on Language and Literacy, 43,* 35–41.

Schatsneider, C., Fletcher, J. M., Francis, D. J., Carlson, C. D., & Foorman, B. R. (2004). Kindergarten prediction of reading skills: A longitudinal comparative analysis. *Journal of Educational Psychology, 96*(2), 265–282.

Share D. L., & Stanovich, K. E. (1995). Cognitive processes in early reading development: Accommodating individual differences into a model of acquisition. *Issues in Education, 1*(1), 1–57.

6

Reading Fluency Among English Learners

Coleen D. Carlson

By completing this chapter, the reader will

- Learn the components of reading fluency
- Understand evidence-based reading fluency instruction for English learners (ELs)
- Determine the components necessary for measuring fluency
- Design fluency instruction for ELs

Bernardo was a bit nervous about his reading lesson. He knew that Mrs. Garcia, his third-grade teacher, was going to ask him to read a passage and determine if he had made any progress with his reading fluency. Bernardo reviewed the high-frequency word lists that Mrs. Garcia provided each day. He also looked at the word wall for the vocabulary words from previous lessons. He practiced the phonics workbook that she suggested for him to complete. Although he was determined to succeed and make progress, he was feeling somewhat frustrated because he really did not understand what more he could do to improve his fluency skills or his deep understanding of the passages like the other kids in the class.

INTRODUCTION

As you read through this chapter, keep the vignette of Bernardo in mind and consider what information you would gather to inform yourself about his reading fluency and related skills and the instructional methods/strategies from which he might benefit.

Reading fluency has long been considered one of the critical features of skilled reading (Hasbrouck & Tindal, 1992; Huey, 1968; LaBerge & Samuels, 1974). Reading research and theory have consistently documented a relationship between reading fluency and reading comprehension (Chall, 1996; Crosson & Lesaux, 2010; Slocum, Street, & Gilberts, 1995; Torgesen, Rashotte, & Alexander, 2001). This chapter begins by defining reading fluency and describing the components that make up fluency. It goes on to explore the features of evidence-based fluency instruction, discussing a variety of strategies to meet the needs of and build skills for English learners (ELs).

FLUENCY

Definitions for fluency vary and are primarily based on the components that are emphasized. Some experts believe that the accuracy with which the words are read and the automaticity (effortlessness) of the reading should be of primary focus (e.g., Hudson, Pullen, Lane, & Torgesen, 2009). Others think that the primary emphasis should be on the prosodic (expressive) features of oral reading (Daane, Campbell, Grigg, Goodman, & Oranje, 2005; Rasinski, Rikli, & Johnston, 2009) or the ability to read accurately and comprehend at the same time (Samuels, 2006). Regardless, most definitions acknowledge three primary contributors of fluency:

1. *Accuracy:* reading words correctly

2. *Rate:* reading with speed and effortlessness (automaticity)

3. *Prosody:* reading with good expression

In other words, it is the ability to accurately read words in text, seemingly effortlessly and quickly (seemingly automatically), with appropriate patterns of expression (e.g., rhythm, sound, stress, intonation) that enhance the meaning of the text.

In addition to variations in the definition of fluency, thinking about how fluency and comprehension are related has also changed over time. Although it was once thought that fluency was a prerequisite for comprehension, some studies suggest that fluency and comprehension are complex yet related skills that develop side by side, consist of some similar and interrelated underlying skills, and continually influence one another (Kuhn, Schwanenflugel, & Meisinger, 2010; Paige, Rasinski, & Magpuri-Lavell, 2012).

This chapter uses Kuhn et al.'s (2010) proposed definition of fluency: "Fluency combines accuracy, automaticity, and oral reading prosody, which, taken together, facilitate the reader's construction of meaning. It is demonstrated during oral reading through ease of word recognition, appropriate pacing, phrasing, and intonation" (p. 242). This definition focuses on the common characteristics of fluent readers (accuracy, rate, and prosody) while acknowledging the essential relationship of fluency to comprehension. Thus, fluency is viewed as a component skill of comprehension and something that can facilitate or impair comprehension of the text being read.

There is a long history of the influence of automaticity theory on thinking about the role of fluency in reading comprehension (LaBerge & Samuels, 1974). This theory posits that reading (decoding) requires the use of cognitive resources. Readers who are unable to easily and accurately decode words are thought to be using most of their cognitive resources for the decoding process itself, leaving few resources for comprehending the text being read. Thus, laborious and inefficient reading will make it more difficult for the reader to remember what has been read, gain access to background knowledge, and relate ideas from the text. Alternately, those readers who are able to accurately and effortlessly decode words in text are thought to have more available cognitive resources, allowing them to allocate these resources to attending to other features of the text, incorporating their background knowledge, relating ideas from the text, and ultimately comprehending the text being read (Linan-Thompson, Vaughn, Hickman-Davis, & Kouzekanani, 2003; Lingo, 2014; Marchand-Martella, Martella, Modderman, Peterson, & Pan, 2013). As such, fluent reading is also thought to lead to fewer misunderstandings of the text being read (Hudson, Lane, & Pullen, 2005). It is important to understand that although weak fluency can certainly impede understanding of the text being read, fluent reading does not guarantee comprehension. In other words, if the process of decoding words is challenging for the reader, then most of the reader's available cognitive resources may be focused solely on the task of decoding words. As a result, there are not enough cognitive resources available to the reader for processing information related to text comprehension (e.g., word grouping, syntax, background knowledge).

Reading accuracy and speed (automaticity) are thought to develop concurrently (Logan, 1997). As one's ability to decode improves, reading typically becomes faster and less labored. For many, reading eventually becomes an effortless process. Yet, decoding accurately and effortlessly alone does not necessarily produce readers with comprehension of the text they are reading. Some readers can read quite accurately and at a quick rate, but they fail to comprehend what they have read and/or are unable to read aloud with appropriate expression. Thus, they have acquired a level of automaticity, yet they are unable to comprehend what is read. At the same time, some disfluent readers are able to comprehend the text they have read. Thus, it is clear that fluency entails many skills beyond decoding accurately and quickly. Fluent reading requires the processing of information from multiple sources in different ways. One's ability to multitask in this manner requires efficiency, and fluency is essentially the key to this efficiency.

Reading with good prosody (expression) is also an important component of reading fluency (Kuhn et al., 2010). Reading with appropriate expression requires the reader to vary his or her pitch and place stress on certain words or phrases in a manner appropriate to the text being read. Research has shown that, minimally, young fluent readers pause in grammatically appropriate places (Benjamin & Schwanenflugel, 2010) and stress appropriate syllable patterns within words (Gutierrez-Palma & Palma-Reyes, 2007). This expression illustrates a level of understanding of the text that is often not seen with nonfluent readers. Struggling readers, on the other hand, are often characterized as reading in monotone voices with little expression or appropriate phrasing. Skilled reading prosody is believed to emerge once some level of automaticity has developed, thus allowing the reader to use more cognitive resources for expression and comprehension (Schwanenflugel, Hamilton, Kuhn, Wisenbaker, & Stahl, 2004).

Fluency and Comprehension

A critical aspect of fluency lies in its influence on the process of comprehension. Fluency can facilitate or impede the ability to comprehend the text being read as well as the depth of understanding gleaned from the text. Research has consistently documented a positive relationship between fluency and comprehension among monolingual English speakers. This relationship is relatively strong, especially in the elementary years, and is found across a variety of fluency measures with different formats (Kim, Petscher, Schatschneider, & Foorman, 2010; Lai, Benjamin, Schwanenflugel, & Kuhn, 2013; Reschly, Busch, Betts, Deno, & Long, 2009; Valencia, Smith, Reece, Li, Wixson, & Newman, 2010).

It is important to note that increased reading rate is not limitless. The largest gains in accuracy and rate are typically seen early on, whereas less gain is seen as a student's reading rate trajectory begins to flatten out (Fuchs, Fuchs, Hamlett, Walz, & Germann, 1993). This pattern suggests that the relationship between reading rate and comprehension should be stronger in the elementary and junior high grades than in older individuals (Jenkins & Jewell, 1993).

Although most research fails to address the expressive component of fluency, there is evidence of the importance of its role in comprehension above and beyond simply reading accuracy and rate. Including measures of expression in examinations of the relationship between reading accuracy and rate and comprehension have indicated that measures of reading expressiveness significantly contribute to the relationship between fluency and comprehension (Benjamin et al., 2013; Valencia et al., 2010).

FLUENCY AND ENGLISH LEARNERS

A large portion of research has focused on students whose native language is English. There is a rapidly growing area of research, however, extending the focus to the process of reading in second language learners. This research has shown similar relationships to those seen with monolingual learners, in that word reading accuracy and reading comprehension skills are highly correlated (Crosson & Lesaux, 2010; Quirk & Beem, 2012) as are word reading fluency and reading comprehension. Yet, this research also suggests an important difference between monolingual and second language learners. Specifically, the relationship between reading fluency and comprehension is moderated by English oral language skills (Crosson & Lesaux, 2010), meaning oral language is an important foundation that supports the role of fluency as a bridge to comprehension. Given that by definition ELs have less well-developed English oral language skills than monolingual learners, the importance of building these skills will necessarily affect reading fluency.

Reading fluency has shifted into the spotlight of necessary and important skills that together determine a reader's proficiency and ability to comprehend written text. Our understanding of the role of fluency in the reading and understanding process is continually being refined and expanded, especially for ELs.

PRINCIPLES OF ORAL READING FLUENCY INSTRUCTION FOR ENGLISH LEARNERS

The past few decades have seen a dramatic increase in the time spent on direct fluency instruction in the classroom. Although educators believe fluency to be a critical component of reading development, fluency instruction in many classrooms is often constrained by the assessments being used to assess fluency (Rasinski, Blachowicz, & Lems, 2006; Samuels & Farstrup, 2006). Many of the most commonly adopted fluency assessments focus solely on accuracy and rate/speed. As a result, much of fluency instruction seen in classrooms models techniques that focus solely on timed reading, emphasizing increased rate without necessarily focusing on a more comprehensive set of fluency-related skills that support comprehension development.

Common sense tells us that the best way to become a more fluent reader is to practice, and practice, and still practice. In fact, some believe that a student will develop into a skilled, fluent reader only with extensive practice with a large amount of texts (Allington, 1983; Snow, Burns, & Griffin, 1998). More research has found that it is engaged and repetitive reading practice that is embedded with systematic support that is most effective in the early grades (Chard, Vaughn, & Tyler, 2002; Denton, Fletcher, Anthony, & Francis, 2006; Kuhn & Stahl, 2003; Mathes et al., 2005; Meyer & Felton, 1999; National Reading Panel, 2000; Therrien, 2004; Wolf & Katzir-Cohen, 2001). Instruction that incorporates a focus on the prosodic features of the text being read has also been shown to be a valuable component of interventions with struggling readers (Rasiński et al., 2009).

Fluency instruction can be especially beneficial for ELs because the instructional activities designed to develop fluent reading can also promote oral language development in English and reading comprehension. Students who practice reading English text with accuracy, automaticity, and appropriate prosody can gain valuable information about the sounds and cadences of the English language, which supports the development of oral language fluency and reading comprehension as well as listening comprehension.

Fluency instruction for ELs should be explicit and systematic, which means the learning goals of the tasks are clearly delineated in a comprehensible manner and the process and completion of the task is specifically modeled. Explicit and systematic instruction provides ELs with clear guidelines and easy to follow, comprehensible instructions, thus increasing their ability to successfully engage in and complete the learning tasks (Calderón, Hertz-Lazarowitz, & Slavin, 1996).

STATEGIES AND TECHNIQUES FOR TEACHING FLUENCY TO ENGLISH LEARNERS

The following sections introduce common research-based strategy techniques used for fluency instruction in the classroom. Regardless of the specific techniques employed, fluency instruction should always begin as early as possible but take different forms at different levels of the reading process. As students are learning to decode, substantial practice is necessary for decoding to become automatic. The decoding process is facilitated by knowledge of letters and sounds, phonological awareness, vocabulary, and morphological knowledge. Strong foundational skills provide a base upon which fluency develops; thus, students need to have solid basic phonological and orthographic skills to support the development of fluency. As students are learning to decode, vocabulary and morphological knowledge can assist with decoding words and understanding their meaning. Knowledge of syntax and semantics can also assist with quickly and efficiently deciphering words and meanings.

Instruction that focuses solely on the development of accurate reading speed should not be a primary focus. With markedly less fluent students, the primary focus should be on further development of the foundational skills that they are lacking and that are interfering with their ability to develop some level of automaticity. For the most part, all students can benefit from practicing reading connected text.

Fluency instruction with connected text should always include ample practice, include repeated reading (exposure), allow for self-correction, provide corrective feedback, be relatively brief, be implemented consistently and frequently, and include tracking of reading accuracy and rate as well as ratings of prosody and monitoring of comprehension. No one technique will typically afford the opportunity to address all of these components. Using a combination of techniques, however, will assist in addressing each component on a consistent basis. In addition, a combination of techniques will lessen task repetitiveness and student boredom.

The National Reading Panel report (2000) endorsed the use of supported, guided, and repeated reading techniques in the classroom as a means for improving students' reading fluency (among other skills). Specifically, the report supported repeated reading procedures that have students reading passages orally multiple times while receiving guidance or feedback from peers, parents, or teachers as being effective in improving a variety of reading skills. Many of these techniques are relatively easy to implement in the classroom and do not require extensive materials. These techniques/procedures have been shown to improve all students' reading ability, at least through primary grades. Research has shown that effective instructional techniques for monolingual learners is also effective for ELs. Although these techniques provide a foundation for ELs, they are not sufficient alone. Adaptations or enhancements to the techniques are often required to promote ELs' development (Goldenberg, 2013).

Repeated Oral Reading

Repeated oral reading is a broad term for oral reading fluency instructional techniques designed to increase the confidence of students with low reading fluency while increasing reading accuracy and speed, the ability to process words automatically, reading with meaningful expression, and comprehending the material being read. Repeated oral reading can be done individually, in pairs, or in small and large groups. Although this method was originally proposed as an intervention for students with learning disabilities, research has shown that all students can benefit from this approach, including ELs.

Several studies on repeated reading intervention techniques concluded that repeated reading is positively related to increases in reading accuracy and rate (Kubina, Amato, Schwilk, & Therrien, 2008; O'Connor, White, & Swanson, 2007; Welsch, 2007), with many also showing gains in comprehension, which is the main goal of such interventions (O'Connor et al., 2007; Oddo, Barnett, Hawkins, & Musti-Rao, 2010; Staubitz, Cartledge, Yurick, & Lo, 2005; Welsch, 2007; Yurick, Robinson, Cartledge, Lo, & Evans, 2006).

Some findings also indicated that gains seen in repeated reading seem to transfer to new texts (Ardoin, Williams, Klubnik, & McCall, 2009; Chafouleas, Martens, Dobson, Weinstein, & Gardner, 2004; Daly, Bonfiglio, Mattson, Persampieri, & Foreman-Yates, 2005; Welsch, 2007). Thus, gains may not only be seen with the text that has been repeatedly read but also with new texts being read.

The following components of repeated reading intervention promote student gains (Chard et al., 2002; Morgan & Sideridis, 2006; Stevens, Walker, & Vaughn, 2014; Therrien, 2004):

- Rereading multiple times

- Allowing for self-correction and providing error correction feedback

- Using progressively more difficult text

- Including an adult model of fluent reading prior to group or independent practice

In the event that an adult is not available or feasible, a more proficient peer is also beneficial, followed by a same ability level peer (Ardoin et al., 2009; Daly et al., 2005; Decker & Buggey, 2014; Oddo et al., 2010; Sáenz, Fuchs, & Fuchs, 2005). Same ability level peers were less beneficial than more proficient peers or adults, but they were significantly more beneficial than no model at all (Musti-Rao, Hawkins, & Barkley, 2009; Staubitz et al., 2005; Yurick et al., 2006).

Based on this information, the following guidelines are suggested for implementing reading practice in the classroom:

- Repeated reading instruction should be implemented consistently (multiple times per week).

- Choose texts (e.g., songs, poems, portions of books) that are approximately 100–200 words in length. Longer texts can be used as students become more proficient readers.

- Ensure that the selected text is decodable to the reader—on or near his or her instructional level. If the student reads the passage for the first time with an accuracy rate less than 90%–95%, then an easier story should be selected.

- Preread the passage to yourself to identify any words you think the student will not know. Briefly teach the student the identified words, including the correct pronunciation and a student-friendly definition.

- Model fluent reading of the text for the student—reading in a fluid manner with appropriate expression.

- Prior to student reading, instruct the student to focus on the accuracy of his or her reading as well as appropriate expression and comprehension.

- Have students read the selected passage aloud.

- Record and chart the student's reading accuracy, reading rate, and appropriate expression (see the Measuring Fluency section). Allow the student to participate in the tracking of his or her progress so he or she can see and be proud of his or her achievements.

- If the student misreads a word, then provide the correction.

- If a student asks for the pronunciation of a word, then provide it.

- If the student stumbles on a word and is unable to move on, provide him or her with the word and encourage him or her to continue. The goal is for the student to increase his or her ability to self-monitor and self-correct.

- Text comprehension is important to include and should focus on deeper understanding of the text rather than simple recall. Comprehension should focus on summarizing, questioning motives, predicting (if using portions of texts that will eventually be read in full), linking to personal experiences, and so forth.

- Have the student reread the passage as many times as needed until the reading of the text is fluent (as determined by a prescribed criterion for rate, speed, and prosody—see the Measuring Fluency section) and the student shows good comprehension of the text.

Although the previous steps are important for all readers, identifying words that may be unknown or less known and explicitly teaching the words is especially important for ELs (August & Shanahan, 2006). No text should include more than five words that are unfamiliar to the student. Building fluency is about the students increasing their automaticity, prosody, and, ultimately, their comprehension of the text. Reading texts at too high a level or with too many unknown words will make this process more difficult. For EL students, drawing attention to unknown words during the initial presentation of the text, providing appropriate levels of definitions (e.g., providing English labels for words for which concepts and labels in one's native language are understood, quick definitions or demonstrations for simple words), and tying to background knowledge is critical. No amount of simply reading and rereading words will produce knowledge of unknown vocabulary. In addition to teacher identification of vocabulary challenges, teaching students to identify and become comfortable with identifying unknown words is also beneficial and can promote increased ownership over their own reading.

Choral Reading

Choral reading is a repeated oral reading technique that allows students to experience a fluent model of text reading while also gaining practice in reading aloud. Choral reading is implemented with groups of students in which they read text aloud at the same time and then again in different groups.

Choral reading can be a nonthreatening way for reluctant readers to practice reading because it allows them to hear what they are seeing without drawing attention to themselves individually. Choral reading can reduce anxiety in ELs over mispronunciations and provide a comfortable way to practice reading and hearing fluent reading. Because choral reading involves a group reading simultaneously, ELs' mistakes are not the primary focus of the group reading. This type of repeated reading allows ELs to hear their own errors in comparison with what is being said by their peers as well as to hear models of fluent reading. Thus, choral reading provides models and practice in a more comfortable setting, especially for struggling readers and ELs. To implement choral reading in the classroom, the teacher should do the following:

- Introduce the text to students by reading it aloud to them while they follow along silently. Texts that lend themselves to active emphasis are especially good with this technique (e.g., poems, songs).

- Have students read through the text aloud and in unison.

- Reread the text multiple times, breaking the larger group into smaller groups and asking different groups to take turns reading portions of the text aloud in unison. Students can be grouped in many ways (e.g., boys/girls, brown/blue eyes, favorite colors).

Some people extend this experience to include an actual performance with a script. Portions of the text are assigned to different groups of students, and the script indicates how certain words or phrases should be read (e.g., bold words are read with more emphasis, italic words are spoken softly). Students practice their portions repeatedly and the process ends with a performance of the entire group. This extended choral reading is typically completed over multiple days and often incorporates movement.

Some research has shown the benefit of choral reading in that it seems to increase students' willingness to practice and engage in the reading process (Jennings, Caldwell, & Lerner, 2014). If students find choral reading enjoyable, then they may be more motivated and focused when reading.

As with any form of repeated oral reading, it is important for ELs to draw attention to unknown vocabulary or concepts and build knowledge of these words or phrases and background knowledge during the initial presentation of the text. Chunking the text into meaningful units (e.g., phrases, clauses, meaningful portions of a sentence) can be especially useful for ELs. These units are often associated with places where pauses, emphasis, or changes in intonation would occur and thus provide opportunities to emphasize those transitions for the EL (Hasbrouk, 2006).

Partner Reading

Partner reading is a research-based instructional strategy that is often used to successfully assist students in building reading fluency (Vaughn,

Gersten, & Chard, 2000). Partner reading developed out of programs taking a cooperative framework approach to learning and combines repeated reading with peer-assisted learning strategies. Partner reading is an efficient technique for keeping students engaged regardless of their ability level and providing immediate feedback and correction (Fuchs, Fuchs, Mathes, & Simmons, 1997). Several studies have found that partner reading is especially beneficial for ELs because it allows them the opportunity to engage in a linguistically complex interaction with a fluent model, engage in collaborative experiences constructing and sharing text meaning, and hear and practice appropriate prosody (Calderón, Hertz-Lazarowitz, & Slavin, 1998; Calhoun, Otaiba, Cihak, King, & Avalos, 2007; Wright, 2015). Partner reading also helps teachers assist students at all levels simultaneously and removes the need to sit one to one with each student for a period of time. As such, it is a valuable tool to assist the teacher in addressing the need for individualized instruction (Rathvon, 2008). Research has shown positive effects on student fluency and comprehension as a result of partner reading interventions (Fuchs et al., 1997).

In contrast to choral reading, students read consecutive portions of the text rather than the same text in unison during partner reading. In this approach, both students in the partnership play the role of reader and supporter alternately throughout the text. During partner reading, students most commonly alternate roles page by page. One student reads the first page aloud while the other plays a supporting role, following along and providing corrections and assistance with unknown or misread words. The students switch roles on the next page.

A number of suggestions about how to teach, organize, and manage the partner reading process have been developed. First, studies have shown that this technique can be effective whether the partners are of a similar ability level or moderately different in their ability levels (Griffin, 2002). For EL students, a variety of pairings have been recommended, including pairing the student with a monolingual English partner, pairing the student with another EL with stronger English language skills, and allowing them the experience of coaching another EL with somewhat weaker English language skills. Although it is important that ELs are exposed to a fluent model, balancing this practice and exposure with the opportunity to play a coaching role can also boost the student's confidence in his or her own skills.

Another important facet of partner reading is the existing relationship among the students—their ability to work together and get along. Teacher monitoring and observation during partner reading sessions also plays an important role, although this monitoring can be periodic and does not have to be constant. Regrouping students periodically and allowing students to play different roles in the partnerships in also recommended to enhance collaborations and relieves redundancy (Griffin, 2002).

Instructing students on the partner reading process is important to its success and should include discussion of the following:

- The basic procedure of paired reading
- How to listen to their partners
- How to provide positive, productive feedback to their partners

Echo Reading

Research has shown that echo reading with a fluent adult model can improve reading accuracy rates on familiar passages. Echo reading is a repeated reading technique that is designed to assist students struggling with fluent, expressive reading. The teacher models the reading of a short segment of text out loud while the student follows along with his or her finger. Once the teacher stops reading, the student then rereads the segment out loud. In his or her repetition, the student attempts to read the words accurately with the same expression as the model. This pattern progresses through the entire selected text.

Echo reading is a particularly useful strategy for students just learning to read, including ELs with very low English proficiency levels. Research has shown that echo reading with a fluent adult model improved reading accuracy rates on familiar passages.

MEASURING FLUENCY

The ability to measure ELs' level of accurate and fluent reading with appropriate prosody and monitor their progress in these areas is key to planning successful instruction. Teachers need to be able to identify each student's area of need as well as gauge the effectiveness of their instruction. To effectively accomplish this, teachers need ways to assess fluency validly and efficiently.

First, it is critical that the assessments used to assess fluency are reliable and valid. This means that the assessment results provide a consistent measure of fluency and do not vary because of problems in the assessment itself (reliability). In addition, the assessments should measure what is intended (validity).

Fluency involves far more than simply reading fast. Yet, in many U.S. school systems, the assessment of fluency has been reduced to recording the number of words read correctly per minute (WCPM). The appeal of this approach is that it is easy to implement and takes little away from classroom instructional time. This type of assessment, however, simply measures the accuracy and speed of reading with no attention provided to the student's ability to read with prosody or comprehend the text being read. Thus, these assessments provide an incomplete view of fluency, one that is focused on speed at the detriment of meaning (Kuhn et al., 2010).

The following section illustrates common methods for assessing a student's fluency. Regardless of the specific method or metric being assessed, it is important to know that a student's fluency level may not always appear consistent. Fluency can be influenced by characteristics of text and the student's familiarity with the text. Specifically, fluency can vary based on the type of text being read, the readability of the text for the specific student, familiarity with the topic of the text, knowledge of the meaning of words in the text, and overlap in words across texts and contexts (National Reading Panel, 2000).

When assessing components of fluency, it is always important to interpret results within the context of other, related skills. Fluency should not be interpreted and acted upon in isolation. In addition, it is important to distinguish between nonfluent reading and reading with an accent. Many ELs will read and speak English with an accent as they are beginning to learn English, and some will retain an accent throughout their lives. Students can read English fluently with a native language accent.

Measuring Accuracy

Assessment of word reading accuracy can be accomplished in numerous ways. In its most simple form, listening to oral reading and counting the number of errors per 100 words can provide valuable individual or group instructional information. Alternately, a more in-depth analysis of a student's miscues can provide more detailed information about the student's strategy use as well as his or her strengths and weaknesses. For example, observing a student who is trying to read an unknown word could provide useful information about phonological knowledge, ability to use context cues, the ability to relate unknown words to known words, and so forth. Whatever the level of assessment specificity, the use of contextual and oral reading has been shown to be a better measure of reading rate than reading words in a list or silent reading (Jenkins, Fuchs, van den Broek, Espin, & Deno, 2003).

Reading rate and accuracy are often assessed simultaneously using one assessment. Although accuracy can be assessed without also assessing rate, rate requires the assessment of accuracy. In its most basic form, reading accuracy is simply a measure of the number of words read correctly in the text. The number of words read correctly is also part of the equation for calculating reading rate (see the rate section). By itself, knowing the total number of words read correctly is not very useful. It must be compared with the total number of words the student could possibly have read correctly in order for it to become useful information. For example, a student read two passages (A and B), and the student accurately read 50 words on both passages. Without knowing how many words were possible in the passages read, just knowing the student read 50 words correctly reveals very little. Consider, however, a situation in which passage A consisted of 50 words and passage B consisted of 100 words. Now we know that the student read 50/50 words correctly in passage A and 50/100 words correctly in passage B. We also know that passage A was easier for the student to decode than passage B.

This information can be used to calculate the readability of the passage for this student (Gunning, 2002). Readability is typically calculated by taking the total number of words read correctly, divided by the total number of words in the text being read.

Total number of words read correctly/total number of words in the text = percent accuracy

Using the previous example, the student's percent accuracy would be 50/50 = 100% for passage A. For passage B, the student's percent accuracy would be 50/100 = 50%. For ease of interpretation, the percent accuracy is then typically assigned one of three categorical values that indicate the level of text readability for that student:

1. Independent

2. Instructional

3. Frustrational

Independent level text is one the student can read with an accuracy of 95%–100%; in other words, ≤ 1 in 20 words are misread. Instructional level text is one in which the student can read with an accuracy of 90%–94%, or about 1 in 10 words are misread. Frustrational level text is one that the student can read with an accuracy of < 90%, or more than 1 in 10 words are misread. Independent level texts are those most often targeted for use in fluency instruction because they allow students to work on increasing their reading fluency, practice reading with appropriate expression, and focus on gleaning meaning from what they are reading. Texts at the instructional level require more attention and cognitive resources to be used for decoding. This level of text can also be used for fluency instruction but is most useful when there is a lot of additional support provided. Frustrational level texts are rarely a focus for reading fluency practice because the cognitive load required is significantly more demanding. Referring back to the example, passage A was read at the independent level, whereas passage B was read at a frustrational level.

Although not used as often in an educational setting, diagnosticians and clinicians frequently also examine reading accuracy by tracking and examining the types of errors that are made while reading. Thus, the focus is on words read correctly as well as words read incorrectly. This type of information is useful in helping to determine the strategies students are using or are to use while reading, and patterns of errors can also help inform intervention. Adding more specific aspects of reading accuracy can help focus fluency-based intervention. In-depth discussion of error analysis is beyond the scope of this chapter, but a useful first resource is Johnston's (2000) book on running records.

Accent is one of the more common difficulties encountered when assessing ELs' reading accuracy. Fluency should not be confused with reading with an accent. Many ELs will read and speak English with an accent, especially as they are beginning to learn English. Students can read English fluently with a native language accent.

Other common errors in reading accuracy encountered with ELs, especially those with less developed English skills, are word reading error patterns involving sounds and sound combinations that are unfamiliar to the student or are not as frequently encountered in his or her native language.

Measuring Rate

Reading rate (or speed of reading accuracy) is most often measured using timed readings of connected text. When assessing reading rate, it is critical to use text that is at a student's independent reading level (i.e., text the student can read with 95%+ accuracy).

Reading rate is typically expressed in terms of the number of WCPM, although many also use the number of words read correctly in an entire passage. Calculating the number of WCPM is typically seen as more efficient and economical because it can be calculated in a shorter period of time. This method provides a good snapshot of the student's rate of reading accuracy that is highly correlated to their reading accuracy rate with longer passages. Some also argue, however, that calculating rate using a full passage (of appropriate grade level) provides a more accurate picture of reading rate because it allows for more reading time and a more natural view of the student's reading (e.g., providing more time for the student to increase and decrease pace during a reading).

Reading accuracy rate is calculated using the total number of words read correctly and the total number of seconds spent reading the text. Depending upon the specific approach, the formula to calculate reading rate varies slightly. Reading rate is most commonly assessed using one of two methods—reading of a full passage or 1-minute probes of passage reading. In both methods, students read the passage and the teachers (using a copy of the passage) mark each word the student reads incorrectly by drawing a line through the word. Self-corrections are typically counted as words read correctly.

In the full passage method, the teacher times the student using a stopwatch from the beginning of reading of the first word to the end of reading of the last word. The teacher then records the total number of seconds of reading and totals the number of words read incorrectly. The additional piece of information the teacher needs is the total number of words in the passage that was read. The following formulas are then used to calculate reading rate:

Words read correctly = total words in passage - total words read incorrectly

WCPM = words read correctly/total number of seconds X 60

In the 1-minute probe method, the teacher times the student using a stopwatch from the beginning of reading of the first word to the end of 60 seconds, marking words read incorrectly as previously described. At the end of 60 seconds, the teacher circles the last word read. The student can then either be asked to stop reading, or the teacher can have the student read the remainder of the passage without tracking errors. The number of words read correctly (not slashed) from the beginning of the passage to the end of the 60 second probe are then totaled, which is the WCPM. When using 1-minute probes, it is recommended that the teacher complete multiple probes with different level texts and then use the average rate obtained. These results provide a more stable estimate of the student's fluency rate at a given point in time.

As previously noted, assessments of fluency should focus on students who read at an independent level. Assessing reading fluency with independent level text allows the teacher to determine the student's relative fluency rate on text that the teacher would expect him or her to read without difficulty.

Hasbrouck and Tindal (2017) (see Figure 6.1) have developed a set of oral reading fluency norms by grade level (1–6) and time of year (fall, winter, and spring). These norms are based on native English readers. This does not, however, diminish their usefulness with ELs. It should be expected that ELs' oral reading fluency rates will be lower than that of a native EL, especially for early learners. These norms, however, serve as a gauge for progress and a reference for where ELs are in relation to monolingual learners

Grade	Percentile	Fall WCPM	Winter WCMP	Spring WCPM	Grade	Percentile	Fall WCPM	Winter WCMP	Spring WCPM
	90		97	116		90	153	168	184
	75		59	91		75	125	143	160
1	50		29	60	4	50	94	120	133
	25		16	34		25	75	95	105
	10		9	18		10	60	71	83
	90	111	131	148		90	179	183	195
	75	84	109	124		75	153	160	169
2	50	50	84	100	5	50	121	133	146
	25	36	59	72		25	87	109	119
	10	23	35	43		10	64	84	102
	90	134	161	166		90	185	195	204
	75	104	137	139		75	159	166	173
3	50	83	97	112	6	50	132	145	146
	25	59	79	91		25	112	116	122
	10	40	62	63		10	89	91	91

Figure 6.1. Oral reading fluency norms by grade level (1–6) and time of year (fall, winter, and spring). (From Hasbrouck, J., & Tindal, G. [2017]. *An update to compiled ORF norms* [Technical Report No. 1702]. Eugene: Behavioral Research and Teaching, University of Oregon; reprinted by permission.) (*Key:* WCPM, words correct per minute.)

in their peer group. Thus, the Hasbrouk and Tindel norms are a useful reference for identifying the relative standing of the EL to other students and to mean expectations for students in that grade at that time. The utility of the Hasbrouk and Tindel norms are that they retain the distributive nature of oral reading fluency scores. Meaning, they do not require the use of an arbitrary cut score to determine the adequacy of the fluency score. Instead, the authors noted the limited evidence in research supporting the benefit of intervention for students with fluency scores above the 50th percentile. Intervention with students whose fluency is at or below the 50th percentile, however, is well supported in the literature.

For example, if a student in the fall of second grade read a grade-level passage with a fluency rate of 84, then the percentile score for that student would be 75 (see Figure 6.1). Thus, the fluency rate is above average for beginning-of-the-year second graders. If another student in the fall of second grade read a grade-level passage with a fluency rate of 42, then the percentile score for that student would be below the 50th percentile—falling somewhere between the 25th and 50th percentile (see Figure 6.1). This student's fluency is below average for his or her grade level at the beginning of the year. As such, additional examination of other skills should be completed to determine how best to address the student's needs.

Notes of Caution on Interpreting Rate   Interpretation of student skill performance should be completed by looking across all skills to identify strengths, weaknesses, and patterns of need. Although reading accuracy (fluency) rate seems to reflect a student's development of decoding automaticity and has been shown to be related to reading comprehension, fluency rate should never be interpreted in isolation. Furthermore, a poor fluency rate should not be interpreted as meaning that students should simply receive explicit and intense instruction and practice that is focused on developing faster readers. Although reading rate can be developed through practiced and assisted readings, this should not be the only or primary focus of instruction for nonfluent readers. A more comprehensive and balanced approach that includes instruction on phonology (if needed) and prosody will be more beneficial in the long run. If teachers provide instruction in fluency that addresses the areas of weakness or the areas causing the slower rate, then fluency, comprehension, and rate will all improve. If teachers primarily focus on developing reading accuracy rate (speed) at the expense of core weaknesses, as well as reading with expression, meaning, and comprehension, then students may end up reading quickly but without comprehension of what is being read.

Along the same line, caution should be taken when using reading rate to assess ELs' reading abilities. Many ELs learn to decode quickly and accurately, yet understand little of what they have read. Thus, educators cannot assume that if a student reads text accurately and with relative fluency that he or she is progressing as desired. The prosody of ELs (and other students) with solid accuracy and fluency rates and low comprehension is often not that of a strong reader or one who seems to be understanding the nuances of what is being read.

Measuring Prosody

Readers who use appropriate volume, tone, emphasis, phrasing, and other elements in oral expression are showing that that they are able interpret or construct meaning from the text. Measurement of reading prosody can only be completed through observation of a student reading text orally. Unlike reading accuracy and rate, assessment of reading prosody is more subjective and requires general knowledge of the sound of good reading prosody for the age range being assessed.

Current ratings schemes measuring reading prosody vary significantly in regard to the specific dimensions that are rated and how they are rated. Some assessments rate multiple dimensions of prosody in a single rating scale (e.g., National Assessment of Educational Process [NAEP] Oral Reading Fluency Scale) (Daane et al., 2005), whereas others address specific dimensions of prosodic reading separately. Assessments addressing separate dimension also vary substantially, with some including two (Comprehensive Oral Reading Scale) (Benjamin et al., 2013), three (Multidimensional Fluency Scale) (Zutell & Rasinski, 1991), or four (Multidimensional Fluency Scale) (Paige et al., 2012).

Difficulties with oral reading prosody, if not addressed, can sustain throughout adulthood for struggling readers. In turn, it is critical to assess a student's skill with this component of fluency (Paige et al., 2012). Selecting the specific measure to be used depends on multiple factors, including time available and level of detail desired. Assessments using rating scales that include multiple dimensions of prosody can be useful when the scale shows good reliability and validity and can be used to compare students within and across classes or populations. Rating scales such as these, however, can be limiting if the goal is to determine the specific areas of weakness. For example, the NAEP Oral Reading Fluency Scale rates a student in one of four levels, and descriptions of the levels follow (Daane et al., 2005):

- Level 1: Reads primarily word by word. Occasional two- or three-word phrases may occur, but these are infrequent and/or they do not preserve meaningful syntax.

- Level 2: Reads primarily in two-word phrases with some three- or four-word groupings. Some word-by-word reading may be present. Word groupings may seem awkward and unrelated to larger context of sentence or passage.

- Level 3: Reads primarily in three- or four-word phrase groups. Some small groupings may be present. The majority of phrasing, however, seems appropriate and preserves the syntax of the author. Little or no expressive interpretation is present.

- Level 4: Reads primarily in larger, meaningful phrase groups. Although some regressions, repetitions, and deviations from text may be present, these do not appear to detract from the overall structure of the story. Preservation of the author's syntax is consistent. Some or most of the story is read with expressive interpretation.

Students reading at levels 1 or 2 are categorized as nonfluent readers, whereas those reading at levels 3 and 4 are considered fluent readers. Multiple dimensions of prosody are embedded in each rating, including phrasing, adherence to sentence/word structure, and expressiveness. Student ratings on this assessment were found to be significantly related to their reading accuracy and rate. Specifically, students with lower level ratings also showed lower accuracy and speed ratings, in general, whereas those with higher ratings (3 and 4) showed greater accuracy and speed.

This type of assessment (single rating scale of multiple dimensions) can be very useful for grouping and comparing student groups. If the goal is to gather information that provides a profile of prosody skills to direct student instruction, however, then a more detailed assessment of prosody (one that separates and rates dimensions independently) may be more beneficial. Regardless of the specific instrument used, the following are some of the primary components of prosody that should be considered. These descriptions apply to monolingual learners and ELs; the errors typically seen in nonfluent learners include the common errors seen in ELs with less well-developed English skills.

- *Phrasing* is the way readers put words together in groups (e.g., clauses, sentence units) to represent the meaningful units of language. Sometimes phrases are cued in text by punctuation (e.g., commas), but often they are not. Nonfluent readers tend to frequently read in a choppy manner (e.g., word by word, in two- or three-word phrases), with run-ons and/or inappropriate pauses midsentence. Fluent reading exhibits phrasing that is appropriate to the clause and sentence structure of the text being read.

- *Pacing* is represented by steady, consistent reading of the text that is not too fast and not too slow. Pace in regard to prosody should not be confused with reading rate or speed. The pacing of fluent reading is consistent and conversational—although somewhat more formal than casual conversation. Nonfluent readers pacing is typically slow and laborious or very uneven.

- *Smoothness* is represented by the easy resolution of word and structure difficulties while reading text. More fluent readers tend to resolve word or structure difficulties quickly without much interruption to the reading of the text (i.e., self-corrections). Nonfluent readers will exhibit frequent pauses and hesitations and false starts that are very disruptive to the reading of the text.

- *Expression* is text reading that sounds like natural language, in which tone, pitch, and volume are varied to convey appropriate text meaning. Nonfluent reading is often characterized by expressionless reading with little to no variation in tone, pitch, or volume, whereas fluent reading conveys appropriate meaning and sounds like natural language.

Overall, well-developed prosodic oral reading is a strong indicator that the reader has at least adequate comprehension of the material being read. Furthermore, reading that is characterized by good prosody enhances the experience and listening comprehension of the listener. Thus, prosodic readers not only understand what they read, but they also make it easier for others to understand what they are reading out loud. ELs who lack prosody may demonstrate features such as incorrect interpretation of the tone and the appropriate phrasing, which may be due to decreased understanding of the text or familiarity with the typical expressive language patterns of monolingual English speakers. For example, Spanish-speaking ELs' tone may not rise at the end of a question as much as a native English speaker. This may be related to the fact that words such as *how* or *why* are accented in Spanish and the tone rises at the beginning of the question much more than at the end of the question. Once again, ELs who have difficulty with prosody may also be experiencing difficulty with interpreting the text and will require direct instruction on what many have termed the *suprasegmental features* of language, which include tone, phrasing, and accent patterns.

DESIGNING FLUENCY INSTRUCTION FOR ENGLISH LEARNERS

After assessing a student's oral reading fluency, educators should review the information to identify area of need and craft fluency instruction to address these needs. For instance, students whose level of accuracy is very low (who likely also have low rate and prosody levels as well as low comprehension) will likely benefit from skill practice and learning at the word level (e.g., phonemic awareness, word reading skills) as well as group-based repeated reading practice (e.g., choral reading). Students with moderate to high accuracy levels but low rate and prosody (and likely low comprehension) levels will likely benefit most from repeated reading practice (e.g., partner reading, echo reading, choral reading). Students with high accuracy and rate but low prosody and comprehension will likely benefit from repeated reading practice that focuses more heavily on prosody. It is always important to pay attention to the types of errors each student is making. Patterns of errors become apparent when carefully listening to the student (i.e., errors involving specific letter or sound patterns, specific prosodic features that are less developed). These patterns of errors will help the teacher determine the needs of each student and group students by need to facilitate instructional organization and development.

For instance, consider the following case: Juan was reading 95 words per minute in the fourth grade. According to the previous scale, he is at approximately the 25th percentile. His oral reading was somewhat laborious and he read in two- to three-word phrases, had several false starts, often did not self-correct, and read with little variation in tone. His oral language proficiency in English is described as capable of speaking in sentences with some grammatical errors. It will be important to monitor Juan's accuracy and rate and also determine the language and grammatical features present in the passage. Some questions to ask include the following:

- Can the student read the types of words present in each passage? In other words, does the student understand the specific sound and syllable patterns in the passage?

- Are there some words that will require explicit instruction and guided practice prior to reading the passage?

- In regard to vocabulary, will the student understand the majority of words within the text?

- Do the words require a quick explanation, or will the student need a significant amount of background knowledge to read the text? The use of visuals and demonstrations or quick videos have been found effective among ELs (Armon & Morris, 2008; Baker et al., 2014).

- Are the grammatical structures simple or complex within the text? Will the student require multiple opportunities for reading particular sentence structures? For example, sentences with conjunctions and prepositions are included, and these sentences could be challenging for the student at this level of oral proficiency.

- How much practice has the student had to work on expression and appropriate oral reading intonation?

CONCLUSION

Reading fluency is a critical feature of skilled reading. To achieve the ultimate goal of reading for understanding, reading fluency must include an individual's ability to read not only accurately and effortlessly but also with expression. This chapter provided evidence-based practices for reading fluency assessment and instruction, with special consideration for teaching

ELs. The following questions are provided to check for understanding and ability to incorporate this knowledge during fluency instruction.

◇◇

STUDY QUESTIONS

1. What are the three primary components of fluency? Describe each component.

2. Which of the reading instructional strategies reviewed in the chapter has been shown to increase a student's willingness to practice rereading?

3. Which instructional strategy reviewed in this chapter is especially useful for students just beginning to read or those with very low English proficiency levels?

4. Describe the procedures for measuring 1) accuracy, 2) rate, and 3) prosody.

5. What are the four primary components of prosody that should be addressed during an assessment?

◇◇

EXTENDED READING AND APPLICATION ACTIVITIES

1. Think back to the vignette about Bernardo at the beginning of the chapter. Given what you know from reading the chapter and the fluency assessment data provided in the following table, discuss what questions you would ask and how you would go about developing an instructional plan for him. *Note:* This example uses the NAEP Oral Reading Fluency Scale for prosody previously described.

Date	Accuracy	Rate	Prosody
9/1	25%	40 (10th percentile)	1
10/15	35%	48 (25th percentile)	1
10/13	45%	60 (25th percentile)	1
12/14	60%	65 (25th percentile)	2

Source: Daane et al. (2005).

2. Read the case example about Emilio in Box 6.1.

BOX 6.1.   Case Example: Emilio

Emilio is a fifth-grade student who has had the opportunity to learn English during the past year. Emilio is a fluent Spanish speaker and is trying to make progress with his English reading skills. He was asked by his teacher to read the following passage. An example of Emilio's reading about the Milky Way during the second month of the school year follows the passage.

Sample Passage

The Milky Way galaxy is a fusion of millions of stars, planets, meteors, and asteroids. The beautiful stars sparkle like treasure in the night sky. Many of the stars are grouped into constellations, such as Orion, who ensures our safety from the bull constellation. The sun is a star and is featured in the center of our solar system. Our solar system is a mixture of many planets and moons. Scientists in our nation are always discovering new information because we have only seen a fraction of what is really out there. Making the decision to look through a telescope is always an adventure!

Emilio's Reading of Passage (in 1 minute)

The Milk Way galax is a fission of millions of estars, planets, meters, and asteroides. The beautiful estars, sparkle, like tressures in the night ski. Many of the estars are groupes into consellations, such as Orion who ensuress our safety from the bul consellation. The sun is estar and is featured in the center of our solar esystem. Our solar esystem is a mixur of many planetas and moons. Science in our nation are always discover new information because we haved only seen a fiction of what is really there. Make the decision to look through a telescope.

---

3. With a partner, discuss the following questions about Emilio's reading:

    • How well is Emilio reading the words in the passage?

    • What is Emilio's reading fluency percentile according to the chart provided in this chapter?

    • What error patterns are observed during reading?

    • What explicit instruction is necessary for Emilio at this time?

    • Do you think Emilio understands each of the vocabulary words in the passage based on the accuracy of his reading?

    • Will Emilio need explicit vocabulary instruction?

    • Describe the type of vocabulary instruction you would plan for Emilio.

    • What electronic resources could you use to enhance Emilio's understanding?

    • Are there some grammatical features of the English language that will be beneficial for Emilio to understand? Describe them.

REFERENCES

Allington, R. L. (1983). Fluency: The neglected reading goal. *Reading Teacher, 36,* 556–561.

Ardoin, S. P., Williams, J. C., Klubnik, C., & McCall, M. (2009). Three versus six re-readings of practice passages. *Journal of Applied Behavior Analysis, 42,* 375–380.

Armon, J., & Morris, L. J. (2008). Integrated assessments for ELL. *Science and Children, 45*(8), 49-53.

August, D., & Shanahan, T. (2006). *Developing literacy in second-language learners: Report of the National Literacy Panel on Language-Minority Children and Youth.* Mahwah, NJ: Lawrence Erlbaum Associates.

Baker, S., Lesaux, N., Jayanthi, M., Dimino, J., Proctor, C. P., Morris, J., . . . Newman-Gonchar, R. (2014). *Teaching academic content and literacy to English learners in elementary and middle school* (NCEE 2014-4012). Washington, DC: National Center for Education Evaluation and Regional Assistance (NCEE), Institute of Education Sciences, U.S. Department of Education.

Benjamin, R. G., & Schwanenflugel, P. J. (2010). Text complexity and oral reading prosody in young readers. *Reading Research Quarterly, 45*(4), 388–404.

Benjamin, R. G., Schwanenflugel, P. J., Meisinger, E. B., Groff, C., Kuhn, M. R., & Steiner, L. (2013). A spectrographically grounded scale for evaluating reading expressiveness. *Reading Research Quarterly, 48*(2), 105–133.

Calderón, M. E., Hertz-Lazarowitz, R., & Slavin, R. (1996). *Effects of bilingual cooperative integrated reading and composition on students transitioning from Spanish to English reading.* Unpublished paper for the Office of Educational Research and Improvement, U.S. Department of Education, Washington, DC.

Calhoon, M., Otaiba, S. A., Cihak, D., King, A., & Avalos, A. (2007). Effects of a peer-mediated program on reading skill acquisition for two-way bilingual first-grade classrooms. *Learning Disability Quarterly, 30*(3), 169–184.

Chafouleas, S. M., Martens, B. K., Dobson, R. L., Weinstein, K. S., & Gardner, K. B. (2004). Fluent reading as the improvement of stimulus control: Additive effects of performance-based interventions to repeated reading on students' reading and error rates. *Journal of Behavioral Education, 13*(2), 67–81.

Chall, J. S. (1996). *Stages of reading development* (2nd ed.). Fort Worth, TX: Harcourt-Brace.

Chard, D. J., Vaughn, S., & Tyler, B. J. (2002). A synthesis of research on effective interventions for building reading fluency with elementary students with learning disabilities. *Journal of Learning Disabilities, 35,* 386–406.

Crosson, A. C., & Lesaux, N. K. (2010). Revisiting assumptions about the relationship of fluent reading to comprehension: Spanish-speaker's text-reading fluency in English. *Reading and Writing, 23,* 475–494.

Daane, M. C., Campbell, J. R., Grigg, W. S., Goodman, M. J., & Oranje, A. (2005). *Fourth-grade students reading aloud: NAEP 2002 special study of oral reading. The nation's report card* (NCES 2006469). Washington, DC: U.S. Department of Education, Institute of Education Sciences.

Daly, E. J., Bonfiglio, C. M., Mattson, T., Persampieri, M., & Foreman-Yates, K. (2005). Refining the experimental analysis of academic skills deficits: Part I. An investigation of variables that affect generalized oral reading performance. *Journal of Applied Behavior Analysis, 38,* 485–497. https://doi.org/10.1901/jaba.2005.113-04

Decker, M. M., & Buggey, T. (2014). Using video self- and peer modeling to facilitate reading fluency in children with learning disabilities. *Journal of Learning Disabilities, 47*(2), 167–177. https://doi.org/10.1177/0022219412450618

Denton, C. A., Fletcher, J. M., Anthony, J. L., & Francis, D. J. (2006). An evaluation of intensive intervention for students with persistent reading difficulties. *Journal of Learning Disabilities, 39*(5), 447–466.

Fuchs, L. S., Fuchs, D., Hamlett, C. L., Walz, L., & Germann, G. (1993). Formative evaluation of academic progress: How much growth should we expect? *School Psychology Review, 22,* 27–48.

Fuchs D., Fuchs L. S., Mathes P. G., & Simmons, D. C. (1997). Peer-assisted learning strategies: Making classrooms more responsive to diversity. *American Educational Research Journal, 34,* 174–206.

Goldenberg, C. (2013). Unlocking the research on English Learners: What we know—and don't yet know—about effective instruction. *American Educator, 37*(2), 4–11, 38.

Griffin, M. L. (2002). Why don't you use your finger? Paired reading in first grade. *The Reading Teacher, 55,* 766–774.

Gunning, T. G. (2002). *Assessing and correcting reading and writing difficulties* (2nd ed.). Boston, MA: Allyn & Bacon.

Gutierrez-Palma, N., & Palma-Reyes, A. (2007). Stress sensitivity and reading performance in Spanish: A study with children. *Journal of Research in Reading, 30*(2), 157–168.

Hasbrouck, J. (2006). For students who are not yet fluent, silent reading is not the best use of classroom time. *American Educator, 30*(2).

Hasbrouck, J. E., & Tindal, G. (1992). Curriculum-based oral reading fluency norms for students in grades 2 through 5. *Teaching Exceptional Children, 24,* 41–44.

Hasbrouck, J., & Tindal, G. (2017). *An update to compiled ORF norms* (Technical Report No. 1702). Eugene: Behavioral Research and Teaching, University of Oregon.

Hudson, R. F., Lane, H. B., & Pullen, P. C. (2005). Reading fluency assessment and instruction: What, why, and how? *Reading Teacher, 58*(8), 702–714.

Hudson, R. F., Pullen, P. C., Lane, H. B., & Torgesen, J. K. (2009). The complex nature of reading fluency: A multidimensional view. *Reading and Writing Quarterly, 25,* 4–32.

Huey, E. B. (1968). *The psychology and pedagogy of reading: A review of the history of reading and writing and of methods, texts, and hygiene in reading.* Cambridge. MA: The MIT Press.

Jenkins, J. R., Fuchs, L. S., van den Broek, P., Espin, C., & Deno, S. L. (2003). Sources of individual differences in reading comprehension and reading fluency. *Journal of Educational Psychology, 95*(4), 719–729. http://dx.doi.org/10.1037/0022-0663.95.4.719

Jenkins, J. R., & Jewell, M. (1993). Examining the validity of two measures for formative teaching: Reading aloud and maze. *Exceptional Children, 59,* 421–432.

Jennings, J. H., Caldwell, J., & Lerner, J. W. (2014). *Reading problems: Assessment and teaching strategies* (7th ed.). Boston, MA: Pearson.

Johnston, P. (2000). *Running records: A self-tutoring guide.* Portland, ME: Stenhouse.

Kim, Y., Petscher, Y., Schatschneider, C., & Foorman, B. (2010). Does growth rate in oral reading fluency matter in predicting reading comprehension achievement? *Journal of Educational Psychology, 102*(3), 652–667. https://doi.org/10.1037/a0019643

Kubina, R. M., Amato, J., Schwilk, C. L., & Therrien, W. J. (2008). Comparing performance standards on the retention of words read correctly per minute. *Journal of Behavioral Education, 17,* 328–338.

Kuhn, M. R., Schwanenflugel, P. J., & Meisinger, E. B. (2010). Aligning theory and assessment of reading fluency: Automaticity, prosody, and definitions of fluency. *Reading Research Quarterly, 45*(2), 232–253.

Kuhn, M. R., & Stahl, S. A. (2003). Fluency: A review of developmental and remedial practices. *Journal of Educational Psychology, 95*(1), 3–21. https://doi.org/10.1037/0022-0663.95.1.3

LaBerge, D., & Samuels, S. (1974). Toward a theory of automatic information processing in reading. *Cognitive Psychology, 6,* 293–323.

Lai, S. A., Benjamin, R. G., Schwanenflugel, P. J., & Kuhn, M. R. (2013). The longitudinal relationship between reading fluency and reading comprehension skills in second grade children. *Reading and Writing Quarterly, 30*(2), 116–138. https://dx.doi.org/10.1080/10573569.2013.789785

Linan-Thompson, S., Vaughn, S., Hickman-Davis, P., & Kouzekanani, K. (2003). Effectiveness of supplemental reading instruction for second-grade English language learners with reading difficulties. *Elementary School Journal, 103*(3), 221–238.

Lingo, A. S. (2014). Tutoring middle school students with disabilities by high school students: Effects on oral reading fluency. *Education and Treatment of Children, 37*(1), 53–75.

Logan, G. D. (1997). Automaticity and reading: Perspectives from the instance theory of automatization. *Reading and Writing Quarterly, 13*(2), 123–146.

Marchand-Martella, N. E., Martella, R. C., Modderman, S. L., Peterson, H. M., & Pan, S. (2013). Key areas of effective adolescent literacy programs. *Education and Treatment of Children, 36*(1), 161–184.

Mathes, P. G., Denton C. A., Fletcher J. M., Anthony J. L., Francis D. J., & Schatschneider C. (2005). The effects of theoretically different instruction and student characteristics on the skills of struggling readers. *Reading Research Quarterly, 40,* 148–182.

Meyer, M. S., & Felton, R. H. (1999). Repeated reading to enhance fluency: Old approaches and new directions. *Annals of Dyslexia, 49*, 283–306.

Morgan, P. L., & Sideridis, P. D. (2006). Contrasting the effectiveness of fluency interventions for students with or at risk for learning disabilities: A multilevel random coefficient modeling meta-analysis. *Learning Disabilities Research and Practice, 21*(4), 191–210.

Musti-Rao, S., Hawkins, R. O., & Barkley E. A. (2009). Effects of repeated readings on the oral reading fluency of urban fourth-grade students: Implications for practice. *Preventing School Failure, 54*(1), 12–23.

National Reading Panel. (2000). *Report of the National Reading Panel: Teaching children to read.* Rockville, MD: National Institute of Child Health and Human Development.

O'Connor, R. E., White, A., & Swanson, H. L. (2007). Repeated reading versus continuous reading: Influences on reading fluency and comprehension. *Exceptional Children, 74*(1), 31–46.

Oddo, M., Barnett, D. W., Hawkins, R. O., & Musti-Rao, S. (2010). Reciprocal peer tutoring and repeated reading. *Psychology in the Schools, 47*(8), 842–858.

Paige, D. D., Rasinski, T. B., & Magpuri-Lavell, T. (2012). Is fluent, expressive reading important for high school readers? *Journal of Adolescent and Adult Literacy, 56*(1), 67–76.

Quirk, M., & Beem, S. (2012). Examining the relations between reading fluency and reading comprehension for English Language learners. *Psychology in the Schools, 49*(6), 539–553.

Rasinski, T. V., Blachowicz, C., & Lems, K. (Eds.). (2006). *Fluency instruction: Research-based best practices.* New York, NY: Guilford Press.

Rasinski, T. V., Rikli, A., & Johnston, S. (2009). Reading fluency: More than automaticity? More than a concern for the primary grades? *Reading Research and Instruction, 48*(4), 350–361.

Rathvon, N. (2008). *Effective school interventions: Evidence-based strategies for improving student outcomes* (2nd ed.). New York, NY: Guilford Press.

Reschly, A. L., Busch, T. W., Betts, J., Deno, S. L., & Long, J. D. (2009). Curriculum-based measurement oral reading as an indicator of reading achievement: A meta-analysis of the correlational evidence. *Journal of School Psychology, 47*, 427–469.

Sáenz, L. M., Fuchs, L. S., & Fuchs, D. (2005) Peer-assisted learning strategies for English language learners with learning disabilities. *Exceptional Children, 71*(3), 231–247. https://doi.org/10.1177/001440290507100302

Samuels, S. J. (2006). Reading fluency: Its past, present, and future. In T. Rasinski, C. Blachowicz, & K. Lems (Eds.), *Fluency instruction: Research-based best practices* (pp. 7–20). New York, NY: Guilford Press.

Samuels, S. J., & Farstrup, A. E. (2006). *What research has to say about fluency instruction.* Newark, DE: International Reading Association.

Schwanenflugel, P. J., Hamilton, A. M., Kuhn, M. R., Wisenbaker, J., & Stahl, S. A. (2004). Becoming a fluent reader: Reading skill and prosodic features in the oral reading of young readers. *Journal of Educational Psychology, 96*, 119–129.

Slocum, T. A., Street, E. M., & Gilberts, G. (1995). A review of research and theory on the relation between oral reading rate and reading comprehension. *Journal of Behavioral Education, 5*, 377–398.

Snow, C. E., Burns, M. S., & Griffin, P. (1998). *Preventing reading difficulties in young children.* Washington, DC: National Academies Press.

Staubitz, J. E., Cartledge, G., Yurick, A. L., & Lo, Y. (2005). Repeated reading for students with emotional or behavioral disorders: Peer- and trainer-mediated instruction. *Behavioral Disorders, 31*(1), 51–64.

Stevens, E. A., Walker, M. A., & Vaughn, S. (2014). The effects of reading fluency interventions on the reading fluency and reading comprehension performance of elementary students with learning disabilities: A synthesis of the research from 2001 to 2014. *Journal of Learning Disabilities, 50*(5), 576–590. https://doi.org/10.1177/0022219416638028

Therrien, W. J. (2004). Fluency and comprehension gains as a result of repeated reading: A meta-analysis. *Remedial and Special Education, 25*, 252–261.

Torgesen, J., Rashotte, C., & Alexander, A. (2001). The prevention and remediation of reading fluency problems. In M. Wolf (Ed.), *Dyslexia, fluency, and the brain* (pp. 333–355). Cambridge, MA: York Press.

Valencia, S. W., Smith, A. T., Reece, A. M., Li, M., Wixson, K. K., & Newman, H. (2010). Oral reading fluency assessment: Issues of construct, criterion, and consequential validity. *Reading Research Quarterly, 45*(3), 270–291.

Vaughn, S., Gersten, R., & Chard, D. J. (2000). The underlying message in LD intervention research: Findings from research syntheses. *Exceptional Children, 67*, 99–114.

Welsch, R. G. (2007). Using experimental analysis to determine interventions for reading fluency and recalls of students with learning disabilities. *Learning Disability Quarterly, 30*(2), 115–129.

Wolf, M., & Katzir-Cohen, T. (2001). Reading fluency and its intervention. *Scientific Studies of Reading, 5*, 211–239.

Wright, W. E. (2015). *Foundations for teaching English language learners: Research, theory, policy, and practice* (2nd ed.). Philadelphia, PA: Caslon Publishing.

Yurick, A. L., Robinson, P. D., Cartledge, G., Lo, Y., & Evans, T. L. (2006). Using peer-mediated repeated readings as a fluency-building activity for urban learners. *Education and Treatment of Children, 29*(3), 469–506.

Zutell, J., & Rasinski, T. (1991). Multidimensional Fluency Scale. In M. F. Opitz & T. V. Rasinsk (Eds.), *Good-bye round robin*. Portsmouth, NH: Heinemann.

7

Vocabulary Instruction Among English Learners

Sharolyn D. Pollard-Durodola

By completing this chapter, the reader will

- Learn about the national expectations for English learners' (ELs') vocabulary learning, which emphasize an integrated instructional approach that embeds language development during content-enriched learning

- Understand how word learning strategies should enable ELs to become independent learners

- Explore how content-enriched vocabulary instruction builds a strong foundation for text comprehension and academic success

- Learn and apply evidence-based strategies for vocabulary instruction among ELs

Mr. Lopez is preparing a third-grade instructional unit based on a Common Core social studies standard of "movement in our world" in which he will highlight the impact of food on history. He brainstorms ideas and creates a semantic map of key concepts that will be included in this unit with the end goal that his English learners (ELs) will have a broader understanding of how our ways of life can be transformed by the introduction of new crops. He includes plants (e.g., maize, sugar cane, sweet potatoes) that historically originated from other geographical locations (e.g., Hispaniola, Cuba, Dominican Republic, South America, Africa) and people (e.g., Native Americans, Aztecs) who originally raised these plants. He brainstorms other content-related vocabulary and academic terms (e.g., immigrants, migrants, transform, culture, the Atlantic*) and related concepts that can be reinforced during science (e.g., growing labor-intensive crops) and English language arts (e.g., shared book reading,* Corn Is Maize *[Aliki, 1986]). In general, he considers how to inspire English word consciousness by selecting vocabulary that can be used to build knowledge about word parts (e.g.,* transform *vs.* transforma<u>tion</u>*) and Spanish-English cognates (e.g.,* inmigrante/immigrant*). These instructional decisions are based on his knowledge that content-enriched vocabulary practices benefit ELs by simultaneously accelerating language and academic knowledge.*

INTRODUCTION

The term *content-enriched vocabulary practices* refers to teaching content-specific vocabulary words that are "primarily used in domain-related contexts" (Purpura & Reid, 2016, p. 260) such as language arts, mathematics, science, and social studies. These are the words that children should know to be able to discuss, read, and comprehend content-related text (e.g., children's trade books, domain-specific curricula) to support academic learning (Neuman & Wright, 2013). The preceding vignette depicts the reflective process that Mr. Lopez draws on as he considers the potential language demands (critical vocabulary) of the academic tasks that ELs will engage in while using a second language (English) to communicate their ideas on the historical impact of food in society.

It is evident that Mr. Lopez is a reflective teacher who engages in a conscious decision-making process around instruction and ELs' learning. John Dewey distinguishes between teachers who are guided by routine and tradition and those who are guided by self-reflection (Grant & Zeichner, 1984). The consequence of routine-driven actions is that teachers can lose sight of broader goals that should shape daily instructional decisions and planning. In contrast, a reflective teacher like Mr. Lopez carefully considers an instructional practice in relation to its long-term impact and consequences on children's academic success.

Specifically, a reflective teacher of ELs designs effective instruction by intentionally planning for their diverse needs while considering the heterogeneity of ELs and immigrant students who arrive to school with varied educational backgrounds and native and second language abilities (Gutiér-rez, Zepeda, & Castro, 2010). Because vocabulary knowledge, more than any other factor (e.g., sociohistorical, sustained poverty, inadequate school instruction), is attributed to ELs' academic success or struggles (August, Carlo, Dressler, & Snow, 2005; Calderón, Slavin, & Sánchez, 2011; Gersten et al., 2007), thoughtful planning around their language development (e.g., vocabulary knowledge) can affect daily subject-area learning (e.g., English language arts, mathematics, science, social studies).

Reflective teachers, especially during the early years, must remain cognizant of the cumulative consequences for ELs when curricular tasks and critical thinking opportunities are made inaccessible via unanticipated vocabulary barriers. Overall, the time needed for ELs to learn new academic content in a second language may exceed the time that is generally available in school settings. High-quality instruction, however, can actually reduce the amount of time needed and increase the probability of in-depth learning for children acquiring vocabulary and new conceptual understandings in an unfamiliar language (Carroll, 1963).

The goal of this chapter is to assist teachers of ELs during the early childhood years to be reflective of ways to bolster their typical vocabulary-building practices to ensure more in-depth word learning opportunities and integrative experiences that reinforce text comprehension, analytical thinking, and academic discussions during content-enriched vocabulary practices. This chapter is organized around nine self-reflection questions with recommendations for how teachers can maximize their daily instructional time so that ELs learn more in less time as their English language proficiency develops.

VOCABULARY AND ENGLISH LEARNERS: WHAT DOES IT MEAN TO KNOW A WORD?

A reflective teacher may initially ask, "What does it mean to know a word?" when designing more effective vocabulary instruction for ELs. Developmental psychologists and speech and communication scientists provide answers to this question because they study language and the nature of its development to better understand the best approaches for stimulating and building children's oral language competencies. Language development research suggests that vocabulary, also referred to as the *lexicon,* is one subcomponent of oral language development that facilitates communication or self-expression via word meanings and understanding how words are formed (Hoff, 2014). Pragmatics (understanding socially acceptable ways of communicating information to others), phonology (the specific sound system of a language), morphology (understanding the system for combining words and word parts in a language), and syntax (the grammatical system for combining words in a specific order in a sentence) are the other subcomponents of oral language development. These subcomponents of a language system also contribute to how young children acquire and use words.

Experts suggest that knowing a word implies knowing its literal meaning in addition to understanding its syntactical or grammatical construction (placement of the word in a sentence), its morphological variations (root derivations), and its semantic variations (synonyms, antonyms) within a language system (August et al., 2005; Nagy & Scott, 2000). This means that knowing a word is dependent on knowing how the word can be used within the structure of a specific language system (Hoff, 2014).

Furthermore, knowing a word also implies knowing the specific concepts, ideas, and knowledge associated with the word because word meanings do not exist in isolation but provide a lens through which we can understand the surrounding world in nuanced ways (Hirsch, 2006; Neuman, 2006; Scarcella, 2003). Basically, as children learn more words, they learn more about the world and are better prepared to discuss academic content, make connections between school and life experiences, and comprehend challenging text (Catts, Fey, Zhang, & Tomblin, 1999; Hart & Risley, 1995). Building a strong language foundation is integral to academic engagement and subject-area text comprehension because vocabulary concepts are the true "carrier of meaning" (Verhoeven & Perfetti, 2011, p. 2) and assume a critical role in learning to read in any language (Adams, 1990; August & Shanahan, 2006; *Eunice Kennedy Shriver* National Institute of Child Health and Human Development [NICHD], 2000).

Why Is Vocabulary Acquisition Important for English Learners?

Bolstering ELs' comprehension abilities via content-enriched vocabulary practices provides daily opportunities to build children's linguistic knowledge (e.g., semantic, syntactic, morphological knowledge) in the second language to reinforce deeper conceptual understandings of texts that increase in vocabulary complexity across the grades. ELs require rich and deep word processing opportunities because they may lack English word depth even for words that are frequently encountered in the second language (Verhallen & Schoonen, 1993). Content-enriched vocabulary practices focus on explicit exposure to content-related words that are important for children to be able to independently read and comprehend academic texts (Neuman & Wright, 2013). For ELs, this content-related word exposure can occur during the second language acquisition process.

Traditional vocabulary routines have utilized decontextualized word-building practices in which students memorize word lists, terms, and their meanings in isolation from the interesting ideas that situate the word within a broader network of world knowledge (Beck, McKeown, & Kucan, 2013; Graves, August, & Mancilla-Martinez, 2013; Scarcella, 2003). This type of "thin instruction" (Graves et al., 2013, p. 22) disregards the notion that vocabulary development is indeed a complex, multidimensional process that relies on priming students' background knowledge, exposing them to important features of the English language, and evaluating their ability to use contextual knowledge (Honig, Diamond, & Gutlohn, 2000) to support comprehension of texts that increase vocabulary complexity across the grades.

Vocabulary knowledge serves as a critical component in all children's language development and plays an important role in the development of conceptual knowledge growth (literacy, science, social studies, mathematics) (Boals, Kenyon, Blair, Wilmes, & Wright, 2015; Gersten et al., 2007), which strengthens and builds background knowledge essential for comprehension of text materials (August & Shanahan, 2006; Hirsch, 2006; Nagy, 2005; NICHD, 2000; Verhoeven & Perfetti, 2011). Specific knowledge domains such as the "worlds of nature and culture" (science, social studies) (Hirsch, 2006, p. 17) can provide the concepts or background knowledge and associated terms that are commonly understood by mature readers and contribute to text comprehension. In general, text comprehension is facilitated when 85%–90% of the words are known in a paragraph or text (Stahl & Fairbanks, 1986), reinforcing the importance of exposing ELs to contextualized vocabulary practices during content-related instruction (science, English language arts, social studies, mathematics). Furthermore, this ability to learn new vocabulary from context increases as children become older and their word formation process improves (Hoff, 2014).

Evidence from literacy and neuroscience studies conducted with native English-speaking children further suggest that early (e.g., kindergarten) vocabulary knowledge is associated with later comprehension gains (Grades 1–4) (Spira, Bracken & Fischel, 2005), and being able to gain access to word meanings in a text keeps the reading process from deteriorating (McKeown, Deane, Scott, Krovetz, & Lawless, 2017). The same holds true for ELs in that vocabulary knowledge supports text comprehension (August & Shanahan, 2006; International Literacy Association, 2017), but the instructional process may require more intentionality and scaffolding.

ELs are not only learning new words or labels that represent new conceptual understandings, but they are also acquiring the academic language used in oral discussions and written curricular materials in a second language (Scarcella, 2003). For this reason, schooling becomes primarily a "linguistic experience" (Gottlieb, 2013, p. 5) for ELs who are continuously exposed to unfamiliar contexts through a new language (e.g., oral, written) during the instructional day (Halliday, 1993).

Within a second language acquisition framework, the term *academic language* refers to academic terms and school language that facilitates a deeper understanding of core curriculum content and enables ELs to actively participate in content-related discussions (e.g., English language arts, mathematics, science, social studies) (Nagy & Townsend, 2012; Teachers of English to Speakers of Other Languages [TESOL], 2006). Academic language for ELs in pre-K–12 settings includes the word level (vocabulary), the sentence level (grammar), and the text level (discourse) (Gottlieb, 2013).

The World-Class Instructional Design and Assessment (WIDA) consortium provides a teacher-friendly framework that explicates the three features of academic language that deepen understanding of the language that ELs process during school interactions—linguistic complexity (the cohesive organization of ideas expressed in sentences), language forms and conventions (the grammatical structures that support sentence meaning), and vocabulary usage (words, phrases, multiple meanings, and cognates used in sentences to convey meaning) (Gottlieb, 2013). Although these three features are collectively intertwined, this chapter focuses on the word level or vocabulary usage, which includes academic vocabulary encountered in content classes and content-related terms (e.g., social studies: *industry, union, factory*) that facilitate communication during academic learning. Specifically, explicit instruction on high-priority content-related words with opportunities to use these words in scaffolded discussions (e.g., using sentence starters, clarifying visuals, implementing English as a second language strategies) can build and extend ELs' academic language use and academic thinking that depend on words (Nagy & Townsend, 2012).

In addition to providing a platform for text comprehension, there is some evidence that academic vocabulary development can make it easier for students to become problem solvers while learning new domain knowledge and its associated terminology (McKeown et al., 2017). Overall, ELs who develop expertise in a domain are able to categorize information and solve problems in new ways. ELs learn new labels and processes (e.g., science: *This is photosynthesis;* math: *Let's compare and contrast two quadrilaterals—a rhombus and a rectangle*) to communicate their ideas during content-related discussions. By developing academic language and vocabulary, ELs acquire the critical tools that promote analytical thinking and talking (Teacher: *What is the difference between a pond and a puddle? What do you think could happen to a pond in the winter?*). This approach to content-enriched vocabulary instruction, however, requires a shift from decontextualized word-building practices to utilizing a more integrative instructional design framework.

VOCABULARY DEVELOPMENT

Vocabulary acquisition begins in the home, where children have opportunities to acquire and use their developing oral language abilities through conversations with their parents and siblings who can scaffold and extend their responses as they learn to talk about the world around them (Farkas & Beron, 2004; Hirsch, 2006; Weigel, Martin, & Bennett, 2006). Infants initially communicate nonverbally via gestures in the early stages of language development, which is a precursor for understanding that spoken words can serve as labels for objects and concepts in the environment (Hoff, 2014; Phythian-Sence & Wagner, 2007). Again, children's first words are representative of their lived experiences (e.g., daily routines, household objects, body parts) (Hoff, 2014). These early vocabularies are also indications that children understand how to link different types of words (e.g., nouns, verbs) to different types of meanings or properties (e.g., counting nouns, adjectives for different properties) (Waxman & Lidz, 2006). Although English-speaking children primarily acquire nouns first, this may not be the case for speakers of other languages (e.g., Japanese, Korean) in which communication is guided by a syntax or grammar that uses verbs more frequently than nouns in the sentence structure (Hoff, 2014; Tardif, Gelmann, & Xu, 1999).

As such, this "verbal environment" (Kucan, 2013, p. 280) may differ from home to home, so children arrive to school with differences in the depth and breadth of their vocabulary knowledge (Lareau, 2003), which influences their ability to understand and benefit from the materials that are introduced in school (Hoff, 2014). Specifically, research documents sizeable differences between families' home language use in the quality and quantity of language used with their children (elaborate and rich vs. more restrictive language use and vocabulary) (Hart & Risley, 1995; Lareau, 2003).

Because talk is the greatest tool parents can use to develop their child's intellectual skills, early home language experiences and opportunities for using rich and varied vocabulary may be affected by inequitable socioeconomic opportunities that influence a family's access to important resources (e.g., literacy materials, stimulating life experiences) that can be used to stimulate adult–child conversations (Neuman & Celano, 2001), especially adult–child conversations in a second language (e.g., English). Specifically, some families may be unable to provide the quality of second language modeling in the home that is sufficient to promote second language vocabulary growth (Hammer, Davison, Lawrence, & Miccio, 2009).

Therefore, native language support and maintenance in the home should be prioritized and encouraged as ELs engage in adult–child conversations using linguistic (code switching) and cultural (e.g., family stories, realia) capital that are more readily available for families to stimulate oral language and knowledge development in culturally relevant ways (Gonzalez, Moll, & Amanti, 2005). Overall, the majority of ELs are Spanish speakers, with 60% of these children residing in homes that employ a range of native and second language use (García & García, 2012). Therefore, a large percentage of Latino children continue to speak their native language at home while acquiring English as their second language in school settings. This native language maintenance is grounded on substantial evidence that maintaining native language use does not deter from English language learning (Yoshida, 2008) or delay an EL's cognitive development (Lopez, Zepeda, & Medina, 2012). Furthermore, knowledge-building talk and experiences (e.g., reading and talking about books) in the primary language can encourage respect for one's own culture as a means to support academic success (Montero-Sieburth & Barth 2001; Tijunelis, Satterfield, & Benkí, 2013).

Most immigrant families, however, will continue to depend on school systems to provide a quality of instructional explicitness that can extend and deepen their child's English vocabulary use while developing a conceptual knowledge base in English beyond what they are able to accomplish at home. The instructional implication is that early vocabulary knowledge differences may increase across time without high-quality and targeted content-enriched vocabulary instruction in school settings, which place ELs at risk for future comprehension difficulties (August & Shanahan, 2006).

NATIONAL STANDARDS FOR ENGLISH LEARNER VOCABULARY LEARNING

Before planning instruction, teachers should review standards that specify expectations for vocabulary learning within the context of second language development. In backward design curriculum mapping, one begins with the "end in mind" (Covey, 2013, p. 102; McTighe & Wiggins, 1998, p. 7). This approach to vocabulary instruction identifies domains of knowledge or big ideas that are beneficial for ELs and facilitates knowledge building and second language vocabulary acceleration. Overall, big ideas are those concepts that should be prioritized and taught more thoroughly than others to maximize learning and instructional time in school (Simmons, Pollard-Durodola, Gonzalez, Davis, & Simmons, 2008).

Many states and school districts are guided by standards or expectations that were originally designed for native English-speaking children and do not take into consideration the language and subject area needs of ELs (Calderón et al., 2011). Two national organizations, however, provide guidance on the big ideas or expectations for vocabulary knowledge acceleration for ELs. TESOL (http://www.tesol.org) and WIDA (https://wida.wisc.edu/) have been instrumental in establishing national standards for children with varying levels of English language proficiency. Collectively, these organizations advocate for best practices and help educators understand what to teach as children progress in school and grow in their English language proficiency. The following abbreviated WIDA-based English language proficiency stages suggest how content-enriched vocabulary instruction for ELs is driven by their second language development (MacDonald, Cook, Lord, & Ramirez, 2014):

- *Low proficiency in English:* ELs can learn to use simple, common vocabulary in short expressions. It is appropriate to explicitly introduce vocabulary that can serve as language connectors (e.g., *so, then, because, but, and, or*) to show logical thinking. Student language arts talk: I like the *comic book* because the girl is the *hero.*

- *Intermediate proficiency in English:* ELs can use sentences that contain more than one idea. It is appropriate to explicitly teach broader language connectors (e.g., *although, even though, since*) to show logical relationships between ideas. Student mathematics talk: I will make a *tally* mark for each player's *hoops, although* the final score on the *scoreboard* appears to be correct.

- *High proficiency in English:* ELs can use complex sentences. Opportunities should be provided to talk about ideas and concepts indirectly without the use of personal pronouns. Student social studies talk: *Economic migration* is the result of believing that life *quality* can *improve* by *relocating* to another city for better *housing* and *employment options.*

National expectations concur with researchers for a type of vocabulary pedagogy that is "rich and varied" (Graves et al., 2013, p. 18), including multiple opportunities for oral vocabulary development during the initial stages of English language acquisition via listening as well as reading text. Attention to more complex vocabulary-building strategies can occur in second grade and beyond (Honig et al., 2000) with opportunities to use more complex synonyms, antonyms, and morphological knowledge (e.g. prefixes, suffixes) to unlock the meaning of words that can deepen text comprehension. These objectives can be addressed by intentionally integrating content-enriched vocabulary practices throughout the daily instructional sequence.

PRINCIPLES OF INSTRUCTIONAL DESIGN TO TEACH VOCABULARY TO ENGLISH LEARNERS

The term *instructional design* refers to the way that information is organized, sequenced, and scheduled within a series of lessons that constitute a course of study to ensure high-quality learning (Simmons & Kame'enui, 1998). The instructional designer (e.g., practitioner) is concerned with developing the architecture for communicating the information to prevent misconceptions and learner error (Tennyson & Christensen, 1986). Therefore, instructional designers provide an essential blueprint that provides sufficient supports, especially for children with diverse learning needs (Simmons et al., 2008).

The following three recommended instructional design principles have been utilized in intervention research to build vocabulary experiences during content-enriched practices for second and native language learners (Pollard-Durodola, Gonzalez, Simmons, & Simmons, 2015; Pollard-Durodola et al., 2016; Simmons et al., 2008). These principles provide guidance on how to intensify typical practices to ensure deeper learning and contextual vocabulary use.

Instructional Design Principle 1: Build Vocabulary Knowledge by Combining New Information With What the Learner Already Knows to Produce Higher Cognitive Learning

Instructional planning should ideally sequence vocabulary concepts within the context of building extensive knowledge networks to broaden children's ability to talk about the world around them and engage in academic discussions in school (Anderson & Freebody, 1981; Hadley, Dickinson, Hirsch-Pasek, & Golinkoff, 2018; Nagy, 2005; Neuman, 2006). Therefore, in this approach, vocabulary instruction is intensified when guided by the instructional design principle of "integration" (Nagy, 1988, p. 10).

Strategic integration purposefully combines new information with what the learner already knows to foster higher cognitive learning (Pollard-Durodola et al., 2015; Simmons et al., 2008). Integration emphasizes critical and explicit connections important for comprehension and academic learning. Strategic integration in vocabulary instruction implies thoughtful sequencing of instructional tasks to accelerate vocabulary development (Baker, Simmons, & Kame'enui, 1998) so that vocabulary concepts are taught in meaningful contexts as opposed to isolated word meanings (Hirsch, 2006; Nagy, 1988). This approach to designing instruction allows second language learners to see associations between new English vocabulary with related concepts (Nagy, 1988). Following are examples of how vocabulary concepts can be intentionally integrated or connected to existing or new concepts to accelerate content knowledge. Two of these examples derive from research-based vocabulary interventions for children acquiring academic English.

- **Instructional application:** Prior to teaching the word *crater* while reading and discussing the storybook *The Stories Julian Tells* (Cameron, 1989), children engage in a conversation about the moon's surface. They all know something about the moon but learn that large holes can be created when a large meteorite falls on the moon. The concept of *crater* is taught in the context of building background knowledge about the moon's surface (Seals, Pollard-Durodola, Foorman, & Bradley, 2007a, 2007b).

- **Instructional application:** Prior to teaching three thematically related words (*twig*, *branch*, and *woods*), children engage in a conversation about the broad theme of living things. They know that living things are plants, animals, and people. They discuss how living things need air, water, and sunlight to survive and grow. The discussion continues about trees and why they are living things. The teacher uses visuals that depict the essential characteristics of the three thematic target words that are examples of living things. This preview activity takes place before reading and talking about *Owl Babies* (Waddell & Benson, 2002), a text about an owl family who lives on a tree branch in the woods (Pollard-Durodola et al., 2015).

Instructional Design Principle 2: Integrate Multiple Opportunities for Using New Vocabulary to Make Connections to Concepts and Lived Experiences

The term *multiple exposures* refers to opportunities for children to use new vocabulary and the associated concepts in a variety of contexts to facilitate in-depth word knowledge (Nagy, 1988). Teachers can intentionally plan sufficient practice opportunities for children to master newly learned concepts in a carefully constructed scope and sequence (Simmons et al., 2008). In-depth word knowledge is specifically generated through frequent opportunities for children to think deeply about taught information and then articulate perceived word and concept associations across networks of knowledge. This instructional design principle is supported by strong evidence that ELs benefit from an intense academic vocabulary regimen that is distributed across several days using a variety of instructional activities (e.g., word associations, themes and topics, multimedia supports) so that children engage in frequent opportunities to use new words during content learning (Carlo et al., 2004; Silverman & Hines, 2009; What Works Clearinghouse, 2014).

- **Instructional application:** In planning a social studies lesson on water scarcity, ELs in a third-grade classroom read an informational text about farmers in another country who face a water shortage. In a whole-class discussion, children learn and use the terms *advantage, disadvantage, problem, solution,* and *effective(ness),* which are visually represented on picture/concept cards that are later placed on a word wall. Students who are Spanish speakers brainstorm words from their language for each term: *advantage/la ventaja, disadvantage/la desventaja, problem/el problema, solution/la solución,* and *effective/eficaz (effectiveness/la eficacia).* The teacher and students use a Spanish/English dictionary to write meanings for the words on the word wall and then discuss similarities and differences in orthography (spelling). The teacher and students decide which words are cognates and why. Knowing these terms in Spanish equips ELs with vocabulary and concepts that may facilitate student discussions. Students then work in pairs, depending on their language ability, to conduct research across the week to discover potential solutions to farming practices when there is water scarcity. The following week, students work in teams with lively discussions in English and Spanish as they share their findings and make lists of potential advantages and disadvantages of potential solutions to farming when water is scarce. During the final week of the project, teams create and perform a simple skit in which they demonstrate the effectiveness of their solution to the water scarcity problem.

Instructional Design Principle 3: Integrate Intentional Opportunities for Adult–Child Language Interaction Around New Vocabulary During Content Learning

Intentional language opportunities allow explicit tasks and time for children to respond, discuss, and engage in academic content (Simmons et al., 2008). Basically, children's responses vary according to the language demand of the task. Furthermore, engagement rate is the percentage of time that children are actively involved in the learning process and can be maximized through small-group formats, group and individual turns, and planned opportunities for discussing and responding (Pollard et al., 2015; Simmons et al., 2008).

- **Instructional application:** During a science lesson on the seasons, the class participates in an I Want to Be the Teacher activity. "Seasons" is the theme of the game. The teacher shows two visuals that depict the four seasons: spring, summer, fall, and winter. The teacher asks what is the same or different about the two visuals. First, the entire class describes how the leaves are changing colors. The teacher expands on the class's summary and provides more information about what is happening by using vocabulary introduced in previous lessons: The leaves on the trees are changing colors because the weather is changing. Individual children have an opportunity to be the teacher to talk about what is happening in the two visuals as the teacher monitors language use by scaffolding with open-ended questions: Can you tell us how the leaves are becoming different? Why are they changing? Last, the teacher points to both visuals and models how to talk about what is the same or different. Children participate in this game every day, sometimes focusing on social studies concepts or even mathematics. Multiple opportunities are provided across the week for whole-class and individual turns in the game as well as small-group discussions with those children who require the most support to participate in these interactive discussions (Pollard et al., 2015). Collectively, these three instructional design principles provide a starting place for thinking about how to sequence instruction that builds vocabulary cumulatively.

STRATEGIES FOR TEACHING VOCABULARY SKILLS TO ENGLISH LEARNERS

This section presents strategies for teaching vocabulary skills to ELs. These approaches are discussed in the following subsections: engaging in shared book reading, making connections across languages, providing instruction on cognates to promote text comprehension, promoting native language vocabulary learning, and encouraging deep processing and analytical thinking during content-enriched vocabulary instruction.

Shared Book Reading

Shared book reading is a well-known practice referred to as *read-alouds* and *storybook reading* (Ezell & Justice, 2005). It is the primary instructional approach to stimulating young children's oral language and vocabulary knowledge whether they are native English speakers (Ezell & Justice, 2005; Hargrave & Sénéchal, 2000; Hindman & Wasik, 2015; Neuman & Dwyer,

2011; Whitehurst & Lonigan, 1998) or ELs (Collins, 2010; Roberts & Neal, 2004; Silverman, 2007; Spycher, 2009). Shared book reading is the process of talking about books between an adult and a child or children when reading or looking at books (What Works Clearinghouse, 2015) and can be used to accelerate oral vocabulary development via interactive adult–child conversations. In the early school years, vocabulary acceleration occurs around rich adult–child conversations around books during shared book reading experiences. Researchers have investigated how specific strategies can be embedded in the shared book reading process to promote children's early language and literacy abilities via prereading instruction, comprehension skills, and word meaning discussions (Diamond, Justice, Siegler, & Snyder, 2013).

Although more than 20 years of shared book reading research has been conducted with native English speakers in classroom settings, the benefits of shared book reading with ELs is still being investigated, specifically when children are in the initial stages of second language development and may require considerable adult scaffolding during book discussions to using words in an emerging language. Emerging evidence suggests that ELs benefit from explicit instruction on a set of words across multiple days (Cohen, Kramer-Vida, & Frye, 2012; Roberts & Neal, 2004).

Furthermore, there are emerging shared book reading intervention studies implemented in preschool and kindergarten that suggest that the following practices intensify vocabulary learning while reading and talking about books:

- Shared book reading content is organized by content-related themes (e.g., science) (Spycher, 2009). Hirsch (2006) referred to this approach as "topic immersion" (p.19).

- Repeated readings of texts (e.g. two readings distributed across 2 consecutive days) provide multiple exposures to new words and concepts and opportunities to frequently engage in adult–child interactions and discussions (Espinosa, 2010; McGee & Schickedanz, 2007; Pollard-Durodola et al., 2017).

- Strategic use of nonlinguistic visual supports (e.g., pictures of target words, book illustrations) (Cohen et al., 2012; Silverman & Hines, 2009).

- Opportunities to use language to discuss science and social studies concepts (Pollard-Durodola et al., 2016, 2017; Spycher, 2009).

The following 5-day shared book reading scope and sequence is a recommended approach that has been studied scientifically in Project Words of Oral Reading and Language Development (Gonzalez, Pollard-Durodola, & Saenz, 2011–2014) with Spanish-speaking ELs acquiring English as a second language in a dual language program model (see Pollard-Durodola et al., 2016, 2017). This daily 20-minute routine is implemented in preschool and utilizes a weekly storybook (e.g., social studies: *Five Little Sharks Swimming in the Sea* [Metzger & Bryant, 2006]) paired with a complementary informational text (e.g., social studies: *The Ocean* [Ring, 2004] by a broad science or social theme (e.g., social studies: The Earth) with opportunities to engage in challenging analytical talk and thinking (*Could you swim across an ocean? Why or why not? What would happen if there was a storm over an ocean?*). Three semantically related content words (e.g., *ocean, river, sea*) that are visually represented in the text are selected from each book for a total of six words that are explicitly taught during shared book reading interactive small-group discussions. This approach has also been implemented with kindergarten in a whole-class format in Spanish. Box 7.1 offers an abbreviated summary of how to organize interactive, content-enriched discussions with intentional

---

BOX 7.1. Example of a Content-Enriched Vocabulary Shared Book Reading Approach

Day 1: Build thematic background knowledge (e.g., science: what water can do) and preview new theme-related words with visuals that provide naturalistic representations to support a back-and-forth discussion about the new concepts and children's lived experiences. Words should also be visually represented in the text. Read the storybook for the first time, stopping briefly to discuss the words in the context of the story when they first appear on the book page. Ask open-ended questions using the vocabulary about the big thing that happened in the story.

Day 2: Read the storybook again and discuss previously taught concepts using new vocabulary. Ask open-ended challenging questions that connect the words to children's daily experiences.

Day 3: Preview three new theme-related words with visuals that provide naturalistic representations to support a back-and-forth discussion that extends knowledge about the broad theme introduced on Day 1. Words should be visually represented in the text. Read the informational text for the first time, stopping briefly to discuss the words in the context of the story when they first appear in the book. Ask open-ended questions about what additional information was learned about the theme.

Day 4: Read the informational text again and discuss previously taught concepts using new vocabulary. Ask open-ended challenging questions that connect the words to children's daily experiences.

Day 5: Cumulatively review the words and concepts by discussing similarities and differences across the two thematically paired texts. Use English as a second language scaffolds (e.g., sentence frames) and pages from the books to assist students in sharing their ideas about the conceptual similarities and differences.

vocabulary exposures that are distributed across the 5-day weekly unit (see Pollard-Durodola et al., 2015, for a more detailed description.)

Make Connections Across Languages: The Structure and History of English Should Inform Word Learning Strategies and Instruction

The history of the English language indicates that some words were derived or borrowed from other languages. Basically, after the Battle of Hastings in 1066, Norman French was the official and literary language of England for 3 centuries (Nagy & Townsend, 2012). Although English replaced French and Latin as the language of the educated classes, many academic Greek and Latin words remained, along with words of German origin, and are still used to date. The instructional implication is that some aspect of vocabulary instruction will focus on words that derive from Greek and Latin roots, and this expectation is often specified in national standards.

Furthermore, the English language can be described as "morphophonemic" (Kucan, 2013, p. 282, which means the English orthography or language system is based on phonemes, the smallest unit of sounds, and morphemes, the smallest unit of meaning (Carlisle & Stone, 2005; Kucan, 2013). Students learning to read must be taught to attend to phonemes to decode words and morphemes to understand the meanings of new words (Carlisle & Stone, 2005). As children progress in their English language proficiency, they should also progress in their morphological awareness, which is the ability to identify and manipulate morphemes or units of meaning to form new words. Morphological awareness plays an important role in reading development for all children and is related to reading comprehension and vocabulary acceleration (Carlisle, 2000; Laufer, 2000).

The structure of the English language determines the word-building strategies that ELs should learn as they continue to grow and develop in their second language abilities. These strategies primarily teach students to attend to the units of meaning within a word—separating words into smaller parts to understand the meaning of the whole word. Teaching students to use word parts is important because more than 60% of unfamiliar words encountered in texts can be broken down into smaller word parts (Nagy, Anderson, Schommer, Scott, & Stallman, 1989). Specifically, knowledge of word parts such as prefixes, suffixes, and roots can be used to increase children's ability to recognize related words in word families so that their networks of knowledge and conceptual understandings are expanded (Carlisle, 2000, 2007; Carlisle & Stone, 2005; Kucan, 2013; Wright, 2010). Word-part instruction derives from what is known about the English language.

All words are composed of one or more morphemes. For example, the word *vessels* is composed of two morphemes, or small meaningful units: *vessel* (single noun) + *s* (plural). If students understand the meaning of vessel—a large ship or boat—and have been taught that the *s* ending refers to a plural word, then this knowledge allows the reader to comprehend that there is more than one vessel referred to in a written passage or discussion. Instruction that attends to these smaller units of meaning within words is referred to as *morphological awareness* and can support students in reading complex words (Nagy, Berninger, & Abbott, 2006).

The instructional implication is that explicit vocabulary instruction for ELs should prioritize opportunities for learning important suffixes, prefixes, and so forth so that students have a tool for understanding meanings of new words. Explicit instruction on derivational affixes and suffixes can increase students' ability to read and understand unfamiliar words. Basically, the study of morphology can be divided into two categories—inflectional morphology and derivational morphology (Wright, 2010). *Inflectional morphology* refers to changes to a word, such as the number or quantity, verb tense, and degree.

- Changes in quantity: liquid (singular noun), liquids (plural noun); meadow (singular noun), meadows (plural noun)

- Changes in verb tense: stroll, strolled, strolling

- Changes in degree: wide, wider, widest

In contrast, *derivational morphology* refers to how words are formed or derived from other words by the use of word parts such as suffixes and prefixes.

- Prefixes: *dis*agree—absence of agreeing; *pre*view—before viewing

- Suffixes: live*ly*—in a manner that is full of life and energy; cheer*ful*—in a manner that is full of cheer or joy

Overall, teachers of ELs should provide multiple opportunities to assist students in understanding how to construct plurals, verb tense changes, contractions, superlatives, comparatives, possessives, and compound words (Wright, 2010).

The following word-building learning experience and discussion can occur in a shared book reading activity using *Donovan's Word Jar* (Degross, 1994), with explicit opportunities to talk about suffixes. ELs have learned that the main character, Donavan, loves to *collect* words. Students have learned and talked about the meaning of the verb *collect*. They now brainstorm examples of objects that they like to collect (e.g., rocks, pin-back buttons, songs, comic books). In the discussion, the teacher points out that Donavan has a special word *collection* because he writes the words on paper and puts the scraps of paper into a jar. Donavan, therefore, is a *collector*, a person who collects things, because it is his hobby.

After this discussion, students discuss how the suffixes *-tion*, *-or*, and *-ible* can be added to the word *collect* to generate new words and expand their existing knowledge. A semantic map can be used to show that the words *collect*, *collection*, *collector*, and *collectible* are connected, deriving from

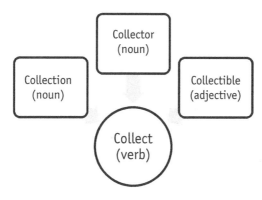

Figure 7.1. Word parts: using suffixes to generate words related to *collect*.

the verb *collect* (see Figure 7.1). Next, the teacher can explicitly use a table to discuss how new words are formed from the word *collect* by adding suffixes (Latin based) to generate new vocabulary (see Table 7.1).

While teaching ELs to use the structure of the English language to decipher unfamiliar words in a content-related text, a broader goal, however, is to develop and reinforce metacognitive awareness in ELs to promote word consciousness and strategies that help them remember words. *Metacognitive awareness* refers to children's ability to think about and consciously regulate their ability to learn, remember, and recall information (Trawick-Smith, 2014). Experts in the field of vocabulary research suggest that teaching specific word learning strategies can increase ELs' metacognitive awareness of how they learn new vocabulary concepts (Nagy & Anderson, 2013). In the context of vocabulary acceleration, metacognitive awareness can be developed by initially discussing the value of using specific word learning strategies followed by a description of the strategy and when it should be used (Nagy & Anderson, 2013). The instructional implication is that reflective teachers can emphasize how word learning strategies can help students make "educated guesses about what a word means" during daily content learning (Nagy & Anderson, 2013, p. 76).

Table 7.1. Word parts: Generating new words with suffixes

New vocabulary	Word part: Suffixes
Collect (verb)	
Collec*tion* (noun)	*-tion* This suffix refers to an action. The act of _____. Example: *Collection* refers to the act of collecting objects.
Collec*tor* (noun)	*-or* This suffix refers to a person who does something. Example: *Collector* refers to a person who collects objects.
Collec*tible* (adjective)	*-ible* This suffix refers to being capable of an action. Example: Words are collectibles because they can be written on paper and collected or stored in a jar. Other examples of collectibles include stamps, photographs, shoes, and marbles.

Following is an example of how one might integrate an opportunity to build word consciousness in a social studies discussion about pollution. During a lesson, ELs engage in a discussion about the importance of maintaining good air quality by eliminating sources of *pollution*. The teacher strategically uses visuals that depict environments with different sources of pollution—smog, smoke from industrial plants, and congested streets with cars that emit exhaust fumes. In this discussion, the teacher inquires, "What do you think the word *pollute* means? For example, in this photograph, we see that factory smoke can *pollute* the air and destroy the air quality. In these pictures, we see many other examples of *pollutants*. What do you think the word *pollutant* means?"

In this discussion, students must first understand what the term *pollution* means before they can make an educated guess about the meaning of *pollutant* and *pollute*. After this discussion, the teacher can use a semantic map or other visual that shows the network of vocabulary concepts that are associated with pollution to generate a deeper understanding of how these words are connected, especially how they are connected to word knowledge that has been previously taught (e.g., word parts: the suffix *-tion*, adding *s* to make a plural). See Figure 7.2 for a sample map.

In general, semantic maps are great for focusing students' attention on key points during vocabulary building. In this approach, the teacher identifies a key word, phrase, or theme and then asks students to brainstorm related words. In the introductory vignette, Mr. Lopez brainstormed different types of plants that historically transformed our ways of living. The teacher can scaffold the discussion by prompting (e.g., asking open-ended questions) students to think deeper or think in a different direction. Last, the teacher can ask students to make connections between the related ideas and their lived experiences (Nagy, 1988).

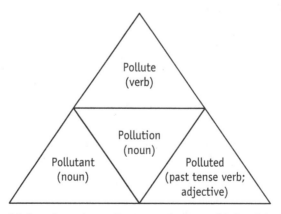

Figure 7.2.   Pollution: using word connections to expand content-enriched vocabulary knowledge.

Provide Instruction on Cognates to Promote Text Comprehension

Cognates refers to words across languages that are similar in spelling, meaning, and etymology or word history/origin (Montelongo, Hernández, Herter, & Cuello, 2011). Explicit instruction on cognates can serve as an important semantic resource for children learning English as a second language (August, Calderón, & Carlo, 2002; August et al., 2005; Bravo, Hiebert, & Pearson, 2007; Calderón et al., 2005; Nagy, García, Durgunoğlu & Hancin-Bhatt, 1993), which enables ELs to utilize native language knowledge to facilitate English vocabulary knowledge development. Therefore, explicit instruction on cognates can provide a foundation for some transfer of vocabulary concepts and conceptual understandings across languages (e.g., from Spanish to English) that share cognate pairs to enhance comprehension (August et al., 2005).

Most studies on cognates related to knowledge transfer have been conducted on older students with mixed results (Hancin-Bhatt & Nagy, 1994). ELs benefit from attending to the linguistic similarities and differences across their native and second language (August & Shanahan, 2006; Graves et al., 2013). For example, it may be a good practice to explicitly point out true cognates and false cognates—words that may be similar in spelling but do not share the same meaning (e.g., Spanish *sopa* means "soup" and not "soap"; Spanish *carpeta* means "folder or file" and not "carpet"), when appropriate. Overall, intentional instruction on important cognates is one way of using the native language as an instructional support for second language learning. Table 7.2 offers examples of English–Spanish cognates in mathematics, science, and social studies.

Promote Native Language Vocabulary Learning

Leveraging an EL's native language as a linguistic and cognitive resource can provide an important conceptual knowledge base for second language vocabulary learning and knowledge acceleration when specific strategies are utilized (e.g., bilingual, teaching English as a second language [TESL]) (Cummins, 2007). This instructional process is known as *teaching to transfer* (Cummins, 2008) and is supported by the conceptual framework that bilingualism is developed and nurtured via the interaction between the child and an "educational treatment" or instruction (Cummins, 1978, p. 226), and native language support does not detract from second language development (Ordóñez, Carlo, Snow, & McLaughlin, 2002; Winsler, Kim, & Richard, 2014). During content-enriched vocabulary instruction, teaching to transfer can include explicitly developing deep content vocabulary knowledge networks in the native language prior to providing instruction to promote English knowledge acquisition and vocabulary depth. This means strengthening native language proficiency so that children can engage in an explicit

Table 7.2. English–Spanish cognates in mathematics, science, and social studies

Subject area	English term	Spanish term
Mathematics	Calendar	El calendario
	Angle	El ángulo
	Area.	El area
	Divided by	Divido por
	Equal groups	Los grupos iguales
	Exponent	El exponente
	Gallon	El galón
	Hexagon	El hexagon
	Triangle	El triángolo
Science	Classify	Clasificar
	Cycle	El ciclo
	Diagram	El diagrama
	Elements	Los elementos
	Electricity	La electricidad
	Galaxia	La galaxia
	Identify	Identificar
Social Studies	Map	El mapa
	Society	La sociedad
	Independence	La independencia
	Community	La comunidad
	Exploration	La exploración
	Immigration	La immigración
	Liberty	La libertad
	Vote	El voto
	Geography	La geografía
	Region	La región

sequence of content-enriched interactive activities, analytical discussions, and deep processing of academic concepts in the native language.

Ordóñez and colleagues (2002) specifically studied the potential of knowledge transfer in ELs. These investigators sought to understand whether ELs' ability to define and talk about vocabulary in Spanish was predictive of their equivalent ability in English. They found that the depth of ELs' knowledge for high-frequency Spanish nouns related to their depth of knowledge for similar English nouns. Basically, these researchers learned that ELs were able to draw from their rich Spanish vocabularies to leverage English vocabulary learning (Ordóñez et al., 2002).

To further exemplify how instructional design can facilitate knowledge transfer, teaching to transfer during content-enriched shared book reading can include book-reading experiences with explicit exposure to high-priority words and concepts in the native language (e.g., Spanish) prior to reviewing and extending the same content-related vocabulary and associated concepts during English interactive book-reading discussions. This pedagogical approach is also known as "bootstrapping on first-language knowledge and skills" (Graves et al., 2013, p. 31) and can include previewing important concepts and words in the student's native tongue prior to learning the labels for the same concepts in a second language (Roberts, 2008; Ulanoff & Pucci, 1999).

Encourage Deep Processing and Analytical Thinking During Content-Enriched Vocabulary Instruction

Deep processing experiences allow students to make semantic connections to other words or concepts to encourage a richer and more nuanced understanding of vocabulary meanings. A semantic feature analysis is an instructional approach that focuses students' attention on conceptual connections or word relationships (Nagy, 1988). In this process, the teacher selects words that are semantically related, including a few familiar words as a starting point for the discussion, in addition to several shared and distinguishing features (e.g., features that are not shared). In Mr. Lopez's instructional unit, he developed a matrix of important plants that were transmitted across cultures (see Figure 7.3). He used this tool to generate a class discussion and prompted students to identify if the plants grew in rows, on vines, were labor intensive, or were used as cash crops.

During this discussion, a plus (+) was placed in the square to indicate if a feature was shared by a word. A minus (–) was placed in the square if a feature was not shared by a word. A question mark (?) was placed in the square if the students were uncertain and needed to learn more about the plant.

A similar matrix was developed in another social studies unit as ELs learned about three kinds of boats:

1. Rowboat: a small boat that is propelled by oars

2. Motorboat: a small boat that is propelled by a motor

3. Sailboat: a boat that is propelled by the wind that moves the sails

After reading and discussing books related to these boats, Mr. Lopez created a matrix that allowed the students to learn about other types of boats, comparing and contrasting their shared and distinguishing features (see Figure 7.4). Again, with scaffolding and further discussion, the class was able to agree on shared features.

Posing open-ended analytical questions that encourage students to interact deeply with words can serve as a culminating experience (Beck et al., 2013). In the unit on the historical impact of foods, Mr. Lopez stimulated

Plants that transformed history	Labor intensive	Row crops	Vine crops	Cash crops
Maize	?	+	–	+
Sugar cane	+	+	–	+
Tea	?	+	–	+
Potato	?	+	–	?

Figure 7.3. Matrix of plants that transformed history.

Boats	Uses oars	Uses paddles	Propelled by the wind	Propelled by a motor	Transports one person	Transports more than one person
Rowboat	+	–	–	–	+	+
Sailboat	–	–	+	–	+	+
Motorboat	–	–	–	+	+	+
Canoe	–	+	+	–	+	+
Yacht	–	–	+	+	+	+
Kayak	–	+	+	–	–	+

Figure 7.4. An analysis of features shared by boats.

deeper thinking with school–world connections by discussing the following questions at the end of his social studies unit:

- Which of the following *crops* can be found in your diet (maize, sugar cane, tea, potatoes)? Why? Which of the following *crops* are not included in your diet (maize, sugar cane, tea, potatoes)? Why?

- Sugar cane is a *labor-intensive crop*. Can you think of other *crops* that require rigorous work to grow and harvest?

- What projects have you completed at school or at home that were *labor intensive*? Why did the project require rigorous work?

- We have studied about crops that *transformed* history. Describe one other event that can *transform* history. Talk about one event that has *transformed* your life.

CONCLUSION: PUTTING THIS INTO PRACTICE

Overall, this chapter's most prominent message is that reflective teachers should intentionally structure the classroom learning environment for frequent explicit and varied vocabulary building throughout the school day so that learning new words in a second language is not left to chance and informal "teachable moments" (Neuman & Wright, 2013, p. 8). These frequent opportunities should encourage ELs to be immersed in listening, speaking, reading, and writing new words during content-enriched instruction (August & Shanahan, 2013; Gersten et al., 2007; TESOL, 2006). Although informal opportunities to use new words are important, they do not provide sufficient robust exposures to new vocabulary use that can only take place through intentional planning that emphasizes deciding which words to teach and which word-building strategy is most appropriate. Teachable moments have a role in instruction, but they cannot replace planned opportunities for maximizing knowledge-building talk around new words and high-priority concepts that are important for future comprehension.

The early years represent an optimal window for vocabulary acceleration and knowledge expansion with daily opportunities to stimulate young children's analytical thinking and talking. It may be beneficial to reflect on some final questions about how typical vocabulary practices can be enhanced and intensified through the use of recommendations provided in this chapter.

STUDY QUESTIONS

1. Define *content-enriched vocabulary instruction.*

2. Why is vocabulary acquisition essential for ELs?

3. Describe the national expectations for ELs' vocabulary learning. How should these inform instructional approaches to teaching vocabulary?

4. What is instructional design, and how can it deepen vocabulary-building practices during content-enriched instruction?

5. What strategies have been shown to be effective and evidence based for vocabulary instruction to ELs?

EXTENDED READING AND APPLICATION ACTIVITIES

Select one content area (English language arts, science, mathematics, social studies) and review a week of your own lesson plans or plans from another educator, whether it be from a teacher you know or from a sample found online. Respond to the questions associated with the following four steps by writing brief responses in a journal or in this text.

1. Which of these strategies are present in your daily vocabulary practices during content instruction?

2. Based on the information that you have acquired in this chapter, select one content lesson (literacy, science, mathematics, social studies) and summarize what might be done differently to integrate content-enriched vocabulary practices. How would you integrate rich vocabulary talk during the lesson in relevant ways (e.g., beyond school connections, connections to important concepts)? Which semantically related words are important to teach and why?

3. Based on the evaluation of the lesson plan modifications, design and implement a new content lesson, noting the successful experiences and those tasks that require further planning to think around potential obstacles.

4. What are your goals moving forward?

Please review the following suggested readings to further your professional growth and abilities.

Beck, I. L., McKeown, M. G., & Kucan, L. (2013). *Bringing words to life: Robust vocabulary instruction* (2nd ed.). New York, NY: Guilford Press.

Gottlieb, M. (2013). *Essential actions: A handbook for implementing WIDA's framework for English language development standards.* Retrieved from https://wida.wisc.edu/resources/essential-actions-handbook

International Literacy Association. (2017). *Second-language learners' vocabulary and oral language development* [Literacy Leadership Brief]. Retrieved from https://www.literacyworldwide.org/docs/default-source/where-we-stand/ila-second-language-learners-vocabulary-oral-language.pdf?sfvrsn=67f9a58e_6

Neuman, S. B., & Wright, T. S. (2013). *All about words: Increasing vocabulary in the common core classroom: PreK–2.* New York, NY: Teachers College Press.

Pollard-Durodola, S., Gonzalez, J., Simmons, D. C., & Simmons, L. (2015). *Accelerating language skills and content knowledge through shared book reading.* Baltimore, MD: Paul H. Brookes Publishing Co.

REFERENCES

Adams, M. J. (1990). *Beginning to read: Thinking and learning about print—A summary.* Urbana-Champaign: University of Illinois, Center for the Study of Reading, The Reading Research and Education Center.

Aliki. (1986). *Corn is maize: The gift of the Indians.* New York, NY: HarperCollins Publishers.

Anderson, R. C., & Freebody, P. (1981). Vocabulary knowledge. In J. Guthrie (Ed.), *Comprehension and teaching: Research reviews* (pp. 77–117). Newark, DE: International Reading Association.

August, D., Calderón, M., & Carlo, M. (2002). *Transfer of skills from Spanish to English: A study of young learners.* Washington, DC: Center for Applied Linguistics.

August, D., Carlo, M., Dressler, C., & Snow, C. (2005). The critical role of vocabulary development for English language learners. *Learning Disabilities: Research and Practice, 20*(1), 50–57.

August, D., & Shanahan, T. (2006). *Developing literacy in second-language learners: A report on the National Literacy Panel on Language-Minority Children and Youth.* Mahwah, NJ: Lawrence Erlbaum Associates.

August, D., & Shanahan, T. (2013). Introduction. In M. F. Graves, D. August, & J. Mancilla-Martinez (Eds.), *Teaching vocabulary to English language learners* (pp. 1–9). New York, NY: Teachers College Press.

Baker, S., Simmons, D. C., & Kame'enui, E. (1998). Vocabulary acquisition: Research bases. In Simmons, D. C. & Kame'enui, E. J. (Eds.), *What reading research tells us about children with diverse learning needs: Bases and basics* (pp. 183–217). Mahwah, NJ: Lawrence Erlbaum Associates.

Beck, I. L., McKeown, M. G., & Kucan, L. (2013). *Bringing words to life: Robust vocabulary instruction* (2nd ed.). New York, NY: Guilford Press.

Boals, T., Kenyon, D. M., Blair, A., Wilmes, C., & Wright, L. (2015). Transformation in K-12 English language proficiency assessment: Changing contexts, changing constructs. *Review of Research in Education, 39,* 122–164. doi:10.3102/0091732X14556072

Bravo, M. A., Hiebert, E. H., & Pearson, P. D. (2007). Tapping the linguistic resources of Spanish-English bilinguals: The role of cognates in science. In R. K. Wagner, A. E. Muse, & K. R. Tannenbaum (Eds.), *Vocabulary acquisition: Implications for reading comprehension* (pp. 140–156). New York, NY: Guilford Press.

Brophy, J. (2004). *Advances in research on teaching: Using video in teacher education.* New York, NY: Elsevier.

Calderón, M., August, D., Slavin, R., Durán, D., Madden, N., & Cheung, A. (2005). Bringing words to life in classrooms with English-language learners. In E. H. Hiebert & M. L. Kamil (Eds.), *Teaching and learning vocabulary: Bringing research to practice* (pp. 115–136). Mahwah, NJ: Lawrence Erlbaum Associates.

Calderón, M., Slavin, R., & Sánchez, M. (2011). Effective instruction for English learners. *The Future of Children, 21*(1), 103–127. Retrieved from www.jstor.org/stable/41229013

Cameron, A. (1989). *The stories Julian tells.* New York, NY: Random House Children's Books.

Carlisle, J. F. (2000). Awareness of the structure and meaning of morphologically complex words: Impact on reading. *Reading and Writing: An Interdisciplinary Journal, 12,* 169–190.

Carlisle, J. F. (2007). Fostering morphological processing, vocabulary development, and reading comprehension. In R. K. Wagner, A. E. Muse, & K. R. Tannenbaum (Eds.), *Vocabulary acquisition: Implications for reading comprehension* (pp. 78–103). New York, NY: Guilford Press.

Carlisle, J. F., & Stone, A. C. (2005). Exploring the role of morphemes in word reading. *Reading Research Quarterly, 40*(4), 428–449.

Carlo, M. S., August, D., McLaughlin, B., Snow, C. E., Dressler, C., Lipman, D. N., . . . White, C. E. (2004). Closing the gap: Addressing the vocabulary needs of English-language learners in bilingual and mainstream classrooms. *Reading, Research Quarterly, 39,* 188–215.

Carroll, J. (1963). A model for school learning. *Teachers College Record, 64,* 723–733.

Catts, H. W., Fey, M. E., Zhang, X., & Tomblin, J. B. (1999). Language basis of reading and reading disabilities: Evidence from a longitudinal investigation. *Scientific Studies of Reading, 3*(4), 331–361.

Cohen, L. E., Kramer-Vida, L., & Frye, N. (2012). Implementing dialogic reading with culturally, linguistically diverse preschool children. *NHSA Dialog: A Research-to-Practice Journal for the Early Childhood Field, 15*(1), 135–141. doi:10.1080/15240754.2011.639965

Collins, M. F. (2010). ELL preschoolers' English vocabulary acquisition from storybook reading. *Early Childhood Research Quarterly, 25,* 84–97. doi:10.1016/j.ecresq.2009.07.009

Covey, R. (2013). *The seven habits of highly effective people: Powerful lessons in personal change.* New York, NY: Simon & Schuster.

Cummins, J. (1978). Bilingualism and the development of metalinguistic awareness. *Journal of Cross-Cultural Psychology, 9,* 131–149. doi:10.1177/002202217892001

Cummins, J. (2007). Rethinking monolingual instructional strategies in multi-lingual classrooms. *The Canadian Journal of Applied Linguistics, 10*(2), 221–240.

Cummins, J. (2008). Teaching for transfer: Challenging the two solitudes assumption in bilingual education. In J. Cummins & N. H. Hornberger (Eds.), *Encyclopedia of language and education: Bilingual education* (2nd ed., Vol. 5, pp. 65–75). New York, NY: Springer.

Degross, M. (1994). *Donovan's word jar.* New York, NY: HarperCollins Publishers.

Diamond, K. E., Justice, L. M., Siegler, R. S., & Snyder, P. A. (2013). *Synthesis of IES research on early intervention and early childhood education.* Washington, DC: U.S. Department of Education, Institute of Education Sciences, National Center for Special Education Research.

Espinosa, L. M. (2010). *Getting it right for young children from diverse backgrounds: Applying research to improve practice.* Washington, DC: Prentice Hall/National Association for the Education of Young Children.

Eunice Kennedy Shriver National Institute of Child Health and Human Development, NIH, DHHS. (2000). *Report of the National Reading Panel: Teaching children to read: Reports of the subgroups* (00-4754). Washington, DC: U.S. Government Printing Office.

Ezell, H. K., & Justice, L. M. (2005). *Shared storybook reading: Building young children's language and emergent literacy skills.* Baltimore, MD: Paul H. Brookes Publishing Co.

Farkas, G., & Beron, K. (2004). The detailed age trajectory of oral vocabulary knowledge: Differences by class and race. *Social Science Research, 33,* 464–497.

García, E. E., & García, E. H. (2012). *Understanding the language development and early education of Hispanic children.* New York, NY: Teachers College Press.

Gersten, R., Baker, S. K., Shanahan, T., Linan-Thompson, S., Collins, P. & Scarcella,R. (2007). *IES practice guide: Effective literacy and English language instruction for English learners in the elementary grades.* Retrieved from https://files.eric.ed.gov/fulltext/ED497258.pdf

Gonzalez, J. (Principal Investigator) & Pollard-Durodola, S., & Saenz, L. (Co-Principal Investigators). (2011–2014). *Project WORLD: Worlds of Oral Reading and Language Development: Goal 3, Efficacy* (Institute of Education Sciences, CFDA: 84.305A 13).

Gonzalez, N., Moll, L. C., & Amanti, C. (2005). *Funds of knowledge: Theorizing practices in households, communities, and classrooms.* New York, NY: Taylor and Francis.

Gottlieb, M. (2013). *Essential actions: A handbook for implementing WIDA's framework for English language development standards.* Retrieved from https://wida.wisc.edu/sites/default/files/resource/Essential-Actions-Handbook.pdf

Grant, C. A., & Zeichner, K. M. (1984). On becoming a reflective teacher. In C. A. Grant (Ed.), *Preparing for reflective teaching* (pp. 103–114). Boston, MA: Allyn & Bacon.

Graves, M. F., August, D., & Mancilla-Martinez, J. (2013). *Teaching vocabulary to English language learners*. New York, NY: Teachers College Press.

Gutiérrez, K. D., Zepeda, M., & Castro, D. C. (2010). Advancing early literacy learning for all children: Implications of the NELP report for dual-language learners. *Educational Researcher, 39*(4), 334–339.

Hadley, E. B., Dickinson, D. K., Hirsch-Pasek, K., & Golinkoff, R. M. (2018). Building semantic networks: The impact of a vocabulary intervention on preschoolers' depth of word knowledge. *Reading Research Quarterly, 54*(1), 1–21. doi:10.1002/rrq.225

Halliday, M. A. K. (1993). Towards a language-based theory of learning. *Linguistics and Education, 5*(2), 93–116. doi.org/10.1016/0898-5898(93)90026-7

Hammer, C. S., Davison, M. D., Lawrence, F. R., & Miccio, A. W. (2009). The effect of maternal language on bilingual children's vocabulary and emergent literacy development during Head Start and kindergarten. *Scientific Studies of Reading, 12*, 99–121.

Hancin-Bhatt, B., & Nagy, W. E. (1994). Lexical transfer and second language morphological development. *Applied Psycholinguistics, 15*(3), 289–310.

Hargrave, A. C., & Sénéchal, M. (2000). A book reading intervention with preschool children who have limited vocabularies: The benefits of regular reading and dialogic reading. *Early Childhood Research Quarterly, 15*, 75–90.

Hart, B., & Risley, T. R. (1995). *Meaningful differences in the everyday experience of young American children*. Baltimore, MD: Paul H. Brookes Publishing Co.

Hindman, A. M., & Wasik, B. A. (2015). Building vocabulary in two languages: An examination of Spanish-speaking dual language learners in Head Start. *Early Childhood Research Quarterly, 31*, 19–33. doi:10.1016/j.ecresq.2014.12.006

Hirsch, E. D. (2003). Reading comprehension requires knowledge of the words and the world. *American Educator, 27*(1), 10–14.

Hirsch, E. D. (2006). Building knowledge: The case for bringing content into the language arts block and for knowledge-rich curriculum core for all children. *American Educator, 30*(1), 8–18.

Hoff, E. (2014). *Language development* (5th ed.). Belmont, CA: Wadsworth/Cengage Learning.

Honig, B., Diamond, L., & Gutlohn, L. (2000). *Teaching reading sourcebook*. Novato, CA: Arena Press.

International Literacy Association. (2017). *Second-language learners' vocabulary and oral language development* [Literacy Leadership Brief]. Retrieved from https://www.literacyworldwide.org/docs/default-source/where-we-stand/ila-second-language-learners-vocabulary-oral-language.pdf?sfvrsn=67f9a58e_6

Kucan, L. (2013). Vocabulary instruction. In B. M. Taylor & N. K. Duke (Eds.), *Handbook of effective literacy instruction: Research-based practice K-8* (pp. 279–297). New York, NY: Guilford Press.

Lareau, A. (2003). *Unequal childhoods: Class, race, and family life*. Berkeley: University of California Press.

Laufer, B. (2000). What's in a word that makes it hard or easy: Some intralexical factors that affect the learning of words. In N. Schmitt & M. McCarthy (Eds.), *Vocabulary: Description, acquisition, and pedagogy* (pp. 140–155). New York, NY: Cambridge University Press.

Lopez, A., Zepeda, M., & Medina, O. (2012). *Dual Language Learner Teacher Competencies (DLLTC) Report*. Los Angeles, CA: Alliance for A Better Community.

MacDonald, R., Cook, H. G., Lord, S., & Ramirez, N. G. (2014). *Doing and talking mathematics: A teachers' guide to meaning-making with English learners*. Retrieved from http://stem4els.wceruw.org/resources/WIDA-Doing-and-Talking-Math.pdf

McGee, L.M. & Schickedanz, J. A. (2007). Repeated interactive read-aloud in preschool and kindergarten. *The Reading Teacher, 60*(80), 742–751.

McKeown, M. G., Deane, P. D., Scott, J. A., Krovetz, R., & Lawless, R. R. (2017). *Vocabulary assessment to support instruction: Building rich word-learning experiences*. New York, NY: Guilford Press.

McTighe, J., & Wiggins, G. (1998). *Understanding by design*. Alexandria, VA: Association for Supervision and Curriculum Development.

Metzger, S. & Bryant, L. (2006). *Five little sharks swimming in the sea*. New York, NY: Scholastic.

Montelongo, J. A., Hernández, A. C., Herter, R. J., & Cuello, J. (2011). Using cognates to scaffold context clue strategies for Latino ELLs. *The Reading Teacher, 64*(6), 429–434.

Montero-Sieburth, M., & Barth, C. M. (2001). An overview of the educational models used to explain the academic achievement of Latino students: Implications for research and policies into the new millennium. In R. E. Slavin & M. Calderón (Eds.), *Effective programs for Latino students* (pp. 331–368). New York, NY: Routledge.

Nagy, W. E. (1988). *Teaching vocabulary to improve reading comprehension*. Newark, DE: International Reading Association.

Nagy, W. E. (2005). Why vocabulary instruction needs to be long-term and comprehensive. In E. H. Hiebert & M. L. Kamil (Eds.), *Teaching and learning vocabulary* (pp. 27–44). Mahwah, NJ: Lawrence Erlbaum Associates.

Nagy, W., & Anderson, R. (2013). Teaching word-learning strategies. In M. F. Graves, D. August, & J. Mancilla-Martinez (Eds.), *Teaching vocabulary to English language learners* (pp. 73–102). New York, NY: Teachers College Press.

Nagy, W. E., Anderson, R. C., Schommer, M., Scott, J. A., & Stallman, A. C. (1989). Morphological families in the internal lexicon. *Reading Research Quarterly, 24*, 262–282.

Nagy, W. E., Berninger, V. W., & Abbott, R. D. (2006). Contributions of morphology to literacy outcomes of upper elementary and middle school students. *Journal of Educational Psychology, 98*(1), 134–147.

Nagy, W. E., García, G. E., Durgunoğlu, A. Y., & Hancin-Bhatt, B. J. (1993). Cross-language transfer of lexical knowledge: Bilingual students' use of cognates. *Journal of Reading Behavior, 25*, 241–259.

Nagy, W. E., & Scott, J. A. (2000). Vocabulary processes. In M. L. Kamil, P. B. Mosenthal, P. D. Pearson, & R. Barr (Eds.), *Handbook of reading research: Vol. III* (pp. 269–284). Mahwah, NJ: Lawrence Erlbaum Associates.

Nagy, W. E., & Townsend, D. (2012). Words as tools: Learning academic vocabulary as language acquisition. *Reading Research Quarterly, 47*(1), 91–108.

National Early Literacy Panel. (2009). *Developing early literacy: Report of the National Early Literacy Panel: A scientific synthesis of early literacy development and implications for intervention*. Washington, DC: National Institute for Literacy.

Neuman, S. B. (2006). The knowledge gap: Implications for early education. In S. B. Neuman & D. K. Dickinson (Eds.), *Handbook of early literacy research* (pp. 29–40). New York, NY: Guilford Press.

Neuman, S. B., & Celano, D. (2001). Access to print in middle- and low-income communities: An ecological study of four neighborhoods. *Reading Research Quarterly, 36*, 8–26.

Neuman, S. B., & Dwyer, J. (2011). Developing vocabulary and conceptual knowledge for low-income preschoolers: A design experiment. *Journal of Literacy Research, 43*, 103–129. doi:10.1177/1086296X11403089

Neuman, S. B., & Wright, T. S. (2013). *All about words: Increasing vocabulary in the common core classroom: PreK–2*. New York, NY: Teachers College Press.

Ordóñez, C. L., Carlo, M. S., Snow, C. E., & McLaughlin, B. (2002). Depth and breadth of vocabulary in two languages: Which vocabulary skills transfer? *Journal of Educational Psychology, 94*(4), 719–728. doi:10.1037/0022-0663.94.4.719

Phythian-Sence, C., & Wagner, R. K. (2007). Vocabulary acquisition: A primer. In R. K. Wagner, A. E. Muse, & K. R. Tannenbaum (Eds.), *Vocabulary acquisition: Implications for reading comprehension* (p. 1–14). New York, NY: Guilford Press.

Pollard-Durodola, S. D., Gonzalez, J. E., Saenz, L., Resendez, N., Kwok, O., Zhu, L., & Davis, H. (2017). The effects of content enriched shared book reading vs. vocabulary-only discussions on the vocabulary outcomes of preschool dual language learners. *Early Education and Development, 29*(2), 245–265. doi:10.1080/10409289.2017.1393738

Pollard-Durodola, S. D., Gonzalez, J. E., Saenz, L., Soares, D., Resendez, N., Kwok, O., . . . Zhu, L. (2016). The effects of content-related shared book reading on the language development of preschool dual-language learners. *Early Childhood Research Quarterly, 36*, 106–121.

Pollard-Durodola, S., Gonzalez, J., Simmons, D. C., & Simmons, L. (2015). *Accelerating language skills and content knowledge through shared book reading*. Baltimore, MD: Paul H. Brookes Publishing Co.

Pollard-Durodola, S. D., Gonzalez, J. E., Simmons, D. C., Simmons, L., & Nava-Walichowski, M. (2011). Using knowledge networks to develop preschoolers' content vocabulary. *The Reading Teacher, 65*(4), 259–269.

Purpura, D. J. & Reid, E. R. (2016). Mathematics and language: Individual and group in mathematical language skills in young children. *Early Childhood Research Quarterly, 36*(3), 259–268.

Ring, S. (2004). *The ocean.* Bloomington, MN: Red Brick Learning.

Roberts, T. (2008). Home storybook reading in a primary or second language with preschool children: Evidence of equal effectiveness for second language vocabulary acquisition. *Reading Research Quarterly, 43*(2), 103–130. doi.org/10.1598/RRQ.43.2.1

Roberts, T., & Neal, H. (2004). Relationships among preschool English language learners' oral proficiency in English, instructional experience and literacy development. *Contemporary Educational Psychology, 29,* 283–311. doi:10.1016/j.cedpsych.2003.08.001

Saunders, W. M., Foorman, B. R., & Carlson, C. D. (2006). Is a separate block of time in programs for English learners needed? *Elementary School Journal, 107*(2), 181–198.

Scarcella, R. (2003). *Academic English: A conceptual framework* [Technical report]. Irvine, CA: University of California Linguistic Minority Research Institute.

Seals, L., Pollard-Durodola, S. D., Foorman, B. F., & Bradley, A. (2007a). *Vocabulary power: Lessons for students who use African American Vernacular English (Level 1).* Baltimore, MD: Paul H. Brookes Publishing Co.

Seals, L., Pollard-Durodola, S. D., Foorman, B. F., & Bradley, A. (2007b). *Vocabulary power: Lessons for students who use African American Vernacular English (Level 2).* Baltimore, MD: Paul H. Brookes Publishing Co.

Silverman, R. D. (2007). Vocabulary development of English-language and English-only learners in kindergarten. *Elementary School Journal, 107*(4), 365–383.

Silverman, R., & Hines, S. (2009). The effects of multimedia-enhanced instruction on the vocabulary of English-language learners and non-English-language learners in prekindergarten through second grade. *Journal of Educational Psychology, 101*(2), 305–314.

Simmons, D. C. & Kame'enui, E. J. (Eds.), *What reading research tells us about children with diverse learning needs: Bases and basics.* Mahwah, NJ: Lawrence Erlbaum Associates.

Simmons, D. C., Pollard-Durodola, S. D., Gonzalez, J. E., Davis, M., & Simmons, L. (2008). Shared book reading interventions. In S. B. Neuman (Ed.), *Educating the other America: Top experts tackle, poverty, literacy, and achievement in our schools* (pp. 187–212). Baltimore, MD: Paul H. Brookes Publishing Co.

Spira, E. G., Bracken, S. S., & Fischel, J. E. (2005). Predicting improvement after first-grade reading difficulties: The effects of oral language, emergent literacy, and behavior skills. *Developmental Psychology, 41*(1), 225–234. https://doi.org/10.1037/0012-1649.41.1.225

Spycher, P. (2009). Learning academic language through science in two linguistically diverse kindergarten classes. *Elementary School Journal, 109*(4), 359–379.

Stahl, S. A., & Fairbanks, M. M. (1986). The effect of vocabulary instruction: A model-based meta-analysis. *Review of Educational Research, 56*(1), 72–110.

Tardif, T. Gelmann, S. A.. & Xu, F. (1999). Putting the "noun bias" in context: A comparison of English and Mandarin. *Child Development, 70*(3), 620–635.

Teachers of English to Speakers of Other Languages. (2006). *Pre-K-12 English language proficiency standards: Augmentation of the World-Class Instructional Design and Assessment (WIDA) consortium English language proficiency standards.* Alexandria, VA: Author.

Tennyson, R., & Christensen, D. L. (1986). *Memory theory and design of intelligent learning systems.* Paper presented at the meeting of the American Educational Research Association, San Francisco, CA.

Tijunelis, V., Satterfield, T., & Benkí, J. R. (2013). Linking service-learning opportunities and domestic immersion experiences in U.S. Latino communities: A case study of the "En Nuestra Lengua" Project. *Hispania, 96*(2), 264–282.

Trawick-Smith, J. (2014). *Early childhood development.* Boston, MA: Pearson.

Ulanoff, S. H. & Pucci, S. (1999). Learning words from books: The effects of read aloud on second language vocabulary acquisition. *Bilingual Research Journal, 23*(4), 409–422.

Verhallen, M., & Schoonen, R. (1993). Lexical knowledge of monolingual and bilingual children. *Applied Linguistics, 14*(4), 344–363. https://doi.org/10.1093/applin/14.4.344

Verhoeven, L., & Perfetti, C. A. (2011). Introduction to this special issue: Vocabulary growth and reading skill. *Society for the Scientific Study of Reading, 15*(1), 1–7. doi:10.1080/10888438. 2011.536124

Waddell, M., & Benson, P. (2002). *Owl babies*. Somerville, MA: Candlewick Press.

Waxman, S. & Lidz, J. (2006) Early word learning. In D. Kuhn & R. S. Siegler (Eds.), *Handbook of child psychology: Cognition, perception and language* (6th ed., pp. 299–335). New York, NY: John Wiley & Sons.

Weigel, D. J., Martin, S. S., & Bennett, K. K. (2006). Contributions of the home literacy environment to preschool-aged children's emerging literacy and language skills. *Early Child Development and Care, 176*(3-4), 357–378.

What Works Clearinghouse. (2014). *Educator's practice guide: Teaching academic content and literacy to English learners in elementary and middle school*. Retrieved from https://ies.ed.gov/ncee/wwc/Docs/PracticeGuide/english_learners_pg_040114.pdf

What Works Clearinghouse. (2015). *Shared book reading*. Retrieved from https://ies.ed.gov/ncee/wwc/EvidenceSnapshot/458

Whitehurst, G. J., & Lonigan, C. J. (1998). Child development and emergent literacy. *Child Development, 69*, 848–872. doi:10.1111/j.1467-8624.1998.tb06247.x

Winsler, A., Kim, Y. K., & Richard, E. R. (2014). Socio-emotional skills, behavior problems, and Spanish competence predict the acquisition of English among English language learners in poverty. *Developmental Psychology, 50*(9), 2242–2254. doi:10.1037/a0037161

Wright, W. E. (2010). *Foundations for teaching English language learners: Research, theory, policy, and practice*. Philadelphia, PA: Caslon.

Yoshida, H. (2008). The cognitive consequences of early bilingualism. *Zero to Three, 29*(2), 26–30.

8

Reading Comprehension Among English Learners

Colleen K. Reutebuch

By completing this chapter, the reader will

- Define reading comprehension
- Explain how reading comprehension develops in English learners (ELs)
- Understand connections across languages
- Identify principles of effective reading comprehension instruction for ELs
- Learn and apply strategies for teaching reading comprehension to ELs

Esme did not look forward to her reading block in class. Some days, Mrs. Norris, her third-grade teacher, posted a list of vocabulary words that needed to be defined using the dictionary. Other days, she lectured about events, people, and places that were new to Esme. On some occasions, Mrs. Norris read aloud before requiring students to do so in pairs or individually. Esme always worked alone, too timid to expose her feeling of being overwhelmed with trying to navigate unfamiliar concepts in a second language. Esme tried so hard to make out the words and think about what they all meant, but by the time she made it to the end of the required reading assignment, she was still unsure of what she was supposed to know or understand about the topic.

INTRODUCTION

The ultimate goal of reading is to understand and learn from text. Reading comprehension is a critical skill for academic success and of particular importance to English learners (ELs), some of whom may be at risk for developing reading difficulties. Although ELs often acquire foundational reading skills, a breakdown in reading comprehension sometimes occurs due to an underdeveloped knowledge and vocabulary base. According to Linan-Thompson and Vaughn (2007), this breakdown may be due to a failure to understand word meaning; inadequate background knowledge; lack of interest in text; or a disconnect between instruction, the text, and the reader. In addition, restricted "access to high-quality teachers, proficient student learners, and curricula" may further impede the achievement of ELs (Vaughn et al., 2016, p. 22). Fortunately, almost 4 decades of reading research on monolingual learners with and without reading difficulties has helped establish the basis for effective reading comprehension practices for ELs. The application of research on English-only students to ELs is pertinent because many monolingual learners share similar struggles with literacy, including weaknesses in academic language and vocabulary (Torgesen et al., 2007).

This chapter begins by introducing and defining reading comprehension. It goes on to provide findings on research as it relates to reading comprehension and ELs, which is followed by ways connections to reading comprehension can be enhanced across languages. The next section presents principles of effective instruction in this component for those engaged in second language acquisition. Subsequent sections provide information on ways to incorporate effective practices that are likely to contribute to the continual improvement of reading comprehension skills of ELs. To conclude, readers are offered the opportunity for self-assessment and to apply information gleaned from this chapter to case studies that bring the reading comprehension challenges faced by ELs to light.

READING COMPREHENSION COMPONENT

The National Reading Panel report (2000) identified five areas of instruction important to an effective reading program. As students progress through the grades, they are increasingly required to draw upon their reading comprehension skills to learn from text (Williams, 1998). Reading comprehension, one of those five essential components and by far the most difficult, is a complex process in which the reader interacts with the text in an attempt to gain meaning (Klinger, Vaughn, & Boardman, 2007; RAND Reading Study Group, 2002). It depends heavily on knowledge about the world as well as language and print.

Comprehension involves understanding and interpreting what is read. In order to understand text, readers must be able to decode words, have knowledge of what those words mean, make connections with those words and what they already know, and reflect on what they read about. The purpose of reading comprehension is to get meaning from written text. Therefore, a major goal of reading comprehension instruction is to help students develop the knowledge, skills, and experiences they must have if they are to become competent and enthusiastic readers.

Regardless of an individual's language, there are actions associated with a reader's overall success with and understanding of reading tasks. Researchers studied reading behaviors and identified that good readers use the following skills and strategies (Baker & Brown, 1984; Paris, Lipson, & Wixson, 1983; Pressley, 2001):

- Read words accurately and quickly.

- Set a purpose for reading, preview the text before reading to make connections with what they already know, and predict what they will learn or discover.

- Monitor and adjust while reading when understanding breaks down, which means that good readers know why they are reading a text and they remain mindful of their understanding while reading. They maintain their focus on the text by questioning, associating ideas in text to prior knowledge, revising their prior knowledge when new ideas conflict with prior ones, and figuring out unknown words using content clues. They also use word knowledge and reference materials, ask for help if they get stuck, make note of important points, reread if necessary, and interpret the text and its quality.

- Reflect on important points at the conclusion of reading and think about how ideas in the text might be applied in the future.

During the elementary grades, effective reading comprehension instruction teaches students to use graphic organizers, generate and answer questions, and monitor their comprehension (Kamil et al., 2008; Mastropieri, Scruggs, Bakken, & Whedon, 1996). Children in the upper grades (i.e., second through fifth) must be strategic comprehenders of increasingly sophisticated text containing complex vocabulary and concepts (Slavin, Lake, Chambers, Cheung, & Davis, 2010). Reading comprehension does not improve by simply reading more, but rather requires explicit instruction on strategy use (Kamil et al., 2008; Pressley, Wharton-McDonald, Mistretta-Hampston, & Echevarria, 1998).

The National Reading Panel (2000) acknowledged and the National Reading Technical Assistance Center's synthesis (Butler, Urrutia, Buenger, & Hunt, 2010) confirmed the effectiveness of various comprehension strategies, some taught as single strategies and others combined into multiple strategy instruction for building comprehension. They include but are not limited to the following:

- *Summarizing.* A process in which a reader synthesizes the important ideas in a text. Teaching students to summarize helps them generate main ideas, connect central ideas, eliminate redundant and unnecessary information, and remember what they read.

- *Questioning.* A way for readers to engage with the text. When readers are taught to ask questions as they read, they are not only interacting with the text to make meaning of it, but they are also monitoring their own comprehension of what they are reading. Readers ask questions before they read to activate their prior knowledge and make predictions about what they will glean from the text in order to connect with the text. Questioning during reading can take the form of self-questioning, questioning the text, or questioning the author. It creates a dialogue in the student's mind as he or she reads. Asking questions after reading the text can stimulate critical analysis and further research on the topic.

- *Story structure instruction (including story maps).* This involves teaching about the plan or structure of a text (i.e., beginning, middle, end) along with the basic narrative story elements (i.e., setting, characters, problem/conflict, events, resolution/solution, theme). Teaching about story structure helps students grasp how stories are organized in order to distinguish between major and minor events and details. Story maps are templates that provide a concrete framework that readers can use for identifying the elements of text.

- *Graphic and semantic organizer use.* These tools develop students' comprehension skills by having them select the most meaningful and important details from text to display using visual representations (e.g., maps, diagrams, tables, charts).

- *Cooperative learning.* Instructors structure students into small groups that work together in such a way that each group member's success depends on the group's success. Small-group work allows for more opportunities for students to practice reading skills and strategies as well as to receive more intense feedback and support.

- *Comprehension monitoring.* Students self-assess their understanding, and if they encounter a barrier to understanding, then they clarify their understanding by using fix-up strategies (e.g., using visuals or content clues, rereading text, figuring out the meaning of unknown words or phrases using knowledge of word parts or a dictionary) to regain a sense of meaning.

A clear grasp and appropriate use of these skills and strategies does not come naturally for many at-risk or struggling readers; however, when weak comprehenders learn these same strategies, their comprehension can improve (Kamil et al., 2008; Paris, Wasik, & Turner, 1991).

Effective practices for teaching reading comprehension skills include providing direct and explicit instruction of vocabulary and comprehension with opportunities built in for students to practice with immediate corrective feedback, opportunities to learn to read for understanding from a variety of text genres, and small-group and paired instruction that provides specific instruction to meet students' needs as well as opportunities to meaningfully discuss text (Denton & Mathes, 2003; Francis, Rivera, Lesaux, Kieffer, & Rivera 2006; Swanson, Hoskyn, & Lee, 1999; Torgesen et al., 2001). Strategies for effective, explicit instruction to teach reading comprehension are discussed later in the chapter.

READING COMPREHENSION AND ENGLISH LEARNERS

Educators must adjust and adapt instruction to meet the unique needs of ELs. Adaptions should include an emphasis on building oral language as well as taking advantage of a student's native language proficiency to facilitate learning to read in English. Research specific to ELs has emphasized a need for developing their oral language and written skills to better support their reading comprehension (Solari & Gerber, 2008; Tutor-Richards, Baker, Gersten, Baker, & Smith, 2016). Furthermore, the updated What Works Clearinghouse practice guide calls for building second language learner's English proficiency while simultaneously building literacy, numeracy skills, and content knowledge of social skills and science for elementary and middle school students (Baker et al., 2014).

Gay (2010) promoted the concept of culturally responsive teaching—a practice that involves knowledge of students' various cultures, past experiences, and frames of reference to make learning relevant and affirming for diverse students. Although connecting with students' background knowledge is generally considered important in content area instruction (e.g., Alexander & Fox, 2011; Spires & Donley, 1998), it is critical for ELs (Goldenberg, 2011; Goldenberg, Rueda, & August, 2006; Hernandez, 1991; Jimenez, 1997). ELs often encounter concepts or events in texts that are outside their cultural and life experiences (Goldenberg et al., 2006; Short, Echevarria, & Richards-Tutor, 2011; Short, Fidelman, & Louguit, 2012); yet, students can grasp many of these concepts (e.g., political conflicts) by identifying examples in their own life experience (e.g., conflict within a family or community). Content texts are often conceptually dense and require students to draw on their background knowledge and make purposeful connections (McNamara, Kintsch, Songer, & Kintsch, 1996). For students who lack background knowledge, instructional routines that require a written or oral response to convey their connections may cue the teacher to explicitly and purposefully build background knowledge before launching into a lesson, something that teachers do not always carry out (Goldenberg et al., 2006; Short et al., 2011, 2012).

Explicit instruction of multistep reading strategies has been shown to increase ELs' direct comprehension of ideas in text (Genesee & Riches, 2006). Berkeley, Marshak, Mastropieri, and Scruggs (2011) examined one example of an active reading strategy. ELs were included in a diverse sample in inclusive middle school social studies classrooms. Students in the treatment condition who received explicit instruction in using a self-questioning strategy when reading their adopted content text outperformed those in the control condition who also used the normal classroom text but had no explicit reading comprehension strategy instruction. When teachers intentionally incorporate strategies to foster active reading of content text in diverse classrooms, students are better able to access the content (Bulgren, Marquis, Lenz, Deshler, & Schumaker, 2011; Lesaux & Kieffer, 2010).

CONNECTIONS ACROSS LANGUAGES

Like all learners, ELs face the challenge of comprehending vocabulary words in content texts, which are often abstract and complex; historians have noted that students often have to read and understand words that are not current (e.g., the Gilded Age) or that need to be understood metaphorically (e.g., Black Thursday) (Shanahan & Shanahan, 2008). In addition, the language of textbooks is more formalized and complex than conversational English (Schleppegrell, Achugar, & Oteíza, 2004). The body of research available on English-only students has identified effective instructional vocabulary strategies such as providing definitional and contextual information about each word's meaning and actively involving students in word learning through talking about, comparing, analyzing, and using targeted words (Beck & McKeown, 2001; Beck, McKeown, & Kucan, 2002; Stahl, 1999). Furthermore, research has shown that students' ability to acquire textbook vocabulary is enhanced when explicit vocabulary instruction is integrated into existing content area curriculum (Baumann, Edwards, Boland, Olejnik, & Kame'enui, 2003; Bos & Anders, 1992). A meta-analysis on struggling adolescent readers found that older students with reading difficulties benefited from improved knowledge of word meanings and concepts (Scammacca et al., 2007). Knowing the meaning of words relates strongly to comprehension and overall academic success (Baumann, Kame'enui, & Ash, 2003; National Reading Panel, 2000).

One instructional practice that may be especially important for developing the vocabulary of ELs includes taking advantage of students' first language knowledge by increasing their awareness of cognates to extend their vocabulary, thereby also improving their comprehension (August, Carlo, Dressler, & Snow, 2005). Words that are common in Spanish are often cognates of less familiar words in English and appear in academic texts (e.g., *infirm, enfermo*) (August et al., 2005). Studies of vocabulary instruction also indicate that ELs are more likely to learn words that are directly taught and embedded in meaningful contexts with many opportunities for repetition and use. Syntheses conducted by the National Literacy Panel (August & Shanahan, 2006) and Center for Research on Education, Diversity, and Excellence (Genesee, Lindholm-Leary, Saunders, & Christian, 2006) concluded that a student's primary language could be used to preview or introduce new vocabulary and concepts prior to a lesson in English.

PRINCIPLES OF EFFECTIVE COMPONENT INSTRUCTION FOR ENGLISH LEARNERS

Although considerably more research on effective instructional practices for ELs is needed, existing research shows that effective instructional practices include the following (Goldenberg 2008, 2013):

- Use native language instruction for literacy and provide instruction for transfer to English language literacy.

- Encourage reading in English with a focus on developing knowledge and word meaning as well as reading associated with students' interests.

- Establish clear instructional goals and learning objectives and communicate these to students with expectations for how these learning goals can be achieved.

- Provide explicit feedback to students on correct and incorrect responses, reteach instructional areas in which learning is not proficient, and use frequent assessment to determine students' progress for reteaching.

- Make instruction clear and meaningful, and provide challenging and motivating content that is clearly structured with appropriate levels of students' participation.

- Provide opportunities for students to productively engage with others using discourse and writing; opportunities include student paired learning and cooperative groups.

- Combine approaches that provide direct instruction from the teacher with interaction between teacher and student and among students.

- Design instruction to target content learning objectives as well as language objectives.

- Provide organized vocabulary building in all activities, including opportunities to use previously taught words as currently taught words orally and in writing.

- Use predictable classroom and language routines.

- Provide redundant cues for key information, including pictures, graphs, visual cues, and graphic organizers.

- Consolidate and summarize text and learning through teacher and student paraphrases and summaries.

The effectiveness of the previous practices depends on their incorporation across content areas in order to systematically build students' English language and literacy skills. An expert panel began convening in 2012, which led to an expansion of practices to be utilized in elementary grades and extend throughout middle school so that ELs have more opportunities to speak, listen to, and write about academic topics ranging from literature to science to history in daily classroom instruction. This panel identified four recommendations with corresponding levels of evidence aimed at enhancing content as well as academic instruction (Baker et al., 2014).

- *Recommendation 1:* Teach a set of academic vocabulary words intensively across several days using a variety of instructional activities (e.g., writing, speaking, listening).

- *Recommendation 2:* Integrate oral and written English language instruction into content area teaching.

- *Recommendation 3:* Provide regular and structured opportunities to develop written language skills.

- *Recommendation 4:* Provide small-group instructional intervention to students struggling in areas of literacy and English language development.

An important consideration for instructional providers is that enhanced instructional practices that target ELs have been found to benefit monolingual students as well (Vaughn et al., 2009). Vaughn and colleagues conducted an investigation to improve vocabulary and comprehension by incorporating content enhancements (e.g., preteaching of vocabulary and concepts, strategic use of video, writing activities with graphic organizers, paired grouping) into seventh-grade social studies instruction and reported that all students, including those identified as ELs, who received the enhancements improved on measures of vocabulary and comprehension.

STRATEGIES FOR TEACHING READING COMPREHENSION SKILLS TO ENGLISH LEARNERS

Although ELs may require targeted instructional strategies to support their language and literacy development, specialized efforts to support improved reading comprehension can easily be incorporated into existing instructional practices and curriculum and are worth the effort to facilitate reading comprehension and learning outcomes. Duke and Pearson (2009) described routines as an integrated set of practices that can be consistently applied across most texts and afford students 1) better understanding of the texts to which the routines are applied as well as 2) development of a set of processes that will advance negotiations with future text, especially texts that students will have to work through on their own. Instructional routines are interactive and designed to engage students and increase their chances for successful learning.

Teach and Model Routines

The following comprehensive routines should be explicitly taught and modeled by teachers who allow for extensive practice with the routines so that students learn to make them their own. The ultimate goal is for students to apply routines independently as they read and immediately after reading is concluded. These three routines can be used throughout the reading process to help make meaning from reading: 1) previewing of text, 2) using content clues and word analysis, and 3) generating questions and answers.

Preview the Text   Previewing the text—that is, taking a tour of the text prior to reading—helps students identify elements that will be helpful in overall understanding. The goals of previewing are 1) to build and activate students' background knowledge about the topic, 2) to learn as much about a passage as readers can in a brief period of time, 3) to help students make predictions about what they will learn, and 4) to motivate students' interest in the topic and engage them in active reading from the onset. In preparation for previewing the text, students are taught to look

- At the overall organization of the text, including the structure, so they prepare for how the reading process will need to be adjusted for the type of text (e.g., expository, narrative) being read, the purposes for the reading (e.g., to learn about a concept, to solve a problem), and the format of the content (e.g., the format of instructions for conducting a science lab, a primary document in social studies)

- For words or phrases that are in bold or underlined to emphasize their importance, as well as chapter headings and subheadings that break up the text into meaningful sections organized by topics

- Over photographs, illustrations, charts, and tables as students think about how the details provided in the visuals will relate to the story or content

Apply Context Clues and Word Analysis   As students read, they monitor their reading comprehension by looking for words, phrases, and concepts or ideas that may be confusing or unclear. Students use context clues (i.e., how the word in question is used and the meanings of the words that surround it—to deduce the meaning) and word analysis (i.e., knowledge of morphology) to figure out meaning while reading each section of a passage. Steps include

1. Reread the sentence with the unclear word, phrase, concept, or idea and look for key ideas to help figure it out. Think about what makes sense.

2. Reread the sentences before and after the unclear word, phrase, concept, or idea, looking for clues. Clues are often located in the sentence appearing before or after the sentence containing the confusing or unknown word, phrase, or concept.

3. Break an unknown word apart and look for word parts (e.g., prefixes, suffixes, root words) or smaller words.

4. Look for a cognate (i.e., a similar-looking word in one's first language) that can help figure out meaning of an unknown word or concept.

Generate Questions and Answers   Once a passage is read, students formulate questions about what they have learned (Raphael, 1982). They review the text and what they learned to answer those questions. This assists students in reviewing key ideas from the passage and checking their understanding about those key ideas. Generating questions improves students' knowledge, understanding, and memory of what was read. Ideally, students should be guided to develop not only questions that focus on recall of information and facts but also questions that require higher order thinking. Question types include

•   *Right there:* The answer is easy to find in the reading. The words used to make up the question and the words used to answer the question are right there in the same sentence. Answering "right there" questions is usually easy and requires little thinking or effort. "Right there" questions are appropriate for identifying and recalling facts and key information and are helpful when learning new content.

•   *Think and search:* The answer to the question is in the reading. The answer is made up of information that comes from more than one sentence or paragraph. Readers have to put together information from different parts of the reading to find the answer. "Think and search" questions are useful for recalling facts and learning new content. In addition, "think and search" questions help the reader remember several events in a plot or storyline and require the reader to synthesize information.

•   *The author and you:* The answer to the question is not in the reading and requires the reader to make an inference. The answer to an "author and you" question will not be stated directly in the text, just implied, so the reader must think about what the author has stated, what the reader already knows, and how it all fits together.

Teachers should model how to generate questions using question stems as a scaffold. Some examples of question stems include

- What is_____?
- What was the turning point in _____?
- Who was _____ and what did he (or she) do?
- What were some of the reasons for _____?
- Why is _____ a good or a bad thing?
- Why do you think _____ happened?

Integrate Metacognitive Awareness Strategies

Metacognition involves an awareness, understanding, and control of one's own learning and thought processes. Proficient readers use one or more metacognitive strategies to comprehend text. The use of such strategies develops over time as the reader learns which ones are best suited to aid in comprehension (Pressley et al., 1998). Metacognitive strategies emphasize the monitoring and regulative mechanisms that readers consciously use to enhance comprehension. Examples of specific metacognitive strategies in reading may include 1) establishing a purpose for reading, 2) evaluating reading materials, 3) repairing misunderstanding, 4) evaluating one's ongoing understanding of the text, 5) analyzing the text and paragraph structure to clarify the author's intention, 6) adjusting reading speed and selective cognitive strategies accordingly, and 7) engaging in self-questioning to determine if the purpose for reading has been achieved.

There are several procedures educators can teach that can be used to promote active reading and engagement with text throughout the reading process—before, during, and after reading. These techniques fostering better comprehension and a more thoughtful approach to the text.

Make a Prediction Before Reading   When students make predictions before reading, they must recall what they know about the type of text to be read and anything they might know about the specific text or the topic it covers. A student might predict, "I think I am going to find out why volcanoes erupt" or, "I think this will be mainly about causes of the Mexican War." Making predictions before reading also gives students an opportunity to check and reflect on their predictions while reading as well as after reading. Discussions of predictions that include teacher supports and scaffolds also provide an opportunity for students to gain an understanding of the purpose for reading the text.

Monitor Understanding and Ask Questions During Reading   Monitoring understanding and asking students questions during reading cues students to recognize when their comprehension breaks down and identify the knowledge (e.g., of a vocabulary word or a content concept) they need to repair their comprehension. A teacher might ask about a word or phrase that he or she believes some students might not understand (e.g., What kind of toll is the author referring to?). Asking ELs to explain their processes for making meaning while reading and their strategies used to overcome difficulties is another method to increase opportunities to produce language (e.g., What clues did you use to figure out the meaning of *siege?* Which fix-up strategy helped you figure out that word?).

Create a Main Idea Statement After Reading a Passage   Later, you will read about developing a full summary after reading the entire text. Summarizing requires readers to synthesize what they have read, but it does not have to wait until the reading of the text is completed. To stay engaged in reading and making meaning as one reads, students should develop a main idea statement after reading sections of text. The goal of developing these statements is to 1) teach students to restate in their own words the most important point as a way of making sure they have understood what they read and 2) improve students' memory of what they have learned. Depending on the length of the text, this statement might be written about one or several paragraphs, sections of a chapter in a textbook, or a chapter in a novel. The amount of text chunked together for this activity should be manageable for the student. The text should have one overall main idea and several supporting ideas. Developing a main idea statement requires the reader to distinguish what is important from what is not. The reader must identify who or what the section of text was mainly about along with distinguishing some key information about the who or what from less important information. Once that has been done, the student creates a brief statement (i.e., about 10–15 words) that tells about the main idea of the text. Vaughn and colleagues (2011, 2013) referred to this as "getting the gist." These gist statements can be connected later to produce a full summary after the entire text selection has been read.

According to Francis et al. (2006), these aspects of reading comprehension instruction have been shown to be important for native English speakers and relevant for ELs, who need significant support to navigate and actively make meaning from text and who need opportunities for structured talk about text. Metacognition is a vital skill for learning a second language and is used by highly proficient readers of any language (Alliance for Excellent Education, 2005). The good news is that metacognitive strategies are teachable and can lead to improved achievement (Marzano, 1998).

Scaffold Story Retells for English Learners

Retelling occurs following reading or listening when readers retell what they remember either orally, in writing, or through illustrations (Kalmback, 1986). Recounting story elements aids in language learning. Research suggests that oral retelling of what has been listened to or read results in increased comprehension and recall of discourse (Gambrell, Koskinen, & Kapinus, 1991; Gambrell, Pfeiffer, & Wilson, 1985; Lipson & Wixson, 1997). Students develop language complexity through internalization of text features as they reconstruct text (Brown & Cambourne, 1987) and acquire a sense of story structure (Morrow, 1985), thereby providing the schema for comprehending, learning, and remembering the ideas in stories and texts (Anderson, 1994). Retellings add considerably to our understanding of students' comprehension as they provide an examination of the quantity, quality, and organization of information constructed during reading or listening (Stoicovy, 2004).

Story retelling can be used with narrative and expository text. For narrative text, the teacher first models by identifying key story elements—that is, main characters, setting, problem, and resolution. It is a good idea to teach these mechanisms separately and then assist students in combining them. Provide students opportunities to work in small groups in order to identify retell components and practice retelling parts of the story with peers. Retelling can be used with expository text, and it is essential that teachers ensure that students understand different text types. The differences are highlighted in Table 8.1.

Once students are comfortable retelling narrative text, teachers may introduce expository, or information, text for retelling. In retelling expository text, students see the relationships between key facts and ideas, which contrasts with story recalls that show evidence of sequence and storyline (Lipson & Wixson, 1997). Students soon become skilled at retelling both narrative and expository texts across the subjects. Retelling facilitates literacy learning not only for ELs but also for primary English speakers (Brown & Cambourne, 1987).

Simple retell components involving narrative text include the recounting of story events:

- Beginning (If necessary, prompt with *What happened first?*)

Table 8.1. Differences in story retelling for narrative and expository text

Narrative texts	Expository texts
Tell stories	Explain information or tell about topics
Follow a familiar story structure	Provide a framework for comprehension of content area textbooks
Include short stories, folktales, tall tales, myths, legends, fables, autobiographies, biographies, fantasies, historical fiction, mysteries, science fiction, plays	Include informational books, content area textbooks, newspapers, magazines, brochures, catalogues

- Middle (If necessary, prompt with *What happened next?*)
- End (If necessary, prompt with *What happened last?*)

If a child is unable to retell the story, or if the retelling lacks sequence and detail, then prompt the retelling step by step:

- *Who* was the story about?
- *When* did the story happen?
- *Where* did the story happen?
- *What* was the main character's problem? (if applicable)
- *How* did he or she solve the problem?
- *What* was done first/next?
- *How* was the problem solved?
- *How* did the story end?

To be successful with retelling information text, the reader must be familiar with expository text structure (e.g., sequential order, classification, cause/effect, compare/contrast). The structures should be explicitly taught. Unlike retelling about story plot with narrative text, students retelling informational text must identify information that is important to the topic—who, what, when, where, why, and how. When students are learning to identify information to recall from informational text, the following questions provide a scaffold for the selection of important elements to be retold:

- *Who/what* is the most important subject in this passage/article?
- *What* is important about that subject?
- *When* does/did this take place?
- *Where* does this take place?
- *Why* is the subject important?
- *How* does/did this occur?

Studies on story recall have found that extended use of this technique leads to large improvements in comprehending the story, making inferences, and understanding story structure. Rather than having children answer specific questions about story details, story retelling requires children to focus on the big ideas in the story and subsequently allows the teacher to gain access to how well a child understands what was read. By having students tell the story in their own words, educators can identify children's strengths and specific areas of difficulty that arise for individual students. Retelling helps readers develop important reading skills while allowing the teacher to easily evaluate their progress over time. Incorporating the use of story retelling can improve children's reading comprehension and vocabulary as well as help them become more engaged in the reading process.

Summarizing Procedures

Summarizing involves identifying the most important ideas in a text. It helps students learn to determine essential ideas and consolidate important details that support them. It enables students to focus on key words, ideas, and phrases of an assigned text that are worth noting and remembering. Summarizing teaches students how to take a large selection of text and reduce it to the main points for more concise understanding. The goals for summarization include 1) extracting the important elements from a piece of text for the purpose of comprehending that text; 2) reducing large pieces of text into the bare essentials, including the gist, the key ideas, and the main points worth remembering; and 3) authentically constructing a short paragraph that includes the main ideas of the text.

The information contained in a summary will depend on the type of text read. With narrative text, students recall and explain a sequence of events that includes recapping information about the plot's main events and characters, their relationships, and changes they undergo. When developing a summary with informational text, students describe the following:

- *Who* or *what* the text is about

- *What* happened in the text

- *Where* something occurred

- *When* something occurred

- *How* something looked or was done

- *Why* something happened

Graphic organizers are a key summarizing tool. They are visual and spatial displays of information that are used to highlight important information and help make abstract concepts more comprehensible (Ausubel, 1968). These tools are associated with improving learning and reading comprehension for students of varying academic ability. With the proper instruction, graphic organizers aid in organizing information or depicting relationships and provide the ideal scaffolding for helping students to summarize. Examples of graphic organizers include visual displays such as flowcharts, Venn diagrams, story maps, cognitive maps, semantic maps, matrices, or a sequence chart (Dexter & Hughes, 2011; Kim, Vaughn, Wanzek, & Wei, 2004). Figure 8.1 shows how students can consolidate important information compiled from several paragraphs or sections of a text into one organized and concise summary.

Research proposes that instruction and practice in summarizing improves students' ability to summarize text as well as their overall com-

Main Idea Paragraph/Section 1
Main Idea Paragraph/Section 2
Main Idea Paragraph/Section 3
Main Idea Paragraph/Section 4
Main Idea Paragraph/Section 5

Summary

Figure 8.1.　Sample graphic organizer for consolidating information from several paragraphs or sections of a text.

prehension of text content. Thus, instruction in summarization not only improves students' ability to summarize text, but it also improves their ability to comprehend text and recall. Teaching students to summarize improves their memory for what is read, and summarization strategies can be used across content areas.

CONCLUSION

Teacher knowledge about reading comprehension, the processes and strategies involved in the process of making meaning from text, and the special consideration for ELs, along with the skills to provide effective comprehension instruction, helps ensure that students become strategic readers who self-monitor and understand and learn from what they read. Comprehension instruction involves much more than asking questions to assess if students understand what they read. Students must be taught to think about what they read and monitor their own understanding. Now that you have completed this chapter, test your understanding by responding to the knowledge survey that follows.

◇◇

STUDY QUESTIONS

1. Match the key concept to its definition by writing the letter in the correct blank.

_____ Reading comprehension	A. Helps students identify elements of the text that will be helpful in overall understanding
_____ Summarizing	B. A practice that involves knowledge of students' various cultures, past experiences, and frames of reference to make learning relevant and affirming for diverse students
_____ Questioning	C. Tells stories and follows a familiar story pattern
_____ Preview	D. Students formulate questions and corresponding answers about what they have learned from reading
_____ Metacognition	E. A complex process in which the reader interacts with the text in an attempt to gain meaning
_____ Story retell	F. Knowledge of morphology (word parts, including affixes and roots)
_____ Culturally responsive teaching	G. A similar-looking word in one's first language
_____ Cognate	H. Involves an awareness, understanding, and control of one's own learning and thought processes
_____ Word analysis	I. Readers recount a story they read or listened to
_____ Narrative text	J. A process in which a reader synthesizes the important ideas in a text

2. Describe how reading comprehension develops in ELs. Are all ELs at risk for developing reading difficulties in reading comprehension?

3. What are the three instructional routines described in this chapter that should be used throughout the reading process? Explain each briefly.

4. What other strategies have been shown to be effective for teaching reading comprehension to ELs? Create a sample activity related to one of these strategies.

◇◇◇

EXTENDED READING AND APPLICATION ACTIVITIES

Two case studies follow and are provided as a means to apply knowledge acquired after reading this chapter. The names appearing in the subsequent case studies, although fictitious, are based on real situations. The scenarios provided highlight struggles that can occur as second language learners face the demands of reading for meaning in English.

Consider a typical classroom—several students may come from homes in which a language other than English is spoken, whereas others may speak little or no English at all. In addition, some learners will have academic, behavioral, or other issues. Still, others may require supplementary or accelerated instruction in order to benefit and remain engaged.

1. Review the case example in Box 8.1 about Farah.

BOX 8.1. Case Example: Farah

Farah is a fifth-grade student who moved with her family from Lebanon to Texas. Farah entered second grade when she started school in the United States. She received instruction in Lebanese Arabic and French when she lived in Lebanon. Now Farah is assigned to a typical classroom in which all instruction and reading is done in English. Farah came to the United States with a strong foundation in her first language and easily made the transition into an English-only classroom. For her first 2 years in her Texas school, she did receive some specialized language support in the form of a weekly English as a second language pullout. She likes school, her teachers, and learning, but recently she has started to struggle with reading and writing when it comes to science, social studies, and especially math, which has a heavy emphasis on word problems.

(continued)

BOX 8.1. *(continued)*

Her teacher, Mrs. Banks, has noticed that Farah seems to be able to pronounce the words on a page with ease, but at the end of a passage, she cannot tell what the passage was about or decipher what a word problem is asking her to solve. When Farah is asked about what she does to determine the main idea and what is important, she becomes agitated and insists, "But after I read I still do not know. There is too much to remember." Farah's teacher speaks no Lebanese or French. Although she does encourage her Spanish students to think and discuss things in Spanish with other Spanish-speaking students in the class, there are no other Arabic or French speakers to partner with Farah. Mrs. Banks wishes she could do more to help Farah, but she is not sure what to do. See the following questions about how to best provide instruction for Farah.

---

2. Reflect on Farah's case. Based on your understanding about reading comprehension and ELs, what suggestions to you have for

    - Mrs. Banks

    - Farah

3. Explain why cognate instruction would or would not be an appropriate vocabulary strategy to use with Farah.

4. How could Farah be helped to better retain information that she has read?

5. Identify why word problems are difficult for Farah to understand and suggest what Mrs. Banks should do to help Farah improve her understanding.

6. Review the case example in Box 8.2 about Rubén.

BOX 8.2. Case Example: Rubén

Rubén is an eighth-grade student of Mexican-American descent who lives in California. He was born in California's central valley to migrant farm workers from Mexico. Throughout his 13 years, Rubén has relocated up and down the California coast as his family works as seasonal laborers in the avocado orchards, tomato fields, and lettuce farms. Over the last few years, the family has had to look for work as far away as Illinois because of the California drought. They eventually settled in Texas, but that means

---

(continued)

BOX 8.2.   *(continued)*

Rubén has had to shuffle from one school to another and from program to program. In some years he has been enrolled in immersion classes, whereas other times he has been placed into Spanish-only classes. Now that he is in his teens, placement is usually into English-only classes. Rubén is bilingual (Spanish/English) and according to his teachers, "He sounds like a native English speaker." A closer look, however, reveals that Rubén has limited literacy skills in Spanish, and his academic literacy skills in English are not as well developed as his oral skills.

Rubén is disinterested in school. He finds the work difficult, and because his family does not speak much English, there is little support for schoolwork outside of the school setting. His parents hope he will be the first to complete school and have the skills that will afford him opportunities other than farm labor. Teachers are worried that Rubén may soon drop out because he is performing below grade level in reading and writing and, as a result, struggles in all content areas that require literacy. Because Rubén is a long-term English learner, he is not eligible for newcomer programs and is usually placed in general education classes without the benefit of language support. His schedule does include an English as a second language class, but Rubén states he does not like going to it because it is too easy—"A class for babies." For example, the teacher reads a paragraph and students take dictation, or the teacher spends time teaching everyday English words related to food, clothing, or hygiene.

Content area teachers are sympathetic to Rubén. He is quiet and unassuming. He will speak in Spanish but only to friends outside of his classes. His teachers often try to support him by having other students read aloud to him or summarize text because they know he struggles to comprehend in English. Although the supports are well meaning, they are insufficient.

See the following questions about how to best provide instruction for Rubén.

7. Based on your understanding about reading comprehension and ELs, what opportunities have been missed with Rubén?

8. What suggestions do you have for

   • Rubén's content area teachers

   • The literacy specialist at Rubén's school

   • Rubén

9. Compare what you know about Rubén's oral language abilities in English with his current competencies in literacy in Spanish and English.

10. What vocabulary supports could be used with Rubén to help him gain access to English content area text?

REFERENCES

Alexander, P. A., & Fox, E. (2011). Adolescents as readers. In M. L. Kamil, P. D. Pearson, E. B. Moje, & P. P. Afflerbach (Eds.), *Handbook of reading research* (Vol. IV, pp. 157–176). New York, NY: Routledge.

Alliance for Excellent Education. (2005). *Six key strategies for teachers of English-language learners*. Retrieved from https://all4ed.org/reports-factsheets/six-key-strategies-for-teachers-of-english-language-learners/

Anderson, R. (1994). Role of the reader's schema in comprehension, learning, and memory. In R. B. Ruddell, M. R. Ruddell, & H. Singer (Eds.), *Theoretical models and processes of reading* (pp. 469–482). Newark, DE: International Reading Association.

August, D., Carlo, M., Dressler, C., & Snow, C. (2005). The critical role of vocabulary development for English language learners. *Learning Disabilities Research and Practice, 20*, 50–57.

August, D. L., & Shanahan, T. (2006). *Developing literacy in second-language learners: A report of the national literacy panel on language minority children and youth*. Mahwah, NJ: Lawrence Erlbaum Associates.

Ausubel, D. P. (1968). *Educational psychology: A cognitive view*. Austin, TX: Holt, Rinehart & Winston.

Baker, L., & Brown, A. L. (1984). Metacognitive skills and reading. In P. D. Pearson, R. Barr, M. L. Kamil, & P. Mosenthal (Eds.), *Handbook of reading research* (pp. 353–394). New York, NY: Longman.

Baker, S., Lesaux, N., Jayanthi, M., Dimino, J., Proctor, C. P., Morris, J., . . . Newman-Gonchar, R. (2014). *Teaching academic content and literacy to English learners in elementary and middle school* (NCEE 2014-4012). Washington, DC: National Center for Education Evaluation and Regional Assistance (NCEE), Institute of Education Sciences, U.S. Department of Education.

Baumann, J. F., Edwards, E. C., Boland, E., M. Olejnik, S., & Kame'enui, E. J. (2003). Vocabulary tricks: Effects of instruction in morphology and context on fifth-grade students' ability to derive and infer word meanings. *American Educational Research Journal, 40*, 447–494.

Baumann, J. F., Kame'enui, E. J., & Ash, G. E. (2003). Research on vocabulary instruction: Voltaire redux. In J. Flood, D. Lapp, J. R. Squire, & J. M. Jensen (Eds.), *Handbook of research on teaching the English language arts* (2nd ed., pp. 752–785). Mahwah, NJ: Lawrence Erlbaum Associates.

Beck, I. L., & McKeown, M. G. (2001). Text talk: Capturing the benefits of read-aloud experiences for young children. *The Reading Teacher, 55*, 10–20.

Beck, I., McKeown, M. G., & Kucan, L. (2002). *Bringing words to life: Robust vocabulary instruction*. New York, NY: Guilford Press.

Berkeley, S., Marshak, L., Mastropieri, M. A., & Scruggs, T. E. (2011). Improving student comprehension of social studies text: A self-questioning strategy for inclusive middle school classrooms. *Remedial and Special Education, 32*(2), 105–113.

Bos, C. S., & Anders., P. L. (1992). Using interactive teaching and learning strategies to promote text comprehension and content learning for students with learning disabilities. *International Journal of Disability, Development and Education, 39*(3), 31–42.

Brown, H., & Cambourne, B. (1987). *Read and retell*. Portsmouth, NH: Heinemann.

Bulgren, J. A., Marquis, J. G., Lenz, B., Deshler, D. D., & Schumaker, J. B. (2011). The effectiveness of a question-exploration routine for enhancing the content learning of secondary students. *Journal of Educational Psychology, 103*(3), 578–593.

Butler, S., Urrutia, K., Buenger, A., & Hunt, M. (2010). *A review of the current research on comprehension instruction*. Austin, TX: RMC Research Corporation.

Denton, C. A., & Mathes, P. G. (2003). Intervention for struggling readers: Possibilities and challenges. In B. R. Foorman (Ed.), *Prevention and remediating reading difficulties: Bringing science to scale* (pp. 229–252). Baltimore, MD: New York Press.

Dexter, D. D., & Hughes, C. A. (2011). Graphic organizers and students with learning disabilities: A meta-analysis. *Learning Disability Quarterly, 34*, 1–15.

Duke, N. K., & Pearson, P. D. (2009). Effective practices for developing reading comprehension. *Journal of Education, 189*(1/2), 107–122.

Francis, D. J., Rivera, M., Lesaux, N., Kieffer, M., & Rivera, H. (2006). *Practical guidelines for the education of English language learners: Research-based recommendations for instruction and academic interventions*. Portsmouth, NH: RMC Corporation, Center on Instruction.

Gambrell, L., Koskinen, P. S., & Kapinus, B. A. (1991). Retelling and the reading comprehension of proficient and less-proficient readers. *Journal of Educational Research, 84,* 356–362.

Gambrell, L., Pfeiffer, W., & Wilson, R. (1985). The effects of retelling upon reading comprehension and recall of text information. *Journal of Education Research, 78,* 216–220.

Gay, G. (2010). *Culturally responsive teaching: Theory, research, and practice* (2nd ed.). New York, NY: Teachers College Press.

Genesee, F., Lindholm-Leary, K., Saunders, W., & Christian, D. (2006). *Educating English language learners: A synthesis of research evidence.* New York, NY: Cambridge University Press.

Genesee, F., & Riches, C. (2006). Literacy: Instructional issues. In F. Genesee, K. Lindholm-Leary, W. Saunders, & D. Christian (Eds.), *Educating English language learners: A synthesis of research evidence* (pp. 109–175). New York, NY: Cambridge University Press.

Goldenberg, C. (2008). Teaching English language learners: What the research does—and does not—say. *American Educator, 32*(2), 7–23, 42–44.

Goldenberg, C. (2011). Reading instruction for English learners. In M. L. Kamil, P. D. Pearson, E. B. Moje, & P. P. Afflerbach (Eds.), *Handbook of reading research* (Vol. IV, pp. 684–710). Newark, DE: International Reading Association.

Goldenberg, C. (2013). Unlocking the research on English learners: What we know–and don't yet know–about effective instruction. *American Educator, 37*(2), 4–11, 38.

Goldenberg, C., Rueda, R. S., & August, D. (2006). Sociocultural influences on the literacy attainment of language-minority children and youth. In D. August & T. Shanahan (Eds.), *Developing literacy in second-language learners: Report of the National Literacy Panel on Language-Minority Children and Youth* (pp. 269–318). Mahwah, NJ: Lawrence Erlbaum Associates.

Hernandez, J. S. (1991). Assisted performance in reading comprehension strategies with non-English proficient students. *Journal of Educational Issues of Language Minority Students, 8,* 91–112.

Jimenez, R. T. (1997). The strategic reading abilities and potential of five low-literacy Latina/o readers in middle school. *Reading Research Quarterly, 32*(3), 224–243.

Kalmback, J. (1986). Getting at the point of retellings. *Journal of Reading, 29,* 326–333.

Kamil, M. L. (2004). Vocabulary and comprehension instruction: Summary and implications of the National Reading Panel findings. In P. McCardle & V. Chhabra (Eds.), *The voice of evidence in reading research* (pp. 213–234). Baltimore, MD: Paul H. Brookes Publishing Co.

Kamil, M. L., Borman, G. D., Dole, J., Kral, C. C., Salinger, T., & Torgesen, J. (2008). *Improving adolescent literacy: Effective classroom and intervention practices: A practice guide.* Washington, DC: National Center for Education Evaluation and Regional Assistance, Institute of Education Sciences, U.S. Department of Education.

Kim, A., Vaughn, S. Wanzek, J., & Wei, S. (2004). Graphic organizers and their effects on the reading comprehension of students with LD: A synthesis of research. *Journal of Learning Disabilities, 37,* 105–118.

Klingner, J. K., Vaughn, S., & Boardman, A. (2007). *Teaching reading comprehension to students with learning difficulties.* New York, NY: Guilford Press.

Lesaux, N. K., & Kieffer, M. J. (2010). Exploring sources of reading comprehension difficulties among language minority learners and their classmates in early adolescence. *American Educational Research Journal, 47,* 596–632.

Linan-Thompson, S., & Vaughn, S. (2007). *Research-based methods of reading instruction for English language learners: Grades K–4.* Alexandria, VA: Association for Supervision and Curriculum Development.

Lipson, M., & Wixson, K. (1997). *Assessment and instruction of reading and writing disability: An interactive approach.* New York, NY: Addison-Wesley.

Marzano, R. J. (1998). *A theory-based meta-analysis of research on instruction.* Aurora, CO: Mid-continent Research for Education and Learning.

Mastropieri, M. A., Scruggs, T. E., Bakken, J. P., & Whedon, C. (1996). Reading comprehension: A synthesis of research in learning disabilities. *Advances in Learning and Behavioral Disabilities, 10B,* 201–227.

McNamara, D. S., Kintsch, E., Songer, N. B., & Kintsch, W. (1996). Are good texts always better? Interactions of text coherence, background knowledge and levels of understanding in learning from text. *Cognition and Instruction, 24*(1), 1–43.

Morrow, L. (1985). Retelling stories: A strategy for improving young children's comprehension, concept of story structure, and oral language complexity. *Elementary School Journal, 85*, 647–661.

National Reading Panel. (2000). *Report of the National Reading Panel: Teaching children to read.* Rockville, MD: National Institute of Child Health and Human Development.

Paris, S. G., Lipson, M. Y., & Wixson, K. K. (1983). Becoming a strategic reader. *Contemporary Educational Psychology, 8*(3), 293–316.

Paris, S. G., Wasik, B. A., & Turner, J. C. (1991). The development of strategic readers. In P. D. Pearson, R. Barr, M. L., Kamil, & P. Mosenthal (Eds.), *Handbook of reading research* (Vol. 2, pp. 609–640). New York, NY: Longman.

Pressley, M. (2001, September). *Comprehension instruction: What makes sense now, what might make sense soon. Reading Online, 5*(2). Retrieved from https://pdfs.semanticscholar.org/7585/89eade45b7d230fdd7acca8dd5b65524dc07.pdf

Pressley, M., Wharton-McDonald, R., Mistretta-Hampston, J., & Echevarria, M. (1998). Literacy instruction in 10 fourth- and fifth-grade classrooms in upstate New York. *Scientific Studies of Reading, 2*, 159–194. doi:10.1207/s1532799xssr0202_4

RAND Reading Study Group. (2002). *Reading for understanding. Toward a R & D program in reading comprehension.* Santa Monica, CA: Author.

Raphael, T. E. (1982). Question-answering strategies for children. *Reading Teacher, 36*, 186–190.

Scammacca, N., Roberts, G., Vaughn, S., Edmonds, M., Wexler, J., Reutebuch, C. K., & Toregesen, J. (2007). *Interventions for adolescent struggling readers: A meta-analysis with implications for practice.* Portsmouth, NH: RMC Research Corporation, Center on Instruction.

Schleppegrell, M. J., Achugar, M., & Oteíza, T. (2004). The grammar of history: Enhancing content-based instruction through a functional focus on language. *TESOL Quarterly, 38*(1), 67–93.

Shanahan, T., & Shanahan, C. (2008). Teaching disciplinary literacy to adolescents: Rethinking content-area literacy. *Harvard Educational Review, 78*(1), 40–59.

Short, D. J., Echevarria, J., & Richards-Tutor, C. (2011). Research on academic literacy development in sheltered instruction classrooms. *Language Teaching Research, 15*(3), 363–380.

Short, D. J., Fidelman, C. G., & Louguit, M. (2012). Developing academic language in English language learners through sheltered instruction. *TESOL Quarterly: A Journal For Teachers of English to Speakers of Other Languages and of Standard English as a Second Dialect, 46*(2), 334–361.

Slavin, R. E., Lake, C., Chambers, B., Cheung, A., & Davis, S. (2010, January). *Effective reading programs for elementary grades: A best-evidence synthesis.* Baltimore, MD: Johns Hopkins University, Center for Data-Driven Reform in Education.

Solari, E. J., & Gerber, M. M. (2008). Early comprehension instruction for Spanish-speaking English language learners: Teaching text level reading skills while maintaining effects on word-level skills. *Learning Disabilities Research and Practice, 23*, 155–168.

Spires, H. A., & Donley, J. (1998). Prior knowledge activation: Inducing engagement with informational texts. *Journal of Educational Psychology, 90*, 249–260.

Stahl, S. A. (1999). *Vocabulary development.* Cambridge, MA: Brookline Books.

Stoicovy, C. E. (2004). Using retelling to scaffold English language for Pacific Island students. *The Reading Matrix, 4*(1). Retrieved from http://www.readingmatrix.com/articles/stoicovy/index.html

Swanson, H. L., Hoskyn, M., & Lee, C. (1999). *Interventions for students with learning disabilities: A meta-analysis of treatment outcomes.* New York, NY: Guilford Press.

Torgesen, J. K., Alexander, A. W., Wagner, R. K., Rashotte, C. A., Voeller, K. S., & Conway, T. (2001). Intensive remedial instruction for children with severe reading disabilities: Immediate and long-term outcomes from two instructional approaches. *Journal of Learning Disabilities, 43*(1), 33–58.

Torgesen, J. K., Houston, D. D., Rissman, L. M., Decker, S. M., Roberts, G., Vaughn, S., . . . Lesaux, N. (2007). *Academic literacy instruction for adolescents: A guidance document from the Center on Instruction.* Portsmouth, NH: RMC Research Corporation, Center on Instruction.

Tutor–Richards, C., Baker, D. L., Gersten, R., Baker, S. K., & Smith, J. M. (2016). The effectiveness of reading interventions for English learners: A research synthesis. *Exceptional Children, 82*(2), 144–169. doi:10.1177/0014402915585483

Vaughn, S., Klingner, J., Swanson, E. A., Boardman, A. G., Roberts, G., Mohammed, S., & Still-Spisak, S. J. (2011). Efficacy of collaborative strategic reading with middle school students. *American Educational Research Journal, 48,* 938–964.

Vaughn, S., Martinez, L. R., Linan-Thompson, S., Reutebuch, C. K., Carlson, C. D., & Francis, D. J. (2009). Enhancing social studies vocabulary and comprehension for 7th grade English language learners: Findings from two experimental studies. *Journal of Research on Educational Effectiveness, 2*(4), 297–394.

Vaughn, S., Martinez, L. R., Wanzek, J., Roberts, G., Swanson, E., & Fall, A. (2016). Improving content knowledge and comprehension for English language learners: Findings from a randomized control trial. *Journal of Educational Psychology, 109*(1), 22–34. doi.org/10.1037/edu0000069

Vaughn, S., Roberts, G., Klingner, J., Swanson, E., Boardman, A., Stillman-Spisak, S.J. . . . Leroux, A. (2013). Collaborative strategic reading: Findings from experienced implementers, *Journal of Research on Educational Effectiveness, 6,* 137–163.

Williams, J. P. (1998). Improving comprehension of disabled readers. *Annals of Dyslexia, 68,* 213–238.

9

Spelling Development Among English Learners

Elsa Cárdenas-Hagan and Alessandra Rico

By completing this chapter, the reader will

- Define spelling
- Describe the stages of spelling development
- Explain how spelling development may vary among English learners (ELs)
- Understand the connections across languages
- Identify effective practices for spelling instruction among ELs
- Apply strategies for teaching spelling concepts to ELs

Lourdes has been in school for 3 years. Her school has emphasized English as a second language throughout all grade levels. Lourdes is now able to speak in short but complete sentences. She can read basic words and sentences in English, but her spelling tests are challenging because she does not always process each of the English sounds within the words. Her spelling errors are often unlike those of her English-speaking peers. She gets frustrated because her mistakes are related to using native language spelling concepts. Her teacher may understand her error patterns, yet they could be interpreted as random and unpredictable. Lourdes wonders how she can improve her spelling skills. Lourdes can write sentences; however, her spelling errors make it difficult to understand the content of her writing.

INTRODUCTION

Spelling is the ability to write words correctly by processing the sounds within words and linking the sounds to the symbols in an accurate order while also following the particular patterns and rules that are applicable to the language. A good speller understands how sounds are represented in print and the spelling patterns and rules within the language. The individual may also understand the morphological patterns of the words and know how particular words are derived from other languages. This can be a helpful skill because spelling patterns will vary when the sound and symbol representations are related to the word's origin. Spelling is a complex task, especially for English learners (ELs) who may have difficulty processing the unique sounds of a second language. This chapter describes how spelling typically develops in the native language and the features of second language spelling development. Readers will learn effective practices for teaching spelling to ELs and will also be able to identify typical error patterns to become more diagnostic and prescriptive when teaching spelling.

This chapter begins by introducing spelling development theories whereby the reader can better understand the typical spelling patterns among students. It then describes how ELs may use knowledge of the first language for English spelling. Overgeneralization of the spelling patterns can be predicted among ELs as they acquire a second language and develop second language literacy skills. Readers will understand how to analyze the spelling error patterns.

The next section of the chapter addresses how to teach spelling to ELs in a systematic manner while utilizing native language knowledge. The chapter then introduces case studies to illustrate the concepts discussed and concludes with a test to measure the knowledge gained regarding spelling development among ELs.

SPELLING DEVELOPMENT

English spelling is a challenge because it carries a rich linguistic heritage from a number of other languages assimilated over the course of 1,500 years (Templeton & Morris, 2000). If a speller can understand the heritage of the language, then it is more likely that he or she will achieve consistency in English spelling. English spelling has consistent sound and symbol correlations as well as consistent morphological patterns within words. It is important for the speller to understand the regularities of the languages and the patterns for spelling.

Stages for Spelling

Henderson (1981) proposed developmental stages for spelling. The phases of spelling were labeled as preliterate, letter-name spelling/alphabetic, within-word pattern, syllable juncture, and derivational principles. Henderson proposed that these developmental stages describe how individuals learn conventional spelling. The phases are described next.

Preliterate Writing   Preliterate writing begins as soon as the child uses a writing tool such as a crayon, marker, pencil, or pen. Writing at this stage represents scribbling. The child understands that a scribble is different from a drawing. The child, however, does not yet understand writing as a system to communicate speech.

Letter-Name Spelling/Alphabetic   This stage begins as the child becomes aware of letter–sound correspondences. Children at this stage know the names of the letters of the alphabet, and their spellings are phonetic. They use a sound-based strategy for spelling. A word such as *cake* might be spelled as *kak*. The child processed the sound and used basic phonetic principles to spell the word.

Within-Word Pattern   The spelling in this stage now represents the individual's experiences with words. This stage includes correct spelling of short and long vowels. In addition, patterns such as a vowel-consonant and final silent *e* are understood. This stage is marked by the individual's understanding of phonics and reading. The word *cake* is now spelled correctly as the experience with this pattern of language has been addressed through reading and spelling instruction.

Syllable Juncture   The syllable juncture stage represents the individual's ability to understand when to double the medial and final consonants for spelling. The knowledge of spelling rules and English syllable patterns becomes more evident at this stage. A word such as *mitten* is spelled correctly as the individual understands when to double the medial consonant. The word *glass* is spelled correctly as the individual also understands when to double the final consonant.

Derivational Principles   In this stage, the individual acquires knowledge of word parts such as roots and the understanding of the origin of words. This knowledge may aid the speller at this stage. The word *kilogram* is spelled correctly as the individual understands that the word is Greek in origin and sounds such as /k/ will be spelled with the letter *k* for these words. In addition, the individual understands the two combining forms to spell the word and understand its meaning.

A Secondary Model for Spelling Development

Gentry (1982) also described a sequence for spelling development that was based on the analysis of spelling for young children who began to spell at home without formal instruction. His stages of spelling development include precommunicative, semiphonetic, phonetic, transitional, and correct stages of spelling. Gentry's stages for spelling are described next.

Precommunicative   Students do not have knowledge of letter–sound correspondences. Spellings are represented by random letter strings. A word such as *pencil* is spelled *npls.*

Semiphonetic   The concept of letter–sound correspondence is emerging, and the child has incomplete phonetic representations of words. The word *pencil* may be spelled *pesl.*

Phonetics   Students now have a very basic knowledge of phonetics. Students can apply the sound features of words and represent them in spelling. The word *pencil* may be spelled *pensel.*

Transitional   Children at the transitional stage not only depend on their phonetic knowledge, but they also depend on their previous experience with the words. They rely on the sound structure of the language and are beginning to gain morphological knowledge. The word *pencils* may be spelled as *pensils.* The individual understands that the morpheme -*s* represents the meaning of more than one or the plural form of the word. The individual may not consistently understand that the sound /s/ can be spelled with the letter *c* when it appears before the vowel sound for short *i.*

Correct Stage   The student understands the patterns and rules and can spell conventionally during the correct stage. Now the word *pencils* is spelled correctly.

Ehri (1986) described stages of spelling and only included three stages. These include semi- phonetic, phonetic, and morphemic. They are very similar to Gentry's stages, but Ehri did not begin a description of spelling development until children attempted to write words, nor did she include a final stage of spelling.

In summary, Henderson, Gentry, and Ehri proposed theories of spelling development that outline qualitatively different stages that children pass through when learning to spell. During the early stages of spelling development, the children use their knowledge of letters and sounds. As they progress, they acquire knowledge of orthographic patterns in the language as well as the morphologic patterns of the language. The stages of spelling development are marked by reliance on different types of information.

The second major theoretical approach proposes that spelling development is more continuous (Treiman, 1993; Venezky, 1970). Rather than using certain types of information at specific points in time and other spelling knowledge at a later point in time, children use a variety of strategies from the beginning of spelling development. Treiman described this as the strategy approach. Research suggest that even very young children can use the orthographic patterns and morphological relationships among words to aid their spelling. The ability to use the orthographic and morphologic knowledge improves over time; however, it does emerge earlier than expected under the stage theories of spelling development (Treiman & Cassar, 1996).

Templeton and Bear (1992) proposed that spelling instruction becomes more than mastering conventional spellings of words but extends into using word study as a means for written language and vocabulary development. It will be important for teachers to have knowledge of the spelling patterns and the morphological aspects of spelling. Henry (2010) suggested that educators who understand the origins of the English language can teach useful strategies to their students and assist spellers in understanding the regularities and irregularities of English words. According to Henry, students learning English as a second language can find that language is quite regular and not a language of exceptions.

SPELLING DEVELOPMENT AMONG ENGLISH LEARNERS

ELs experience the challenge of learning a new language and its representation in print for reading and spelling. Educators can expect ELs to demonstrate some of the similar patterns for spelling development as their monolingual English-speaking peers. ELs may experience some additional spelling error patterns, which involve overgeneralization of the native language and English and the concept of a transitional orthography. Transitional orthography is when students use incorrect spelling patterns due to overgeneralization from the native language to the second language. This sort of overgeneralization will occur more frequently in languages that have similar sound–symbol correspondences (Cárdenas-Hagan, 2018). For instance, Zutell and Allen (1988) investigated the effects of Spanish pronunciation and spelling rules on children's English spelling strategies. They proposed that students generate unique patterns of errors based on their own processing and pronunciation of English words and thus tended to use native language sound–symbol relationships. In other words, the native language influenced English spelling. As an individual acquires the second language and has experiences and instruction related to the structure of the second language, then it is likely he or she will learn the conventional spelling patterns.

Educators must be aware of the additional overgeneralization patterns. It may be that the student overgeneralizes from the native language to the second language. This pattern represents a problem-solving approach toward conventional spelling. For example, it may be that the sound–symbol representation in the second language is unfamiliar and the speller will attempt to use a familiar sound–symbol representation from the native language. Therefore, if the student spells the word *boot* as *but*, then it is important for the instructor to understand that the Spanish letter *u* represents the English digraph *oo*. Spelling instruction should include the English sound–symbol correspondence. Another example of overgeneralization may include spelling the word *gush* as *guch*. The student used knowledge of a native language sound /ch/ that was somewhat similar to the English sound /sh/. However, with explicit spelling instruction, the English learner can become familiar with the new sound and its appropriate spelling pattern. Subsequently, the student may also overgeneralize a spelling pattern or a rule from the same language before acquiring conventional spelling through explicit instruction and opportunities for practice (e.g., spelling the word *ski* as *skee*).

These are just a few examples of the types of error patterns instructors may observe from their native Spanish-speaking students. It is important to understand the types of errors these students may demonstrate because the majority of ELs in the United States speak Spanish as their native language (National Center for Education Statistics, 2017). Although the teacher may not speak the native language, the structure of the language can be examined and understood. For example, the Spanish language has five vowel sounds that do not change. The English language has five vowels that produce not only short and long vowel sounds but also the schwa sound, which is the most common vowel sound in English. It is the muffled /uh/ sound that appears at the beginning of a word such as *about*, which may be challenging for ELs to comprehend. Some of the similarities and differences of the vowel sounds in Spanish and English are described in Table 9.1 (Cárdenas-Hagan, 2015).

Table 9.1. Similarities and differences of the vowel sounds in Spanish and English

Spanish vowel	English vowel
A	Similar to the sound for vowel *a* in the word *father* May use *ey* or *ei* for long vowel sound *a* of English
E	Similar to the sound for short vowel *e* in the word *red* May use the letter *i* to represent English long *e* vowel
I	Similar to the long *e* vowel in the words *equate* or *even* May use *ai* or *ay* for long *i* sound
O	Similar to the long *o* vowel sound in the word *ocean* May use the letter *a* for English short vowel *o*
U	Similar to the vowel digraph sound *oo* in the word *boot* May use the *oo* for long *u* and *a* for short *u*

From Cárdenas-Hagan, E. (2015). *Esperanza teacher training manual*. Brownsville, TX: Valley Speech Language and Learning Center; reprinted by permission.

Table 9.2.   Potential error patterns

Spanish	English	Potential error patterns
b	*b*	*v/b* due to some Spanish dialects
c	*c/k*	*q or k/c* as they also represent the sound /k/
d	*d*	similar across languages with exception of medial position
f	*f*	*f/ph* because the ph pattern does not exist in Spanish
g	*g*	direct transfer in initial and medial position
h silent	*h*	*j, g, x/h* because three Spanish letters represent the sound /h/
i	*i*	*e, ai, ay* for long *i* and *e*/short *i* as an approximant
j	*j*	*ch/j* because this is a voiceless approximant
k	*k*	*c, qu/k* because these Spanish letters represent the sound /k/
l	*l*	*el/l* but Spanish does have final *l*
m	*m*	final *m* may be omitted
n	*n*	direct transfer in all positions of words
p	*p*	final *p* may be omitted
q	*q*	*cua, cue, cui, cuo* for /kw/ of English
r	*r*	*err* because *r* is trilled in Spanish
s	*s*	*es/s* blends
t	*t*	*d/t* due to approximants
v	*v*	*b/v* due to some Spanish dialects
w	*w*	*gua* in some cases
x	*x*	direct transfer of *x* for /ks/ but may use *s/x* as *z*
y	*y*	*ll/y* due to Spanish dialect
z	*z*	*s/z* because Spanish *z* represents /s/ sound

From Cárdenas-Hagan, E. & Carreker, S. (2017). *How written language informs instruction: The why and what-to-do.* Paper presented at IDA 68th Annual Conference, Atlanta, GA; reprinted by permission.

A review of the correlations across Spanish and English can assist educators to better understand the spelling error patterns of Spanish-speaking ELs (see Table 9.2). Some examples may include *but* for *boot* and *ti* for *tee.*

CONNECTIONS ACROSS LANGUAGES: SPELLING PATTERNS AND RULES

In addition to cultural and language constraints, ELs experience the cognitive, linguistic, communicative, contextual, and affective constraints that all writers face (Olson et al., 2007). Teachers must know how to reduce and address these constraints through appropriate spelling instructional practices. For example, in order to reduce affective constraints, which relates to students' mood and feeling, teachers can make connections to students' lives by drawing on their current orthographic knowledge in their native language, making language connections, or creating a responsive classroom in which collaboration is encouraged. Teachers may allow students to collaborate and make connections when they are creating a spelling analogy and analyzing or sorting words. Students may also face cognitive constraints when they are unable to retrieve words to express their ideas or are unable to organize these words and ideas to complete meaningful sentences.

English Learners and Cognate Instruction

Students who are learning cognates begin to see spelling similarities and differences between their home language and English. For instance, the Spanish language has consonant sounds that are similar or somewhat like English but, in many cases, are represented with different letters. Teachers can introduce the double–single consonant pattern in which English words with double consonants become Spanish cognates with one consonant (e.g., *aggressive/agresivo, appreciate/apreciar, letter/letra*).

Consonant blends are two consonants that are produced in a rapid manner. Examples that are the same in English and Spanish include /bl/, /cl/, /fl/, /gl/, and /pl/. Those that are slightly different include /br/, /cr/, /dr/, /fr/, /gr/, and /pr/ because the /r/ is not trilled in English as it is in Spanish.

Consonant digraphs are two consonants representing one sound, such as *ph* and *th*. Consonant digraphs can also alert students to cognates. English words that have the *ph* digraph correspond to Spanish words that have the *f* grapheme, as in *photo/foto* and *elephant/elefante*. The same is true with the *th* digraph, which corresponds to the *t* grapheme in Spanish, as in *third/tercero* and *throne/trono*. The use of cognate knowledge can enhance spelling, vocabulary, and writing. See Tables 9.3 and 9.4 for more on consonant blends and digraphs across English and Spanish.

Second language spelling acquisition is both language general (e.g., speech perception, alphabetic rules) and language specific (e.g., phoneme–grapheme conversion rules). Second language spellers, especially those who are literate in the native language, bring knowledge of native orthography to English spelling.

Table 9.3.   Consonant blends

Spanish	English	Potential error patterns
bl	bl	direct transfer
cl	bl	direct transfer
fl	fl	direct transfer
gl	gl	direct transfer
pl	pl	direct transfer
	sl	no *s* blends in Spanish, and therefore a vowel such as *e* will be added to *s* blends by Spanish speakers
	st	est
	str	estr
	sp	esp
	spr	espr
	sc	esc
	sk	esk
	sl	esl
	sm	esm
	sn	esn
	sq	esq
	sw	esw

From Cárdenas-Hagan, E. (2015). *Esperanza teacher training manual.* Brownsville, TX: Valley Speech Language and Learning Center; adapted by permission.

Table 9.4. Consonant digraphs

Spanish	English	Potential error patterns
ch	*ch*	direct transfer
	th	may use the letter *d/th*
	sh	may use *ch* as an approximant
	ng	may use the letter *n* as *n* before *c* is produced as /ng/ sound
	ck	may use c, k, qu

From Cárdenas-Hagan, E. (2015). *Esperanza teacher training manual.* Brownsville, TX: Valley Speech Language and Learning Center; adapted by permission.

Learning to spell in English as a second language requires not only mastering the writing system in English but also differentiating between knowledge of the native language writing system and the English writing system, provided the child is exposed to native language orthography at home or in the community. Children who learn to read and write in English as a second language will produce errors that are influenced by a wider variety of factors, including their native language orthographic patterns.

English Learners and Morphology

The English language is mainly derived from Anglo-Saxon, Latin, and Greek. Understanding the smaller meaning units in a word (morphemes) can enhance spelling and vocabulary (Henry, 2010). Identifying the morphemes within words can assist ELs with using cross-linguistic knowledge to understand a second language and its spelling patterns. The knowledge of morphemes has been described as one of the developmental stages of spelling, and, therefore, ELs can benefit from this instruction. Following is a sample script for a lesson on morphemes:

Say the word telephone, microphone, megaphone.

What did you hear that was the same in each of these words?

Yes, you heard phone *in each of these words.*

Watch as I write the words.

How do we spell phone?

We use the letters ph *to represent the sound /f/.*

Do any of these words look familiar to you from your native language?

In Spanish, the words are teléfono, micrófono, megáfono.

What is the same? What is different?

What is the meaning of phone? *When we speak on the telephone, we can hear the sounds of the voice of another person. When we use a microphone or a megaphone, we can hear the sounds of someone's voice amplified or very loud.*

So phone *means sound.*

Let's use the words in a sentence.

For example, I speak on the telephone.

I needed a microphone in the cafeteria so the students could hear me speak.

The cheerleaders used megaphones at the basketball game.

The teacher could then prompt the students to write this word part and then write as many words that they can think of using the word part. To make connections for meaning and the similarities or differences in spelling, the teacher could also ask students to write the word part in their native language.

PRINCIPLES OF EFFECTIVE INSTRUCTION FOR ENGLISH LEARNERS

Educators should plan and implement explicit and systematic instruction to help ELs gain spelling skills. ELs will require multiple opportunities to gain an awareness of speech sounds in spoken words. Consider teaching phoneme awareness as a basic skill to improve spelling. Phoneme awareness tasks may include activities that promote the recognition or discrimination of specific sounds within words. The use of an activity that addresses the minimal pairs of sounds could be beneficial for the ELs if those similar sounds are challenging.

Teachers must explicitly teach spelling constraints in English, such as certain letters never double, certain letters do not occur in sequence, and words do not end in certain letters. ELs will need to understand that multiple spellings for the same sound and many irregular words exist in English. Understanding these irregularities could benefit the ELs. They can also benefit from cross-linguistic transfer and the use of cognates and morphemes when applicable to English spelling instruction, which creates a strategy that can be helpful. ELs also require immediate corrective feedback with an explanation of the spelling pattern or rule and a rationale for why the error pattern occurs. In summary, successful spelling instruction promotes awareness of these facets.

STRATEGIES FOR TEACHING SPELLING
PATTERNS AND RULES TO ENGLISH LEARNERS

Explicit and systematic spelling instruction of patterns and rules reinforces reading proficiency by improving sounds and letter patterns (Adams, 1990), which ultimately facilitates learning word pronunciation and word meanings (Ehri & Rosenthal, 2007). Common spelling errors for ELs include letters out of order; missing letters; additional letters, although all sounds have been represented; incorrect letters that suggest difficulties with discriminating similar sounds; letters not doubled, dropped, or changed; and an overgeneralization of orthographic patterns or rules within the language or across languages.

Use a Rubric to Identify Spelling Errors

Common spelling errors can be analyzed, and a rubric to categorize the patterns can be helpful. For example, a Spanish-speaking EL named Mario made the following spelling errors in a written language sample:

Fader/father

Closset

Chrayn/train

Misez

Pitk/picked

To analyze his errors, Mario's teacher could use the rubric in Table 9.5, which ranks spelling on a scale from 1 to 5. Using the table, determine the appropriate rubric number for Mario's errors. Once you have completed your review, read the following analysis description.

As you analyze Mario's spelling error patterns, you may have determined that the use of the letters *d* and *th* within the word *father* could represent a reasonable letter for a Spanish-speaking EL. This is the case because the letter *d* in Spanish can represent the voiced /th/ of English. Therefore, on the rubric, the analysis number would be 3.

The use of the double *s* for the word *closet* represents an overgeneralization of the rule for doubling the final consonant in one-syllable words after a short vowel in English. Therefore, on the rubric, the analysis for this error would be 4.

The use of the letters *ch* and *tr* and *ay* and *ai* within the word *train* represents difficulty discriminating sounds and overgeneralization of a pattern. Therefore, on the rubric, the analysis number is 2 for the first error and 4 for the second error within the word. The use of the letters *z* and *s* represents an overgeneralization of a pattern. Therefore, the analysis number is 4 on the

Table 9.5. Sample rubric for evaluating spelling errors

Score	Level of spelling
1	Random strings of letters; letters are out of order or missing
2	Extra letters within the word, but all sounds represented Incorrect letters that represent difficulties with discriminating similar sounds
3	Incorrect but reasonable letters; letters are not doubled, dropped, or changed
4	Overgeneralization of patterns or rules within the language or across languages
5	Correct spelling

From Carreker, S. (2018). Teaching spelling. In J. R. Birsh & S. Carreker (Eds.), *Multisensory teaching of basic language skills* (4th ed., p. 404). Baltimore, MD: Paul H. Brookes Publishing Co.

rubric. The final word *picked* is misspelled and represents a random string of letters, which on the rubric analysis can be described as number 1.

Provide Instruction Based on Identified Areas of Need

By analyzing spelling areas, educators can identify skill gaps and provide instruction accordingly to address those areas of need. For example, in the case of Mario, it is necessary to teach him how to discriminate between similar sounds, which could include an explicit lesson related to the minimal pairs of sounds within a language. Minimal pairs of sounds are those that are similar to one another with the exception of one feature, which is voicing. For example, the sound /s/ is similar to the sound /z/. The only difference between these sounds is that the /z/ sound is voiced and the /s/ sound is not. The minimal pairs of sounds for English are listed in Table 9.6. A teacher could prompt the following to teach minimal pairs of sounds:

Say the sound.

Do your vocal chords vibrate?

If so, this is a voiced sound.

Now say the sound without voicing.

Your vocal chords will not vibrate.

The sound is ___.

Let's see if you can hear and feel the differences between these sounds.

Students can also benefit from a multisensory approach in learning spelling rules and patterns, such as using manipulatives to represent sounds and letters or using a mirror as they repeat the word needed to be spelled.

Integrate Guided Discovery Instruction

An individual must interpret spoken words and sounds and attach a symbol or group of letters or graphemes to that speech sound in order to spell. Therefore, instruction in the sounds that transfer across languages, sound–

Table 9.6. Minimal pairs of sounds within English

Voiced	Voiceless
/d/	/t/
/v/	/f/
/j/	/ch/
/b/	/p/
/z/	/s/
/zh/	/sh/
/th/+	/th/-

symbol correspondences, rules and patterns, and cross-language morphemes presented in an explicit, systematic, and sequential order is crucial in creating successful spellers and building on ELs' orthographic knowledge in their native language. A guided discovery instruction, as described by Carreker (2018), provides formal spelling instruction that results in better spelling performance in ELs.

For example, the teacher will say a few words with a common sound(s) and ask students to identify the sound(s) in the spoken words. (This approach heightens sensitivity to a particular sound in a word.) Once the student has identified the common sound, the teacher will ask for the position the sound was heard. Students respond that the common sound was heard in the initial, medial, or final position of the word (position of a particular sound in a word). The teacher will guide and prompt students to create a spelling analogy to attach the symbol(s) to the common speech sound. Students must have opportunities to analyze and sort words into the appropriate rule or pattern. This guided discovery instruction can be helpful to ELs because it promotes a multisensory procedure to learning spelling patterns and rules and its exceptions.

Instructors can modify this approach by asking students if this sound–symbol correspondence exists in their native language. For instance, a teacher could prompt

Say the words chip, chair, chess, teacher.

What sound was the same in each of the words?

Yes, the sound /ch/ was the same.

In what position did you hear the sound?

Yes, in the initial or medial position of the word.

Watch as I write the word. What letter or letters represent the /ch/ sound?

Ch *is used to represent the /ch/ sound.*

Is this a sound that you recognize in your native language?

Is this a spelling pattern that exists in your native language?

Yes, in Spanish the /ch/ sound is spelled ch.

Are there any similar words in your native language and English with the /ch/ sound?

Yes, chimney *is* chimenea *in Spanish.*

Let's use that key word to help us remember that the /ch/ sound in English is spelled with ch.

Once students learn this connection, they can learn that the /ch/ sound is spelled *tch* in English in a one-syllable word after the short vowel. This is a pattern that does not transfer directly from the native language and English but can be helpful to continue with the routine previously described. ELs will require explicit spelling instruction in order to develop this foundational skill for writing compositions.

Teach About the Irregularities of the English Language

ELs can also benefit from learning the irregularities of the English language. Many words in English do not follow regular sound–symbol correspondences. An example of how to teach irregular words to ELs is described next.

Say the word through.

What sounds did you hear?

The sounds are /throo/.

Watch as I write the word.

What letters follow the sound–symbol correspondence that you understand?

Yes, the letters t-h-r *are regular.*

What letters are not expected and appear to be irregular?

The letters o-u-g-h.

We can mark those in red to help us remember that they do not follow the regular spelling patterns.

The word through *is a preposition. It can be to go between or within.*

A sample sentence is: I went through the tunnel.

Do you have this preposition in your native language?

What is the preposition?

Good job making a connection from your native language and English.

One last time. Say the word through. *Write the word* through *in your spelling notebook and color code the irregular letters in red. Write the meaning and the part of speech and use it in a sentence. Also, write the word that represents this word in your native language.*

You can also draw a picture to help you recall the meaning of the word.

In this example, the EL is provided with the opportunity to explore the sounds of the target word. The student is explicitly taught how the word is spelled and is asked to analyze the regular and irregular letters within the word. The learner is also provided with the opportunity to understand the word's meaning, its grammatical structure, and the use of the word. It is also suggested that the students keep a journal or notebook of irregular words for further reference.

Teaching the regular and irregular spelling of words is necessary for ELs as they develop these foundational skills for writing development. This is helpful because an uncertainty about how to spell a word can interfere with the composing process of writing as well as correct word choice (Graham, Harris, & Hebert, 2011). ELs often use a word in their native language instead of the correct English word or use phrases in place of the word or words and random strings of letters. Graham and Santangelo (2014) found that when 3%–13% of words in a paper are misspelled, scores drop by 0.38 standard deviation compared with a paper with no spelling errors. It is crucial teachers provide explicit and systematic spelling instruction in order to enhance spelling skills, thus enhancing reading proficiency, pronunciation, word meaning, and written language.

CONCLUSION

ELs can benefit from explicit spelling instruction. It is important for instructors to understand typical spelling development as well as the types of overgeneralization patterns that may be experienced by ELs. Using native language letter–sound knowledge as well as cognates and morphemes can enhance ELs' spelling development. ELs will also benefit from learning the irregularities of English. This chapter provided the reader with techniques to incorporate within spelling instruction. Rubrics for analyzing spelling errors can inform instruction and thus provide a metacognitive strategy for spelling development.

STUDY QUESTIONS

1. Describe the stages of spelling development as described by Gentry (1982). How do these differ from the stages described by E. H. Henderson (1981)?

2. What common errors are Spanish-speaking ELs likely to make?

3. What is a pair of minimal sounds? Provide two examples.

4. Use the rubric shared in the example about Mario to describe the following errors:

   Eilien for alien

   Feder for feather

   Rene for rain

   Lest for list

EXTENDED READING AND APPLICATION ACTIVITIES

1. The ELs in your classroom will be reading a passage that includes the irregular word *would*. As the instructor, you will ask them to write a summary and include this irregular word. Therefore, design a lesson that incorporates the irregular word procedure described for ELs in this chapter.

2. Five ELs in your classroom have difficulty spelling words with the /z/ sound spelled with the letter *z*. They substitute the letter *s* for *z*. Describe how you will help this group of ELs using the techniques described in this chapter.

3. Collect writing samples from the ELs in your classroom. Analyze the spelling errors from within the writing samples using the rubric provided in this chapter. Determine the predominant error patterns and design spelling lessons for the students that will address their spelling mistakes.

REFERENCES

Adams, M. (1990). *Beginning to read: Thinking and learning about print*. Champaign: University of Illinois Urbana-Champaign: Center for the Study of Reading.

Arab-Moghaddam, N., & Senechal, M. (2001). Orthographic and phonological processing skills in reading and spelling in Persian–English bilinguals. *International Journal of Behavioral Development, 25*, 140–147.

Calhoon, M. B., Al Otaiba, S., & Greenberg, D. (2010). Spelling knowledge: Implications for instruction and intervention. *Learning Disability Quarterly, 33*, 145–147.

Cárdenas-Hagan, E. (2015). *Esperanza teacher training manual*. Brownsville, TX: Valley Speech Language and Learning Center.

Cárdenas-Hagan, E., (2018). Language and literacy development among English language learners. In J. R. Birsh & S. Carreker (Eds.), *Multisensory teaching of basic language skills* (4th ed., pp. 720–756). Baltimore, MD: Paul H. Brookes Publishing Co.

Cárdenas-Hagan, E., & Carreker, S. (2017). *How written language informs instruction: The why and what-to-do*. Paper presented at IDA 68th Annual Conference, Atlanta, GA.

Carreker, S. (2018). Teaching spelling. In J. R. Birsh & S. Carreker (Eds.), *Multisensory teaching of basic language skills* (4th ed., pp. 389–434). Baltimore, MD: Paul H. Brookes Publishing Co.

Dixon, L. Q., Zhao, J., & Joshi, R. M. (2010). Influence of L1 orthography on spelling English words by bilingual children: A natural experiment comparing syllabic, phonological, and morphosyllabic first languages. *Learning Disability Quarterly, 33*, 211–221.

Ehri, L. (1986). Sources of difficulty in learning to spell and read. In M. L. Wolraich & D. Routh (Eds.), *Advances in developmental and behavioral pediatrics* (pp. 121–195). Greenwich, CT: Jai Publishing.

Ehri, L. C., & Rosenthal, J. (2007). Spellings of words: A neglected facilitator of vocabulary learning. *Journal of Literacy Research, 39*, 389–409.

Figueredo, L. (2006). Using the known to chart the unknown: A review of first-language influence on the development of English-as-a-second-language spelling skills. *Reading and Writing: An Interdisciplinary Journal, 19*, 873–905.

Gentry, J. R. (1982). An analysis of developmental spelling in GNYS AT WRK. *The Reading Teacher, 36*, 192–200.

Graham, S., Harris, K. R., & Hebert, M. (2011). It is more than just the message: Analysis of presentation effects in scoring writing. *Focus on Exceptional Children, 44*(4), 1–12.

Graham, S., & Santangelo, T. (2014). Does spelling instruction make students better spellers, readers, and writers? A meta-analytic review. *Reading and Writing: An Interdisciplinary Journal, 27*, 1703–1743. doi:10.1007/s11145-014-9517-0

Henderson, E. H. (1981). *Learning to read and spell: The child's knowledge of words.* Dekalb, IL: North Illinois Press.

Henry, M. K. (2010). *Unlocking literacy: Effective decoding and spelling instruction* (2nd ed.). Baltimore, MD: Paul H. Brookes Publishing Co.

Myklebust, H. R. (1973). *Development and disorders of written language: Studies of normal and exceptional children* (Vol. 2). New York, NY: Grune and Scratton.

National Center for Education Statistics. (2017). *English language learners in public schools.* Retrieved from https://nces.ed.gov/programs/coe/indicator_cgf.asp

Olson, C. B. & Land, R. (2007). A cognitive strategies approach to reading and writing instruction for English language learners in secondary school. *Research in the Teaching of English, 41,* 269–303.

Templeton, S., & Bear, D. (Eds.). (1992). *Development of orthographic knowledge and the foundations of literacy: A memorial festschrift for Edmund H. Henderson.* Mahwah, NJ: Lawrence Erlbaum Associates.

Templeton, S., & Morris, D. (2000). Theory and research into practice: Questions teachers ask about spelling. *Reading Research Quarterly, 34,* 102–112.

Treiman, R. (1993). *Beginning to spell: A study of first grade children.* New York, NY: Oxford University Press.

Treiman, R., & Cassar, M. (1996). Effects of morphology on children's spelling of final consonant clusters. *Journal of Experimental Child Psychology, 63,* 141–170.

Venezky, R. L. (1970). *The structure of English orthography.* The Hague, Netherlands: Mouton.

Zutell, J., & Allen, V. (1988). The English spelling strategies of Spanish-speaking bilingual children. *TESOL Quarterly, 22*(2), 333–340.

10

Writing Development Among English Learners

Linda O. Cavazos and Elsa Cárdenas-Hagan

By completing this chapter, the reader will

- Learn the developmental progression of written language

- Understand the role of culture and language in learning for English learners (ELs)

- Review second language acquisition and its role in writing development for ELs

- Learn the developmental progression of written language

- Understand the variables associated with writing development among ELs

- Incorporate language strategies for the development of writing

- Identify and use strategies for written language instruction among ELs

Francisco is in the fourth grade and had the opportunity to learn English during the previous school year. His parents have expressed a desire to help Francisco improve his writing in school because his teacher has shared with them that Francisco's written language skills need improvement. Francisco's teacher reports that he exhibits spelling and grammatical errors in print. In addition, his word choice is limited, as he uses few academic words. Francisco's ideas are not fully developed, and they could be elaborated upon with a variety of words. Francisco has agreed to stay after school for tutoring to improve his written language capabilities.

INTRODUCTION

Writing is often described as one of the highest forms of language and takes many years to develop. This is the case for all students, but especially for those students whose native language is not English. This chapter addresses the developmental progression of written language and the special considerations necessary for instruction among English learners (ELs). This is necessary because writing proficiency among a large percentage of students in the United States is below a proficient level. For example, the National Assessment of Educational Progress (NAEP; 2017) reported only 27% of students write proficiently, and Hispanic students score 22 points behind those identified as White students. It is important to note that not all Hispanic students are ELs; therefore, one can conclude that the achievement gap would be greater between White students and ELs. However, this percentage is not reported by NAEP. The writing achievement score gap (avg. 22 points) between Whites and Hispanics has persisted since the inception of NAEP writing in 1998. States recognize the need to improve writing and have incorporated standards to increase writing instruction across all grades. For example, the Common Core State Standards (2010) currently used in 41 states, the District of Columbia, and four U.S. territories recommended writing routinely over extended time frames (time for research, reflection, and revision) and shorter time frames (a single sitting or a day or two) for a range of discipline-specific tasks, purposes, and audiences.

Writing is a process through which people communicate thoughts and ideas. It is a highly complex, cognitive, and self-directed activity driven by the goals writers set for what they want to do and say and the audience(s) for whom they are writing (Graham et al., 2012). To meet these goals, writers must skillfully and flexibly coordinate their writing process from conception to the completion of a text. According to Graham and others (2012), components of the writing process include planning, drafting, sharing, revising, editing, evaluating, and, for some writing pieces, publishing. Subcomponents of writing include knowledge of sentence and paragraph structure. Oral language skills are critical for written language among all students and are especially necessary for those who are learning English as a second language. These students are simultaneously acquiring English and content and must be proficient in listening and speaking to be successful with reading and writing. In order to explore writing skills among ELs, it is important to describe culturally and linguistically responsive instruction in addition to second language acquisition and the typical stages of writing development.

CULTURALLY AND LINGUISTICALLY RESPONSIVE INSTRUCTION

Language and culture shape all learning and play essential roles in human intellectual development (Vygotsky, 1968, 1978). Recognizing the role that language and culture play in student learning and comprehension is essential to provide the necessary academic supports that ELs need. Students' cultural and linguistic resources should be used as the basis for instructional connections to improve student achievement (Gay, 2002; Linan-Thompson, Lara-Martinez, & Cavazos, 2018). For ELs, this means selecting topics familiar to them for writing assignments and discussing associated vocabulary. Teachers can support ELs' linguistic and cultural needs through brainstorming and creating conceptual maps about familiar topics. Background knowledge can be activated and ELs can develop a relational understanding about the topic and its subtopics and the associated vocabulary. It is also important to provide culturally responsive feedback that affirms, clarifies, and improves written work for ELs whose vocabulary and language skills may not be fully developed (Gersten & Geva, 2003). Linan-Thompson and colleagues (2018) suggest that evidence-based practices must be simultaneously combined with culturally and linguistically responsive teaching practices to adequately support ELs' needs.

LANGUAGE DEVELOPMENT

Acquiring a second language follows similar steps as the first language. Students go through five stages of language acquisition: preproduction stage, early production stage, speech emergence, intermediate fluency, and advanced fluency stage. In the intermediate fluency stage, ELs can write more complex sentences with paragraphs, may have fewer grammatical errors, use better verb tenses and conjugations, and have better comprehension. In the advanced fluency stage, ELs generally have mastery of the language with native-like speech (Echevarria & Graves, 2007). Instructors should modify their writing instruction and provide extra scaffolds and linguistic supports to ELs in all of the stages of language acquisition.

English learners are acquiring the second language and learning content at the same time. It is imperative that the instructor know the current levels of language proficiency of each EL to support linguistic needs while teaching writing. ELs' language proficiency levels are measured annually using a state-approved English language proficiency (ELP) assessment.

Most ELP assessments have one to six levels of language proficiency, ranging from basic or entering to advanced high or reaching. Instructors should be providing English language development instruction and differentiated instruction to make language comprehensible (within one level above ELs' current level of understanding). If language is above one level of current understanding, the affective filter will be triggered, and learning will be impacted.

Understanding EL's stages of language acquisition and language proficiency levels can equip instructors with the information needed to improve instruction for ELs and can help them understand why ELs require linguistic scaffolds to achieve native-like levels of writing. Language is the foundation for all learning and essential for writing. The ability to write and the quality of writing is integrally related to language ability.

WRITING DEVELOPMENT

To be able to teach writing effectively, educators must understand the typical progression of writing skills. The stages of writing include precommunicative, semiphonetic, phonetic, transitional, and correct (i.e., conventional) (see Chapter 9; Gentry, 1982).

Spelling is considered one of the foundational skills for writing. Good writers can express their ideas in print and they require good handwriting and good spelling skills. Bloodgood (1999) described the initial stages of writing as preliterate, which include scribbling and drawing. The child can hold a pencil, crayon, or marker and explain orally what the scribbles mean. Next, the child produces letter-like forms and shapes. He or she understands that letter-like shapes or forms can convey meaning. Letter-like forms are in random order; however, when asked, the child will respond orally and describe the printed message. Children distinguish between drawing and writing at approximately 2–3 years of age.

At the next stage, the child is writing letters. Bloodgood (1999) described how children can write their names, and this ability can be correlated with letter production and word recognition. The letters are primarily consonants, and the writing does not have conventional spacing. The letters may represent the first sound of a word; however, they will subsequently represent the specific initial sound of a word. Children recognize that print carries meaning between the ages of 3–4 years. As children grow in their writing abilities, they move into conventional writing and spelling. Conventional writing and spelling occur when the individual is writing words and constructing sentences. Punctuation marks are observed on a more regular basis. The writer can express in print for various reasons with various structures. Handwriting becomes more legible, and few spelling errors are observed.

Throughout the process of writing, it is important to honor the writing efforts of the individual. Educators must find opportunities to expand upon the content of their students' writing while also addressing the structure of sentences and paragraphs. Feedback should be frequent and specific to support improvement and remediate any writing problems. With ELs, it is important to provide specific feedback and offer explicit instructions on how to correct or improve writing. Frequency is important to reduce the cognitive load on ELs. Providing too many corrections at once may activate an EL's affective filter, producing anxiety and low-self-esteem (Krashen, 1981). When this happens, learning is prevented, as the student may shut down.

To develop writing skills, students must have opportunities to write. Children need writing tools such as pencils and pens in order to write. In addition to having the tools and the opportunities, children must also have intact oral language skills. Berninger et al. (2006) described oral language as one of the foundational skills for written language. She described writing as the transcription of one's oral language and discourse.

Graham et al. (2012) noted that the writing process should include time for planning, revising, evaluating, and monitoring with feedback. Graham et al. also described the foundational skills for writing, which include hand-writing, spelling, and keyboarding for drafting compositions. The term *evaluation* revolves around the idea of evaluating the work and continuing to progress monitor until the work is ready for publication. Writers, however, must also know about the various genres for writing. Graham et al. stated that the teacher can help students with the writing process by setting goals. It is also important to create opportunities for students to work collaboratively with others. Students can plan, draft, revise, give and get feedback, and continue the process as needed. Before students can create a written composition, they must understand how to construct a sentence. Sentence structure begins in first grade when teachers work with students to write a complete sentence because most will already have complete thoughts that they express orally. For example, a complete sentence must have a subject and a predicate. Next, students must be able to write a complex sentence that often includes prepositional phrases or a subordinate clause. Once the basic sentence structure is in place, the students must be able to combine sentences. This is a task that many teachers use in their classrooms. Sentence combining will lead to more complex sentences. Good writers must go through the process of brainstorming for an idea, creating a working draft, and revising that draft.

PRINCIPLES FOR TEACHING WRITING SKILLS TO ENGLISH LEARNERS

All students need comprehensive writing instruction to develop the skills for cross-curricular writing for different audiences and purposes. ELs often struggle to become proficient writers because they are simultaneously learning English and academic content while trying to negotiate meaning on culturally and linguistically diverse topics that may be unfamiliar to them. The domains of language include listening, speaking, reading, and writing. Writing is the fourth domain of language acquisition, which presents additional challenges for ELs because of the heavy language demands associated with writing, including cognitive, linguistic, and communicative demands (Graham, MacArthur, & Fitzgerald, 2013). Additional scaffolds should be used to support writing development for ELs. To be successful writers, ELs require a clear understanding of the writing process, ongoing instruction in grammar and developing academic vocabulary (August & Shanahan, 2007), frequent and ongoing monitoring of language, and feedback to reduce the cognitive demand and lower the affective filter (Krashen, 1981).

Strategy instruction and self-regulated strategy development (SRSD) can be used to reduce the cognitive demand of lessons for students (Graham et al., 2013; Harris, Graham, Mason, & Friedlander, 2008). SRSD involves explicitly teaching writing strategies for specific genres with built-in scaffolds and gradual release of responsibility for writing from teacher to student and includes six general stages (Harris et al., 2008):

1. Develop background knowledge

2. Discussion

3. Modeling

4. Memorization

5. Scaffolds

6. Independent writing

These stages can be differentiated or omitted for students who do not need them. See Table 10.1 for strategies to be used at each stage.

Due to the cognitive and language demands of writing, ELs benefit from explicitly taught prewriting strategies using modeling and guided practice and providing ongoing affirming and corrective feedback. These strategies help ELs generate ideas and organize their thinking during the planning and drafting stages of writing. Brainstorming and conceptual mapping are some suggested strategies. Brainstorming is helpful for ELs because related ideas may sometimes seem too similar for students who may not distinguish between similar sounding or meaning words or inflectional use of words. Brainstorming can allow an unrestricted brain dump in which all thoughts are written down and students eliminate information as they review and sort ideas and vocabulary and grammar usage.

Conceptual mapping is a related prewriting strategy that helps ELs group related topics and ideas, identify key vocabulary related to the topic, and begin to develop an advanced organizer for writing. Orthographic awareness is an understanding of writing conventions and can help ELs identify correct and incorrect usage of spelling in writing (Low & Siegel, 2010).

Table 10.1.   SRSD stages: An overview

Develop Background Knowledge

- Read works in the genre being addressed (e.g., stories, persuasive essays) to develop vocabulary ("What is an opinion?"), knowledge ("What are the parts of a persuasive essay?"), concepts ("How does the writer grab the reader's interest?"), and so on that are needed for instruction. Continue development through the next two stages as needed.
- Discuss and explore both the writing and self-regulation strategies to be learned; you may begin development of self-regulation, introducing goal setting and self-monitoring.

Discuss It

- Explore students' current writing and self-regulation abilities.
- Graphing (self-monitoring) may be introduced, using prior compositions; this may assist with goal setting.
- Further discuss strategies to be learned: purpose, benefits, how and when they can be used (begin generalization support).
- Establish students' commitment to learning strategies and acting as a collaborative partner; establish role of student effort.
- May identify and address current negative or ineffective self-talk, attitudes, or beliefs.

Model It

- Use teacher modeling and collaborative modeling of writing and self-regulation strategies, which will result in appropriate model compositions.
- Analyze and discuss strategies and model's performance; make changes as needed.
- Can model self-assessment and self-recording through graphing of model compositions.
- Continue student development of self-regulation strategies across composition and other tasks and situations; discuss use (continue generalization support).

Memorize It

- Though typically begun in earlier stages, require and confirm memorization of strategies, mnemonic(s), and self-instructions as appropriate.
- Continue to confirm and support memorization in the next stage, Support It.

Support It

- Teachers and students use writing and self-regulation strategies collaboratively to achieve success in composing.
- Challenging initial goals established collaboratively; criteria levels increased gradually until final goals are met.
- Prompts, guidance, and collaboration are faded individually until each student can compose successfully alone.
- Self-regulation components not yet introduced may begin.
- Discuss plans for maintenance; continue support of generalization.

Independent Performance

- Students able to use task and self-regulation strategies independently; teachers monitor and support as necessary.
- Fading of overt self-regulation may begin.
- Plans for maintenance and generalization continue to be discussed and implemented.

From Harris, K. R., Graham, S., Mason, L. H., & Friedlander, B. (2008). *Powerful writing strategies for all students* (p. 13). Baltimore, MD: Paul H. Brookes Publishing Co.

STRATEGIES FOR TEACHING WRITING SKILLS TO ENGLISH LEARNERS

ELs will require considerations for their second language capabilities during writing instruction. Troia (2010) described effective writing instruction as that which attends to the multiple levels of language knowledge—word, sentence, and discourse—for all writers, including ELs and those who struggle with writing.

Foster Vocabulary Skills

Instructors must ensure that the writing task is commensurate with students' oral language proficiency level in the second language. Scaffolds such as providing word banks can be beneficial to ELs because they often do not have the academic vocabulary necessary for a written composition (Zwiers, 2008). Essential vocabulary with student-friendly definitions can be introduced with opportunities to understand the words by using several examples and nonexamples. Language components by Bloom and Lahey (1978) can facilitate vocabulary instruction, including reviewing the sounds of vocabulary words, the meaning and word parts within words, the spelling of the word, and the grammatical function and various uses of the word. By following this procedure, instructors will have incorporated phonology, semantics, morphology, syntax, and pragmatics in addition to the written form, which includes spelling. This in-depth review of vocabulary will enhance students' writing (Nelson, Bahr, & Van Meter, 2004). It is also important for educators to understand that not all native languages are represented in print. Some languages exist only in an oral form, which will make writing quite challenging for some ELs, who may benefit from extra and more intensive instruction in handwriting, spelling, and grammar instruction as foundational skills for writing.

Box 10.1 offers an example of individual vocabulary instruction that addresses each of the components of language described by Bloom and Lahey (1978) and incorporates native language word knowledge to make a connection between the native language and English. Making connections between languages and cross-linguistic transfer of language can enhance the understanding of the word and assist with incorporating the word into students' writing.

Address the Foundational Skills of Writing

Writing instruction must address the foundational skills of writing. For example, spelling is a foundational skill for writing, and better spellers tend to be more proficient at writing. (See Chapter 9 for spelling instruction among ELs.)

Fluid handwriting or keyboarding is also a foundational skill for writing and one that must be intact for the students to effectively communicate. Students who lack legible and fluid handwriting skills will need further instruction in this area. In addition, students in upper elementary and middle school should have many opportunities for increasing keyboarding skills.

BOX 10.1.   Teacher Script Template for Individual Vocabulary Instruction

To teach the first word from a particular vocabulary lesson, apply the following script.

We have had several discussions related to the topic of ____.

Today we will explore words related to the topic of _____.

This will help you understand and use these words when you speak and when you write.

The word is _____. It means _____.

In your native language, the word is _____.

Say the word in your native language.

Say the word in English.

How many sounds do you hear in this English word?

How many sounds do you hear in this word from your native language?

Do the words have the same number of syllables?

How many letters are used in English for this word?

How many letters are used in Spanish for this word?

What is the same? What is different between these words?

The part of speech is a _____ for this word.

Let's look at the visual picture that represents this word and discuss any other meanings.

Can we act out the word?

Let's use the word in a sentence in English.

Let's use the word in a sentence in your native language.

Good job. Now we will add this word to our word bank or word wall for use in the future.

We will have many opportunities to practice using our new vocabulary word.

Repeat procedure for remaining words.

From Cárdenas-Hagan, E. (2017). *Working with English learners: Teacher manual* (2nd ed.). Brownsville, TX: Valley Speech Language and Learning Center; adapted by permission.

Provide Instruction on Grammar and Sentence Structure

Another foundational skill for writing includes understanding the parts of speech and how words function within sentences. If an EL understands grammar in his or her native language, then it may be helpful to use cross-linguistic transfer strategies to address the similarities and differences between grammar, capitalization, and punctuation in the two languages. Table 10.2 addresses some of the similarities and differences between English and Spanish. ELs can benefit from understanding the grammatical structures of English and how they may be similar to their native language grammatical structures. Leveraging the first language to support English development through cross-linguistic transfer is an effective strategy that has bidirectional effects on both languages (Linan-Thompson, Vaughn, Prater, & Cirino, 2006).

ELs can also benefit from writing sentences and sentence expansion opportunities. Table 10.3 offers an example activity for this kind of instruction; the teacher prompts the student to repeatedly expand his or her sentence.

Teach About Topic Sentences and Paragraph Structure

Writers need to find the precise words to create a sentence that can express the main idea or serve as a topic sentence. To foster this skill, ELs should

Table 10.2. Similarities and differences between the English and Spanish language capitalization, punctuation, and grammatical rules

English	Spanish
Nouns name a person, place, or thing.	Nouns name a person, place, or thing.
Nouns have gender when something is male or female (*woman/man; tiger/tigress*).	Nouns are masculine or feminine (*perro/perra; gat/gata*).
Subject dropping is not allowed.	Subject dropping is allowed.
Verbs are in present and past tense.	Verbs are in present tense, but past tense has six forms.
Add *-es* when a word ends in *s, sh, ch, v, x,* or *z*.	Add *-s* when a word ends in a vowel.
	Add *-es* when a word ends in a consonant.
Proper nouns are capitalized.	Proper nouns are capitalized except common nouns such as days of the week and months of year.
Verbs are words used to describe action.	Verbs are words used to describe action.
Verbs have tenses such as present and past.	Verbs have tenses such as present and past.
Adverbs are words that modify verbs.	Adverbs are words that modify verbs.
Adverbs are comparative superlative.	Adverbs are comparative superlative.
Adjectives are words that modify a noun.	Adjectives are words that modify a noun.
Adjectives appear before the noun.	Adjectives appear after the noun.
Exclamation point is used at the end of a sentence to alert the reader that something exciting has been stated.	Exclamation point is used at the beginning and the end of a sentence to alert the reader that something exciting has been stated.
Question mark is used at the end of questions.	Question mark is used at the beginning and at the end of questions.

From Cárdenas-Hagan, E. (2018). Language and literacy development among English language learners. In J. R. Birsh & S. Carreker (Eds.), *Multisensory teaching of basic language skills* (4th ed., p. 747). Baltimore, MD: Paul H. Brookes Publishing Co.

Table 10.3. Sentence expansion activity

The student writes . . .	The teacher prompts . . .
I see a man walking.	Good, you have written a complete sentence. Can you tell me something about the man? Is he tall? What are some of his features?
I see a tall, slender man walking.	Good, I have a better visual picture of the man. Where is the man walking?
I see a tall, slender man walking in the park.	Very nice; now I know where he is. Why is he in the park?
I see a tall, slender man walking his dog in the park.	Excellent job. Now I see the man and his dog walking his dog in the park. Why is he walking his dog?
I see a tall, slender man walking his dog in the park for exercise.	Oh, I get it. The dog needs exercise, so the owner who is tall and slender walks his dog in the park. Very good sentence.

have many occasions to practice writing topic sentences. One activity might include providing the details of a paragraph and then asking the student to write the topic sentence. For example, the activity sheet could state

Topic sentence: _____

She helps me with my homework.

She makes delicious home-cooked meals.

Never once have I heard her complain that she is too tired to help me.

Now you may understand why she is so special to me.

Teachers should provide commentary and feedback on the precision of the topic sentence. Feedback can include whether the sentence is grammatically correct and explicitly describes the content of the paragraph and whether the sentence contains correct word choice.

In addition to writing topic sentences, ELs will need to understand some of the more common paragraph structures, including a narrative, which tells a story. The simplest form of a narrative can use the following approach:

State what happened first.

Describe what happened next.

Continue with what happened then.

Close paragraph with what happened finally or in the end.

Use Graphic Organizers to Teach About the Different Types of Paragraphs and Texts

ELs benefit from graphic organizers and other visual tools that help them organize their responses in a systematic and structured way. The kind of graphic organizer or prompt used should be varied based on the kind of paragraph structure or text that is being written.

For instance, writers will need to know how to create a descriptive paragraph. It will be helpful for ELs to have a visual picture and a graphic organizer with sentence stems to facilitate writing a descriptive paragraph. It is extremely helpful for ELs to have the opportunity to orally express and practice describing objects or pictures of places or events. A simple form for a descriptive paragraph is

This is a _____ (object or picture).

It is used for _____.

It is the size of _____.

Its colors are _____ and _____.

It is similar to _____ or _____.

We can compare it with a _____ or _____.

In closing, I find that _____ (object/picture) is _____ (adjective).

For older ELs, a descriptive paragraph is

This can best be described as_____ because of _____.

It is commonly used for _____ and _____, but could also be used for _____.

One way that I can envision using it is _____.

You would likely encounter this through _____ or _____.

It reminds me of _____ in that _____ and _____.

A connection I can make with _____ is _____.

In closing (or in summary), I find that _____ (object/picture) is _____ (descriptive phrase).

ELs will also need instruction for writing expository or informational text. Educators should foster meaningful and structured conversations around the topic to provide the learner with oral language opportunities that can be connected to writing. One strategy is to provide ELs with a simple organizer for creating a draft of an expository text with sentence stems, such as

The topic is _____.

The main idea is _____.

The first detail is _____.

A supporting detail is _____.

The next detail is _____.

A supporting detail is _____.

Another detail is _____.

In closing, _____.

As students progress, sentence stems can be omitted, and students can generate writing with the use of a graphic organizer. The instructor can withhold the use of the graphic organizer once the student can produce many examples of expository text or can allow students choice in using the graphic organizer as an advance organizer for their writing. Advance organizers are often used by good writers for consistent and coherent writing. These are especially useful for ELs, as they develop writing skills and develop deeper understanding of writing structures and craft.

The persuasive paragraph is another common structure for writing. ELs will require a deep understanding of the topics and will need to generate a list of reasons to support a subject. It is important for the instructor to ascertain if ELs have sufficient background knowledge about the topic to write about it (Chang et al., 2017). A quick discussion with visuals or a brief anchor video on the topic can make the language comprehensible (Krashen, 1981) and the topic meaningful for ELs, thus supporting their ability to write about the topic. Figure 10.1 can be integrated to facilitate this kind of writing. See Box 10.2 for additional recommendations for providing effective, explicit writing instruction to ELs.

CONCLUSION

This chapter described the developmental progression of typical writing and explored the principles for effective writing development. In addition, strategies for developing ELs' understanding of sentence and paragraph structures were provided. The goal is to incorporate language instruction with literacy instruction, which includes writing. Graphic organizers were provided for some of the more prevalent paragraph structures with sentence stems to assist ELs. Educators should integrate these techniques during instruction and will be able to reflect on the language and writing skills for each student, especially ELs.

STUDY QUESTIONS

1. What are the foundational skills necessary for good writing abilities?

2. What challenges may ELs experience when learning to write in a second language?

3. How can educators enhance ELs' writing skills?

4. Describe the grammatical concepts that may transfer from a native language to a second language.

Introduction	

Reason 1	Details

Reason 2	Details

Reason 3	Details

Conclusion	

Figure 10.1. Graphic organizer to use for persuasive writing.

From Cárdenas-Hagan, E. (2016). *Practica de escritura-esperanza.* Brownsville, TX:
Valley Speech Language and Learning Center; adapted by permission.
In *Literacy Foundations for English Learners: A Comprehensive Guide to Evidence-Based Instruction,*
edited by Elsa Cárdenas-Hagan. (2020, Paul H. Brookes Publishing Co., Inc.)

BOX 10.2. Writing Instruction Recommendations

1. Provide opportunities for ELs to write each instructional day for a variety of purposes in cross-curricular settings and topics.

2. Support ELs' writing as it relates to a specific topic and expand their background knowledge as necessary.

3. Ensure ELs have the language skills required for the writing task. Use charts with helpful vocabulary terms, use visuals and videos, and provide simplified language when necessary. The goal is to expand language and activate or build current knowledge.

4. ELs will also benefit from instruction related to sentence and paragraph structures. Practicing with sentence expansion and paragraph cohesion will be helpful to ELs. Provide foundational skills of grammatical structures that are not mastered and review those that are.

5. Ensure that ELs have the foundational skills of handwriting and spelling. Provide explicit instruction for these skills. For older students, the use of keyboarding can also be helpful.

6. ELs benefit from routines, and the writing process should include opportunities to plan, draft, revise, edit, and share with others. Provide ample and frequent feedback throughout the process as necessary.

7. As students explore a topic, read model writings of the subject and edit for spelling or grammar; the use of technology can be helpful.

8. Provide a positive and supportive classroom environment for ELs so that they are motivated to write and share their writing with others.

From Cárdenas-Hagan, E. (2017). *Working with English learners: Teacher manual* (2nd ed.). Brownsville, TX: Valley Speech Language and Learning Center; adapted by permission.

EXTENDED READING AND APPLICATION ACTIVITIES

1. Read the Institute for Education Sciences Practice Guide on writing instruction (Graham et al., 2012) and determine the recommendations with significant evidence. Decide which ones can be adapted to meet the needs of ELs.

2. Following is an example of an EL describing a picture. From the information provided in this chapter, determine the foundational skills that are necessary for this learner.

I see a dog runing away of hes honor (hogar/house) um hes haus there is children uriwer and a three is with fire and a fader and the family is callng the firefires cuz their scered and a car is stuck with lives and ranches and is rainy outsind and a pirsons with a rope of water for take of the fire of the three and urithing is wet and is a making a mess in the city. (Cárdenas-Hagan, 2017, p. 77)

REFERENCES

August, D., & Shanahan, T. (Eds.). (2007). *Developing reading and writing in second-language learners: Lessons from the report of the National Literacy Panel on Language-Minority Children and Youth*. Abingdon, United Kingdom: Routledge.

Berninger, V. W., Abbot, R. B., Jones, J., Wolf, B. J., Gould, L., Anderson-Youngstrom, M., . . . Apel, K. (2006). Early development of language by hand: Composing reading, listening, and speaking connections; writing modes; and fast mapping in spelling. *Developmental Psychology, 29*(1), 61–92.

Bloodgood, J. W. (1999). What's in a name? Children's name writing and literacy acquisition. *Reading Research Quarterly, 34,* 342–367.

Bloom, L., & Lahey, M. (1978). *Language development and language disorders*. New York, NY: Wiley.

Cárdenas-Hagan, E. (2016). *Practica de escritura-esperanza*. Brownsville, TX: Valley Speech Language and Learning Center.

Cárdenas-Hagan, E. (2017). *Working with English learners: Teacher manual* (2nd ed.). Brownsville, TX: Valley Speech Language and Learning Center.

Cárdenas-Hagan, E. (2018). Language and literacy development among English language learners. In J. R. Birsh & S. Carreker (Eds.), *Multisensory teaching of basic language skills* (4th ed., pp. 720–756). Baltimore, MD: Paul H. Brookes Publishing Co.

Cárdenas-Hagan, E., Carreker, S., & Tiridas, E. (2017, November). *Errors inform instruction*. Paper presented at the International Dyslexia Association Conference, Atlanta, GA.

Catts, H., Adlof, S., Hogan, T., & Ellis Weismer, S. (2005). Are specific language impairment and dyslexia distinct disorders? *Journal of Speech-Language-Hearing Research, 48,* 378–396.

Chang, S., Lozano, M., Neri, R., & Herman, J. (2017). *High-leverage principles of effective instruction for English learners*. Los Angeles, CA: Center on Standards and Assessments Implementation.

Common Core State Standards Initiative. (2010). *Common Core State Standards for English language arts and literacy in history/social studies science and technical subjects*. Washington, DC: Council of Chief State School Officers and National Governors Association.

Echevarria, J., & Graves, A. W. (2007). *Sheltered content instruction: Teaching English language learners with diverse abilities*. Los Angeles, CA: Pearson/Allyn and Bacon.

Gay, G. (2002). Preparing for culturally responsive teaching. *Journal of Teacher Education, 53,* 106–116.

Gentry, J. R. (1982). An analysis of developmental spelling in GNYS AT WRK. *The Reading Teacher, 36,* 192–200.

Gersten, R., & Geva, E. (2003). Teaching reading to early language learners. *Educational Leadership, 60,* 44–49.

Graham, S., Bollinger, A., Booth Olson, C., D'Aoust, C., MacArthur, C., McCutchen, D., & Olinghouse, N. (2012). *Teaching elementary school students to be effective writers: A practice guide*. Washington, DC: National Center for Education Evaluation and Regional Assistance, Institute of Education Sciences, U.S. Department of Education.

Graham, S., MacArthur, C. A., & Fitzgerald, J. (Eds.). (2013). *Best practices in writing instruction*. New York, NY: Guilford Press.

Harris, K. R., Graham, S., Mason, L. H., & Friedlander, B. (2008). *Powerful writing strategies for all students*. Baltimore, MD: Paul H. Brookes Publishing Co.

Krashen, S. D. (1981). *Second language acquisition and second language learning*. Oxford, United Kingdom: Pergamon.

Linan-Thompson, S., Lara-Martinez, J. A., & Cavazos, L. O. (2018). Exploring the intersection of evidence-based practices and culturally and linguistically responsive practices. *Intervention in School and Clinic, 54*(1), 6–13.

Linan-Thompson, S., Vaughn, S., Prater, K., & Cirino, P. T. (2006). The response to intervention of English language learners at risk for reading problems. *Journal of Learning Disabilities, 39*(5), 390–398.

Low, P. B., & Siegel, L. S. (2010). Spelling and English language learning. In G. A. Troia (Ed.), *Instruction and assessment for struggling writers: Evidence-based practices* (pp. 290–307). New York, NY: Guilford Press.

National Assessment of Educational Progress. (2017). *NAEP reading report card.* Retrieved from https://www.nationsreportcard.gov/reading_2017?grade=4

Nelson, N. W., Bahr, C. M., & Van Meter, A. M. (2004). *The writing lab approach to language instruction and intervention.* Baltimore, MD: Paul H. Brookes Publishing Co.

Troia, G. A. (Ed.). (2010). *Instruction and assessment for struggling writers: Evidence-based practices.* New York, NY: Guilford Press.

Troia, G. (2014). *Evidence-based practices for writing instruction.* Retrieved from http://ceedar.education.ufl.edu/tools/innovation-configuration

Vygotsky, L. S. (1968). *Thought and language* (newly revised, translated, and edited by A. Kozulin). Cambridge, MA: MIT Press.

Vygotsky, L. (1978). Interaction between learning and development. *Readings on the Development of Children, 23*(3), 34–41.

Zwiers, J. (2008). *Building academic language: Essential practices for content classrooms.* San Francisco, CA: Jossey-Bass.

◇◇◇

Using Technology to Adapt and Enhance Instruction for English Learners

Elaine Cheesman

This appendix provides complementary technology resources for the essential literacy skills outlined in the other chapters of this text. Readers will understand technology recommendations for English Learners (ELs) and teachers of English as a second language, also called *English as a foreign language*. Because most computer software, web-based programs, and mobile applications often overlap and are accessible through Apple, Android, and Windows products, these platforms are not specified; the term *apps* is used as an umbrella term for all software, web-based programs, and mobile applications.

INSTRUCTIONAL AND ASSISTIVE TECHNOLOGY

This appendix offers advice on selecting appropriate apps to help a person learn or practice skills, called *instructional technology*, or allow a person to perform a function independently with which he or she would normally have difficulty, called *assistive technology* (AT) (Winters & Cheesman, 2013). Electronic translators or dictionary apps are examples of AT because they enable people to independently gain access to a word's pronunciation or meaning. Using an app or device to broaden academic vocabulary knowledge falls into the category of instructional technology because the technology is helping the user learn new information or practice a previously taught skill. The key for successful educators is to understand student needs and align technology accordingly.

Instructional technology, also called *computer-assisted instruction,* can assist teacher-led instruction or independent student practice for concepts previously introduced by the teacher. Well-designed apps allow students to work at their own pace with interactive, structured, and systematic practice. Programs with immediate corrective feedback increase student engagement and improve academic outcomes (O'Mailey et al., 2013). Some programs also track individual student progress. Effective apps feature activities with a clear focus, are aligned with student needs, and emphasize one or more of the areas identified by science as essential for proficient speaking, reading, spelling, and/or writing.

The key to instruction for the person with reading, spelling, and/or writing difficulties from fourth grade on is to combine instructional technology with assistive technology. In other words, continue to work on building fluent, automatic skills through direct instruction while also providing alternative access to text. When struggling readers and writers reach fourth grade, educators frequently favor accommodations using AT over efforts to build accuracy and automaticity in foundational skills. However, for English learners to become independently literate, it is vital to continue working on fluent, automatic decoding, spelling, and writing skills. AT supports can be used to help students keep up with peers in the increased information demands of the rest of the students' schooling and career (Winters, 2015).

CONVERSATIONAL AND WRITTEN ACADEMIC ENGLISH

Learning English as a foreign language requires the learner to become bilingual—that is, able to engage in conversational listening and speaking) and biliterate, which requires mastery of reading and writing academic text. Oral and written language skills naturally overlap; however, written language instruction includes important differences that should not be overlooked by the educator. To engage in oral conversations, one must understand and use vocabulary to navigate everyday life, but skilled reading and writing involve a deeper understanding of word reading skills and written language structures as outlined in other chapters of this text

The technology discussed in this appendix will align with the needs of conversational English and written academic text, including advanced English orthography (spelling and writing systems) and academic language, which is essential for learning new knowledge and skills (International Dyslexia Association, 2010). To guide educators toward age- and ability-appropriate apps, the app descriptions that follow suggest appropriate level(s) of English language proficiency (ELP) as described by Teachers of English to Speakers of Other Languages (http://www.tesol.org).

- *Level 1:* ELs have limited or no understanding of English and rarely speak or engage in conversations except for a few simple words.

- *Level 2:* ELs can use and understand phrases and simple sentences dealing with everyday life but still make substantial errors in written language.

- *Level 3:* ELs can understand more complex language structures, yet they continue to struggle with English grammar and academic vocabulary. Written language skills vary widely at this level. ELs can comprehend simple texts if they have sufficient vocabulary and background knowledge.

- *Level 4:* ELs' conversational skills are adequate for most situations. In written language, academic vocabulary and complex sentence structures are challenging.

- *Level 5:* ELs have well-developed conversational skills in a variety of situations. They have a good understanding of figurative language (e.g., idioms, metaphors, colloquialisms) and academic language. They are able to read and write academic texts with few errors.

ELs who also have signs of specific learning disabilities in reading and writing, including dyslexia, require more explicit instruction provided in smaller steps and coupled with extensive opportunities to frequently practice skills. Instruction in conversational language and reading and writing for students at risk for reading failure can be effective when delivered by an expert teacher in small-group or individual tutoring sessions. High-quality instructional technology can provide consistent, research-based repetition with immediate, corrective feedback on concepts previously taught by a teacher. It is important to emphasize that knowledgeable teachers, not technology, are the keys to success for students with learning disabilities. Technology provides extra opportunities for individual practice; however, it is not a substitute for good teaching.

SELECTING EFFECTIVE APPS AND DEVICES

The abundance of new apps and devices on the market can be confusing and overwhelming to the busy educator. The following recommendations will help increase the likelihood of successful implementation:

- Whenever possible, take advantage of a trial offer or lite version of a device or app (Winters, 2015).

- After getting a new device or app, be sure to fully explore it and get plenty of practice with it before using it in a real-life or important situation (Winters, 2015).

- Make sure the app has an intuitive and user-friendly interface along with clear written or oral instructions that are appropriate for the intended user (Ishizuka, 2011).

- Ensure instructional apps provide timely corrective feedback.

- Select apps with few unnecessary or distracting images or sounds. This is particularly important for people with attentional difficulties (Winters & Cheesman, 2013).

TECHNOLOGY DEVICES FOR THE CLASSROOM

Technology fits well with the principles of universal design for learning (McLeskey & Waldron, 2007). Several types of devices are useful in any classroom. These include interactive white boards, student responses systems (also known as *clickers*), and mobile devices connected to an overhead projector. Lopez (2010) investigated the use of interactive white boards as a tool to raise ELs' achievement in third- and fifth-grade reading and mathematics. A second aim of the study was to determine if this technology could close the achievement gap between ELs and native English speakers. Results suggested that this technology improved ELs' achievement and narrowed the achievement gap.

Student response systems, or clickers, are interactive technology that allows the teacher to pose a question and immediately collect and view summaries of student responses. The teacher presents multiple choice, true/false, or Likert scale questions with numbers representing particular responses. The students first discuss the problem among themselves and then answer the question using remote transmitters (clickers) or mobile phones using a response app. A histogram shows a summary of the anonymous responses, which can be projected for the class to see and discuss. Individual responses can be downloaded onto a spreadsheet for later analysis. In the English as a second language classroom, clicker technology can be used for many purposes, including—but not limited to—gauging understanding of vocabulary, idioms, and other figurative language; text comprehension; awareness of phonemes; and spelling knowledge.

Computers and mobile devices (i.e., Android, Windows, Apple products) can be linked to a document camera or overhead projector for whole-class instruction. Many brand-name projectors have apps that allow a person to connect via Bluetooth or a wireless network. If wireless is not an option, then an individual can connect via a hard-wired connection using high definition multimedia interface (HDMI) or video graphics array (VGA) cables appropriate for the projector and mobile device. Mobile devices can project photos, movies, music clips, and other web-based content through a wireless network.

Apps for Educators

In this section and the others that follow, each app description includes these details:

- Name of the app
- URL for the app and/or its developer
- Suggested ELP levels
- Reading skills required in one's native language or English

YouTube Educational Videos
URL: http://www.youtube.com/edu
ELP level: 3–5
About: Teachers and parents can search "English language learners" for a variety of videos for English as a second language teachers and ELs.

Colorín Colorado
URL: http://www.colorincolorado.org
About: This an extensive collection of research-based suggestions for teaching vocabulary from pre-K to adult. The phonological awareness activities are limited to rhyme and initial sounds.

English Grammar
URL: http://www.englishgrammar.org
ELP level: 4–5
About: This web site contains extensive lists of downloadable lessons, grammar rules in alphabetical order, online exercises and tools, videos, and writing guides.

ESL Partyland
URL: http://eslpartytown.com/
ELP level: 4–5
About: This web site contains exercises for pronunciation, conversational skills, grammar, and vocabulary. Lesson ideas include video, music, and Internet resources. The companion student site has instructions written in English.

Internet TESL Journal for Teachers of English as a Second Language
URL: http://iteslj.org/
About: This web site contains articles, research papers, lessons plans, questions, games, jokes, classroom handouts, teaching ideas, and links for all levels of ELs.

ESL Videos
URL: http://www.eslvideo.com
ELP level: 4–5
About: This web site provides educational resources for ELs of all levels to improve their listening, speaking, grammar, and vocabulary skills. It includes free quiz activities for use in the classroom or at home. Teachers can build a library of favorites, assign quizzes, view student scores, create new quizzes, and convert the pages to text so that they can customize the lessons to match their locality.

Using English
URL: http://www.usingenglish.com
ELP level: 4–5
About: This is an extensive, searchable interactive resource for lesson plans, idioms, phrasal verbs, irregular verbs, and grammar. It includes many free downloadable resources.

Florida Center for Reading Research
URL: http://www.fcrr.org
About: Although this web site is not specifically for ELs, it has thousands of downloadable center activities in all five components of reading—phonemic awareness, phonics, fluency, vocabulary and comprehension—for kindergarten through sixth grade. It also has research and resources for teachers.

Sound Literacy
URL: https://apps.apple.com/us/app/sound-literacy/id409347075
About: This is a comprehensive collection of electronic tiles for letters, graphemes (e.g., *sh, ay*), and morphemes (prefixes, roots, suffixes) that explicitly show the building blocks of the English writing system. The accompanying web site has instructional videos for educators.

Hemingway App
URL: http://www.hemingwayapp.com
About: This text editing app helps teachers simplify written language when composing for ELs or their parents and caregivers. The user enters text online. Color-coded highlighting identifies sentences that are difficult to read, too long, or in passive voice.

INSTRUCTIONAL TECHNOLOGY

This section describes apps that provide ELs the means to practice skills independently.

Oral Language and Phonological Awareness Skills

Partners in Rhyme
URL: http://www.preschoolu.com
ELP level: 1–2
About: This program is for ELs who need practice in recognizing rhyme in spoken words. It features four intuitive and interactive games with clear enunciation using an adult voice.

Comparative Adjectives
URL: http://www.alligatorapps.com
ELP level: 2–3
About: ELs practice comparative adjectives by tapping the picture that matches the oral word (e.g., bigger truck; tallest man).

Mango Languages
URL: http://www.mangolanguages.com
ELP level: 1–2; requires reading skills in native language and English
About: The mobile app complements the web-based program to provide English instruction in 17 different native languages. Phrases are color coded in English and native languages. It has a built-in voice comparison tool to perfect pronunciation. Variable pronunciation speeds help build awareness of English speech sounds, or phonemes.

Learn English Free
URL: https:/bravolol.com
ELP level: 1–2; requires reading skills in native language and English
About: The mobile app presents words individually and within conversational phrases with matching pictures. It requires some word reading skills, and the user can access phrases offline.

Learn and Speak American English
URL: http://www.mondlylanguages.com
ELP level: 1–2; requires reading skills in native language and English
About: This is a complementary web site and mobile app with a choice of several native languages. The user matches words and phrases with matching pictures in the native language and English. It provides spoken and written verb conjugations within phrases.

Learn English With Lingo Arcade
URL: http://www.alligatorapps.com
ELP level: 1–2; requires reading skills in native language and English
About: The student matches spoken words and sentences with pictures and/or written words in sequential and cumulative instruction. The app tracks progress and automatically branches in response to errors. It is easy to self-select either a review or more advanced level with a variety of games.

Many Things
URL: http://www.manythings.org
ELP level: 2–5
About: This web site provides pronunciation practice with quizzes geared toward precise pronunciation. For example, it contrasts the words *thirteen* and *thirty*. It also includes narrated stories in English with highlighted text.

Word to Word Association, Word to Word Seasons, Word to Word Themes
URL: http://www.mochibits.com
ELP level: 3–5
About: These engaging word association games help users learn synonyms, antonyms, compounds, or words related in subject.

Letter Identification and Handwriting

Live Insights Handwriting Without Tears
URL: http://www.wetdrytry.com
ELP level: 1
About: ELs can practice naming and forming upper- and lowercase letters and numerals; the app records progress and errors.

Writing Wizard/Cursive Writing Wizard
URL: http://www.lescapadou.com
ELP level: 1
About: ELs can practice naming and forming upper- and lowercase letters. Teachers can add words with pronunciation.

iTrace Handwriting for Kids
URL: http://www.itraceapp.com
ELP level: 1
About: ELs can practice naming and forming upper- and lowercase letters with three increasingly difficult tasks. It features manuscript letters, words, and numbers; supports multiple users; and monitors progress. Teachers can add customized words with options that include left-handed and different instructional styles.

Letter Quiz

URL: http://www.tantrumapps.com

ELP level: 1

About: ELs can practice naming and forming upper- and lowercase letters. Four learning games are available to identify and write the letters of the alphabet, match upper- and lowercase letters, and learn the associated sound (not all are the most common sound, though).

Alphabet Dots Game—Build Letter Confidence

URL: http://www.elliesgames.com

ELP level: 1

About: This game provides opportunities for ELs to practice alphabet sequence using lowercase letters.

Letter Case

URL: http://www.elliesgames.com

ELP level: 1

About: This game provides practice in matching upper- and lowercase letters in various fonts.

Dot to Dot

URL: http://www.appsinmypocket.com

ELP level: 1–2

About: This app orally pronounces names of letters and numbers in alphabetical and numerical order. The teacher can adjust settings for older students.

Letter School

URL: http://www.letterschool.com

ELP level: 1–2

About: This site provides three modes of engaging and progressively more difficult letter-forming practice, with mostly correct associated sounds and key words. (*Note:* The *x* keyword and sound is "xylophone" /z/, rather than the most common sound /k-s/ as in "box.")

Conquering Cursive; Powerful Printing

URL: https://writeonhandwriting.wordpress.com/

ELP level: 1–2

About: This site uses simple letter formations and easy-to-understand terminology to explain the letter shapes.

Teachnology
URL: http://www.teach-nology.com/worksheets/language_arts/handwriting
ELP level: 1–2
About: This site provides free, downloadable PDFs of letter formation practice sheets featuring single letters on one sheet with guiding arrows and lined practice area. Worksheets are available in different styles of manuscript and cursive.

KidzType
URL: http://www.kidztype.com
About: This free web site teaches and reviews keyboarding skills in a series of brief, systematic, and cumulative lessons. The intuitive lessons require no reading skills. Color coding links text, keyboard letters, and fingers. Lessons include numbers, symbols, and shift keys. Error feedback is auditory and visual. The lessons progress from isolated letters to real words, nonwords, and phrases. Besides lessons, the site provides games, exercises, and practices. This site is also appropriate for teens and adults.

Linking Letters to Speech Sounds

OG Card Deck
URL: https://apps.apple.com/us/app/og-card-deck/id709418432 (also available on Google Play store)
ELP level: 1–2
About: This app presents written graphemes, associated sounds, key words, and articulation video clips. A spelling drill provides sounds for users to spell and includes multiple spellings for single sounds (e.g., /k/ = k, c, ck, que). It is useful for direct instruction by a teacher or an independent student review.

Alpha-read
URL: http://www.alpha-read.com
ELP level: 1–2
About: This app links letters, key word pictures, and the most common sound. Spelling–sound correspondences are not sequenced in alphabetical order but according to their utility for spelling words (e.g., a, t, m, s). The review mode allows the teacher or EL to select letters to review.

ABC Magic Series
URL: http://www.preschoolu.com
ELP level: 1–2
About: This series of apps matches picture prompts to initial sounds and letters.

Beginning Reading and Spelling

ABC Reading Magic Series
URL: http://www.preschoolu.com
ELP level: 1–2
About: This series of apps includes phonemic awareness activities (blends oral words presented as photographs) and decoding (decoding letters to form words shown as photographs). The mature narration and photographs makes this app suitable for all ages. In a few two-syllable words, vowels in open syllables are pronounced with the short, not long, sound. (*Note*: *c* stands for consonant, *v* for vowel)

- *Reading 1:* CVC words

- *Reading 2:* CCVC, CCCVC, CVCC, CVCCC words

- *Reading 3:* Two-syllable words

- *Reading 4:* Phonograms, digraphs, vowel-*r* and vowel team syllables, and two-syllable words

ABC Spelling Magic Series
URL: http://www.preschoolu.com
ELP level: 1–2
About: This program provides practice segmenting oral words presented as photographs. It has four levels:

- *Spelling 1:* CVC words

- *Spelling 2:* CCVC and CVCC

- *Spelling 3:* Two-syllable words

- *Spelling 4:* Vowel-consonant-silent-*e* words

CVC Words
URL: http://www.alligatorapps.com
ELP level: 1–3
About: This app allows the child to practice reading and phonetically spelling regular words. It is organized by word family, or rime (*hop, pop, mop*). Children can practice reading and spelling words using 14 engaging games. The optional text-to-speech feature reads sentences.

Starfall ABCs/Starfall Learn to Read
URL: http://www.starfall.com
ELP level: 1–3
About: Starfall can be accessed through an identical free (and ad-free) web site and mobile app. It has engaging animations and games for learning letter–sound correspondences. It provides the letter name, not its sound, in the key word for *x* (*x-ray*). A better key word is *box* for /k-s/.

Reading Ninja

URL: http://www.alligatorapps.com

ELP level: 1–3

About: This app promotes overlearning of CVC words. The words fly up from the bottom of the screen. The user taps the word that matches the spoken word among other choices. The narration is a mature voice that is appropriate for all ages.

ABC PocketPhonics

URL: http://www.appsinmypocket.com;
      http:///www.appsinmypocket.com/school

ELP level: 1–3

About: This app combines handwriting practice and spelling graphemes (letters and letter clusters that represent one sound). It presents the alphabetic principle in a logically ordered sequence. After the graphemes are introduced, the app guides the user to apply the target spelling–sound correspondences to spell spoken words. It supports multiple users; school versions are available to enable students to work on different devices. Progress reports are available online or via a weekly e-mail. It is appropriate for learners ages 4 and older.

PocketPhonics Stories

URL: http://www.appsinmypocket.com

ELP level: 1–3

About: This app contains 43 decodable books that are organized by graphemes. An optional text-to-speech feature will narrate the story if activated. If an EL cannot read a word, then a tap will open up a pop-up picture showing the word's spelling. Phonetically irregular words are gradually introduced and are in red type. The app includes quizzes to check for comprehension, which the user must complete before moving to the next book. Progress reports are available online or via a weekly e-mail. It is appropriate for learners ages 4 and older.

Phonics Genius

URL: http://www.alligatorapps.com

ELP level: 1–3

About: This app has a teaching and practice mode. The teaching mode presents basic and advanced phoneme–grapheme associations using a flashcard format. It pronounces words and highlights vowel spellings. The teacher may modify word lists.

Spelling City

URL: http://www.spellingcity.com

ELP level: 2–4

About: Teachers create customized lists on a computer with definitions and sentences. Learning activities are available on the iPad or computer. The web site also includes many learning activities, including alphabetizing and printing handwriting PDFs in manuscript or cursive.

A+ Spelling Test

URL: http://www.alligatorapps.com

ELP level: 2–4

About: The teacher creates custom spelling lists with oral pronunciation. It includes four learning/test modes, and the EL can e-mail the completed tests to the teacher or parent.

Lexia Core5

URL: http://www.lexialearning.com

ELP level: 1–3

About: This program provides instruction and practice in phonemic awareness, reading, spelling, vocabulary, morphology (prefixes, suffixes, Latin roots, and Greek morphemes), and text comprehension. It provides engaging, systematic, and sequential practice starting with very basic levels to advanced reading and vocabulary. It tracks multiple users' progress, provides comprehensive reports, and is suitable for all ages.

Fry Words

URL: http://www.alligatorapps.com

ELP level: 1–3

About: This app provides systematic instruction and practice for 1,000 high-frequency words based on the Fry list. It has a learn mode and an engaging game mode that challenges users to identify high-frequency words from a choice of two to five words.

Fry Words Ninja—Reading Game

URL: http://www.alligatorapps.com

ELP level: 1–3

About: This app promotes overlearning for 1,000 high-frequency words based on the Fry list. The words fly up from the bottom of the screen and the user taps the word that matches the spoken word among other choices. The narration is a mature voice that is appropriate for all ages.

Sight Words
URL: http://www.alligatorapps.com
ELP level: 1–3
About: This app provides systematic instruction and practice for 200 high-frequency words based on the Dolch list grouped by grade level (preschool to third grade). It has a learn mode and an engaging game mode that challenges users to identify high-frequency words from a choice of two to five words.

Sight Words by Photo Touch
URL: http://www.grasshopperapps.com
ELP level: 1–3
About: This app builds automaticity and fluency for 220 Dolch words. The user matches spoken and written words by selecting the correct word from a list of three to 10 words. The app automatically adjusts the number based on user success.

Sight Words by Little Speller
URL: http://www.alligatorapps.com
ELP level: 1–3
About: This app helps the user learn and practice spelling 200 Dolch words. It uses a drag-and-drop letters format. Adjustable options are provided to scaffold task difficulty.

English Words: Everyone Learns, Sight Words: Everyone Learns, and Star Speller: Kids Learn Sight Words Games

URL: https://apps.apple.com/us/developer/teacher-created-materials/id437178006
ELP level: 1–3
About: These three, nearly identical apps have a wide variety of games to practice reading and spelling high-frequency words. The Little Speller is the most economical. Each contains all 300 Dolch words; an individual can buy separate packets for groups of 100 words. This set of apps, however, costs considerably more than comparable apps. It has nine engaging practice games that involve seeing, hearing, recording, and spelling. Although more expensive than other sight word apps, the English Words app is appropriate for ELs and older students.

Stories With Highlighted Narration

Sentence Reading Magic 1 and 2
URL: http://www.preschoolu.com
ELP level: 2–3
About: This program presents 324 two-, three-, four-, and five-word sentences with short vowels (Magic 1) or consonant blends (Magic 2). The user can match spoken and written high-frequency words (Magic 1). The program includes manuscript and cursive fonts.

Rainbow Sentences
URL: http://www.mobile-educationstore.com
ELP level: 1–2
About: Helps students construct grammatically correct sentences. Phrases are color coded to help students understand basic sentence structure. Users can record their sentences in their own voice.

Bob Books—Reading Magic
URL: http://www.bobbooks.com
ELP level: 2–3
About: This program provides decodable, illustrated, and interactive stories. The drag-and-drop feature provides practice for the child to spell spoken words in the story. The program orally reads the sentence after all the words are formed. Each story contains four progressively more difficult user tasks.

Loud Crow Interactive Books
URL: http://www.loudcrow.com
ELP level: 2–3
About: These award-winning narrated e-books include word highlighting for building word recognition and reading fluency.

Dr. Seuss Beginner Book Collection
URL: http://www.oceanhousemedia.com
ELP level: 2–3
About: This company produces apps of narrated text with word highlighting. ELs can tap pictures to reveal words for building vocabulary instruction.

iBooks or Kindle Books and Project Gutenberg
URL: http://www.gutenberg.org
ELP level: 3–5; requires reading skills in native language and English
About: Project Gutenberg is an extensive online collection of out-of-copyright public domain books for children and adults. Follow instructions to download a text into iBooks or Kindle. ELs can tap and hold individual words to hear oral pronunciation and see the definition in English. Tap the "manage" tab to download a non-English dictionary to access definitions in many languages. Tap the "search" tab to access web definitions.

Vocabulary

Right Word App
URL: https://apps.apple.com/us/app/the-right-word/id761529361
ELP level: 4–5; requires reading skills in English
About: This app features four games that challenge advanced ELs to select frequently misused words and phrases within the context of a sentence.

Word Hippo
URL: http://www.wordhippo.com
ELP level: 4–5; requires reading skills in English
About: This web site provides the meaning of a word and also synonyms, antonyms, words that rhyme with it, sentences containing it, the derivatives, and etymology. It includes British and American spellings.

Online Etymology Dictionary
URL: http://www.etymonline.com
ELP level: 4–5; requires reading skills in English
About: This web site is a comprehensive collection of the history of thousands of English words, including slang. Each entry contains the dates of the earliest year for which there is a written record of that word and the word histories. The site also contains an extensive glossary of abbreviations for language terms.

Root Words and Prefixes: Quick Reference
URL: http://www.learnthat.org/pages/view/roots.html
ELP level: 4–5; requires reading skills in English
About: This site contains a list of Greek and Latin morphemes, meanings, and sample words and definitions.

List of English Suffixes
URL: http://www.learnthat.org/pages/view/suffix.html
ELP level: 4–5; requires reading skills in English
About: This site contains a list of Greek and Latin morphemes, meanings, and sample words and definitions.

Irregular Verbs
URL: http://www.alligatorapps.com
ELP level: 3–5; requires reading skills in English
About: This app provides practice reading and use of correct verb forms and presents some homophones in seven engaging games. The optional text-to-speech feature reads sentences. This app is appropriate for younger students and ELs.

Homophones
URL: http://www.alligatorapps.com
ELP level: 3–5; requires reading skills in English
About: This app provides practice using the correct homophone in sentences and opportunities for reading and using the correct homophones. It presents some homophones in seven engaging games, and the optional text-to-speech feature reads sentences.

Wordflex Touch Dictionary
URL: http://www.wordflex.com
ELP level: 4–5; requires reading skills in English
About: This site provides the oral pronunciation of a main word in American or British accents. It shows word relationships as networks of semantic word associations. Word webs are organized by the parts of speech (e.g., noun, verb), phrases, and derivatives. Words listed include phrasal verbs (walk away, pull out). Dynamic word trees can be moved and rearranged. The site is appropriate for older students and teachers.

Neil Ramsden
URL: http://www.neilramsden.co.uk/spelling
About: The mini-matrix maker builds word matrices from a list of word sums the user provides. Example word matrix and word sums for the base sign include

re + de + *sign* + ed = redesigned

sign + al = signal

de + *sign* + ate + ion + s = designations

ASSISTIVE TECHNOLOGY

This section describes apps that assist ELs to perform a function independently with which they would normally have difficulty.

Electronic Translators, Dictionaries, and Thesauri

Google Translate
URL: http://translate.google.com
ELP level: 1–5; requires reading skills in native language and English
About: This app translates oral speech or written text from one language to another, enabling speakers of different languages to converse. It requires Wi-Fi to simultaneously translate oral speech. An individual can download languages for offline use to translate written text. With the mobile app, one can hold the mobile device above the text for instant translation.

Google
URL: http://www.google.com and Siri (Apple products)
ELP level: 3–5; requires reading skills in English
About: To perfect pronunciation, use the microphone icon to ask questions in English. Then read the text to determine accuracy. Use the microphone as a spelling aid and say, "How do you spell _____?" This will produce the word, definition, and a tab to translate the word into several languages. Conversely, one can spell a word orally to hear the word pronounced and defined. Drop-down links provide the etymological roots. Further drop-down links will translate the word to almost any language.

Dictionary.com and Thesaurus.com
URL: http://www.dictionary.com and http://www.thesauraus.com
ELP level: 3–5; requires reading skills English
About: These apps provide user-friendly definitions, synonyms, antonyms, and sample sentences. It also illustrates the etymological roots (language of origin) with words and a world map.

Microsoft Word
ELP level: 3–5; requires reading skills in native language and English
About: ELs can access translations for individual words into numerous languages. Highlight one word. Click Tools > Languages and choose a language. Then click Tools > Thesaurus. The word will be translated into the chosen language. In addition, it will list synonyms and antonyms.

Longman's Dictionaries

URL: http://global.longmandictionaries.com
ELP level: 3–5; requires reading skills in native language and English
About: This collection of dictionaries provides sample sentences using basic vocabulary to complement definitions. Separate volumes include

- Longman Collocations Dictionary and Thesaurus (words plus modifiers such as *heavy rain, pouring rain*)

- Concise English Dictionary

- Phrasal Verbs Dictionary

- Idioms Dictionary

Your Dictionary

URL: http://www.yourdictionary.com
ELP level: 3–5; requires reading skills in native language and English
About: This app provides oral pronunciation, definitions, synonyms, sentences, thesaurus, and quotes on tabs at the top of the screen.

Wordnik

URL: http://www.wordnik.com
About: This site allows the user to enter any word or phrase to reveal definitions, etymologies, and examples in sentences from various sources. It is more appropriate for adults and older students.

Writing Skills: Speech-to-Text Apps

Built-in Speech to Text Applications

ELP level: 3–5
About: Speech-to-text features are becoming standard in several platforms to support office applications, e-mail, social media posts, and many other applications. It allows one to speak and instantly see text on the screen. ELs can use this feature to perfect English pronunciation. To turn on the feature using Apple computers, click System Preferences > Dictation & Speech. To start dictation, place the cursor where you want to start typing, and then tap the *fn* key twice or choose Edit > Start Dictation. This feature works best with headsets that have a built-in microphone. To increase reading fluency skills, read aloud into a headset microphone. The dictation feature will work only if text is read fluently. If the user pauses too long, then the microphone shuts off. Use to compose text without having to worry about spelling. One must also specify the punctuation.

Writing Skills: Text Editing

Ginger Software
URL: http://www.gingersoftware.com
ELP level: 3–5; requires reading skills in native language and English
About: This text editing app integrates with software to correct spelling, grammar, and syntax.

Grammarly
URL: http://www.gramarly.com
ELP level: 3–5; requires reading skills in English
About: This program helps the writer improve his or her writing by checking grammar, punctuation, and spelling. Errors are not corrected automatically; the writer must manually correct each error. Brief explanations of the errors help the user learn about his or her mistakes. The free version of Grammarly supports word documents, e-mail, and social media posts. It corrects contextual spelling (e.g., there, they're, their), punctuation, subject–verb disagreement, grammar, and so forth. School site licenses are available.

CONCLUSION

Incorporating technology into the classroom takes careful planning and resources. Most programs require an Internet connection and/or Wi-Fi. Students with smartphones can access many of the programs with these devices. To use technology to increase student engagement and provide extra teacher time for at-risk students, consider this scenario. Have the more advanced or independent learners use assistive and instructional technology independently. This frees up time for teachers to work with students who are not performing well and are at risk with small-group or individualized instruction. Students who require more repetition to master a concept can use instructional technology at school, in the home, or at the public library. Effective technology can provide extensive practice in research-based skills without undue demands on the teacher's time.

Several obstacles may affect the successful use of technology in the classroom. For one, teachers may not use the program with fidelity. They also may provide access to technology infrequently, thus having to reteach programs, taking up valuable instruction time. Also, teachers may not take advantage of the student tracking features (Lovell & Phillips, 2009). At home, students and parents or caregivers may have limited experience with technology for educational enrichment.

Technology can enhance instruction in many classrooms, increase student engagement, and provide opportunities for extended practice with corrective feedback. There is one thing technology cannot do, however—replace a knowledgeable and skilled teacher. Use technology judiciously, carefully matching the technology with the needs and abilities of the learner.

REFERENCES

International Dyslexia Association. (2010). *Knowledge and practice standards for teachers of reading.* Retrieved from https://dyslexiaida.org/knowledge-and-practices

Ishizuka, K. (2011). *The app squad: SLJ's advisors weigh in on kids' book apps.* Retrieved from https://www.slj.com/?detailStory=the-app-squad-sljs-advisors-weigh-in-on-kids-book-apps

Lexia Learning Systems. (2003). *Early reading.* Concord, MA: Author.

Lexia Learning Systems. (2005). *Primary reading.* Concord, MA: Author.

Lopez, O. S. (2010). The digital learning classroom: Improving English language learners' academic success in mathematics and reading using interactive whiteboard technology. *Computers and Education, 54*(4), 901–915.

Lovell, M., & Phillips, L. (2009). Commercial software programs approved for teaching reading and writing in the primary grades: Another sobering reality. *The Journal of Research on Technology in Education, 42*(2), 197–216.

Macaruso, P., & Rodman, A. (2011). Benefits of computer-assisted instruction to support reading acquisition in English language learners. *Bilingual Research Journal, 34*(3), 301–315. doi:10.1080/15235882.2011.622829.

McLeskey, J., & Waldron, N. (2007). Making differences ordinary in inclusive classrooms. *Intervention in School and Clinic, 42*(3), 162–168. doi:10.1177/10534512070420030501

O'Malley, P., Jenkins, S., Wesley, B., Donehower, C., Rabuck, D., & Lewis, M. (2013, April). *Effectiveness of using iPads to build math fluency.* Paper presented at the Council for Exceptional Children Annual Meeting, San Antonio, TX.

Winters, D. C. (2015, June). *Reading e-text: Alternative strategies using AT.* Retrieved from https://dyslexiaida.org/reading-e-text

Winters, D. C., & Cheesman, E. A. (2013). Mobile instructional and assistive technology for literacy. *Perspectives in Language and Literacy, 39*(4), 49–55.

Index

Page numbers followed by *f*, *t*, and *b* indicate figures, tables, and boxes respectively.